W9-CNX-853

52-Week Football Training

Ben Cook, MA, CSCS

Strength and Conditioning Coach
University of North Carolina

Human Kinetics

Library of Congress Cataloging-in-Publication Data

Cook, Ben
    52-week football training / Ben Cook.
      p.   cm.
    ISBN 0-7360-0085-2
    1. Football–Training–United States.   I. Title. II. Title: Fifty-two week football training.
    GV953.5.C66   1999
    796.332–dc21   99-27996
                                                       CIP

ISBN-10: 0-7360-0085-2
ISBN-13: 978-0-7360-0085-7

Copyright © 1999 by Ben Cook

All rights reserved. Except for use in a review, the reproduction or utilization of this work in any form or by any electronic, mechanical, or other means, now known or hereafter invented, including xerography, photocopying, and recording, and in any information storage and retrieval system, is forbidden without the written permission of the publisher.

Notice: Permission to reproduce the following material is granted to instructors and agencies who have purchased *52-Week Football Training*: pp. 12, 16-25, 30-46, 50-56, 60-73, 78-88, and 92-121. The reproduction of other parts of this book is expressly forbidden by the above copyright notice. Persons or agencies who have not purchased *52-Week Football Training* may not reproduce any material.

Developmental Editor: Julie Rhoda; **Assistant Editors:** Jan Feeney and Sandra Merz Bott; **Copyeditor:** Bob Replinger; **Proofreader:** Sarah Wiseman; **Graphic Designer:** Fred Starbird; **Graphic Artist:** Kimberly Maxey; **Photo Editor:** Clark Brooks; **Cover Designer:** Jack Davis; **Photographer (cover):** Anthony Neste; **Photographers (interior):** Ann B. Cook unless otherwise noted. Photo on p. 226 by Tom Roberts; **Illustrator:** Sharon M. Smith; **Printer:** United Graphics.

Human Kinetics books are available at special discounts for bulk purchase. Special editions or book excerpts can also be created to specification. For details, contact the Special Sales Manager at Human Kinetics.

Printed in the United States of America   10

Human Kinetics
Web site: www.HumanKinetics.com

United States: Human Kinetics, P.O. Box 5076, Champaign, IL 61825-5076
800-747-4457
e-mail: humank@hkusa.com

Canada: Human Kinetics, 475 Devonshire Road, Unit 100, Windsor, ON N8Y 2L5
800-465-7301 (in Canada only)
e-mail: info@hkcanada.com

Europe: Human Kinetics, 107 Bradford Road, Stanningley
Leeds LS28 6AT, United Kingdom
+44 (0) 113 255 5665
e-mail: hk@hkeurope.com

Australia: Human Kinetics, 57A Price Avenue, Lower Mitcham, South Australia 5062
08 8372 0999
e-mail: info@hkaustralia.com

New Zealand: Human Kinetics, Division of Sports Distributors NZ Ltd.
P.O. Box 300 226 Albany, North Shore City, Auckland
0064 9 448 1207
e-mail: info@humankinetics.co.nz

The human body is a vessel of immense intricacy. Its survival teeters on a complex series of chemical on and off switches, a series of positively and negatively charged subparticles. So divinely shaped and patterned by its continuing struggles against stresses of our environment, this flesh and bone is resilient, versatile. The body is a divine creation, but no more so than the human spirit that compels it to perform. What a wonderful gift. Thank you, God.

Thanks for everything, Lisa, Mom, Dad, and Trean!

Contents

Introduction   v

Drill Finder   viii

Part I **Year-Round Training for Football**   **1**

Chapter 1   *Phase 1: Postseason Workouts*   **13**

Chapter 2   *Phase 2: Winter Workouts*   **27**

Chapter 3   *Phase 3: Spring Workouts*   **47**

Chapter 4   *Phase 4: Early Summer Workouts*   **57**

Chapter 5   *Phase 5: Preseason Workouts*   **74**

Chapter 6   *Phase 6: In-Season Workouts*   **89**

Part II **Exercises and Drills**   **123**

Chapter 7   *Flexibility Exercises*   **125**

Chapter 8   *Strength and Power Exercises*   **145**

Chapter 9   *Running Drills*   **197**

Chapter 10   *Speed and Power Exercises*   **206**

Chapter 11   *Football-Specific Agility Exercises*   **225**

About the Author   245

Introduction

Most sports require a variety of skills. Jumping, sprinting, lateral movement, endurance—all are tools of the athlete's trade. An athlete with these skills can more effectively perform his sport. Loss of strength or an inability to continue as a result of fatigue can severely hinder sport performance, but an athlete can correct these deficiencies by developing and completing a proper year-round physical-conditioning program. Resistance training, flexibility training, cardiorespiratory conditioning, speed development, and regulation of body composition are elements that an athlete can exploit to improve performance.

The purpose of this book is to show you, the football player or coach, how to use constructive, progressive exercise to improve playing ability. The book is unique in that it provides a complete 52-week exercise plan for high-performance football. Built on a typical academic and athletic calendar, the plan can be used, with only slight variations, by players in any high school or college program in the country. By using periodization principles that modulate intensity you'll promote maximum muscle growth and, most important, proper muscle recovery.

A major concern in creating strength and conditioning programs is properly addressing *specificity of training*. A well-designed workout plan mimics or parallels specific activities that occur during the actual sporting event, such as blocking an opponent, passing a football, or avoiding a defender. The workouts in this book are exclusively designed to enhance the physical abilities of the football athlete. I've constructed the framework of this program and chosen the exercises and activities by analyzing and recognizing football's requirements for both absolute endurance and absolute power.

This balance of endurance versus power within the sport determines everything about the conditioning program. How long to work out, how long to rest between sets of an exercise, how much weight lifting to do versus running, how far and how long to run—all are factors that the structure of a workout program must address. The athlete who does not consider the balance of endurance versus power may not perform up to his potential.

This book neatly lays out a year-round system of physical training—resistance training, overall conditioning, and fitness and skill abilities.

Part I provides you with detailed resistance, conditioning, and skills workouts for a full year of training from postseason training—which begins after your football season ends (chapter 1)—to the following fall's in-season training (chapter 6). Part II then provides you with illustrated instructions to perform the flexibility exercises (chapter 7), resistance-training exercises (chapter 8), running exercises (chapter 9), speed and power drills (chapter 10), and football-specific agility drills (chapter 11).

Physical training alone, however, will not totally prepare you to succeed in your sport. You must consider other factors that go beyond the scope of this book but still demand mentioning.

- **Nutrition.** Proper nutrition is a critical element in the promotion of recovery. Without taking in the proper amount of calories as nutrients, the muscles you have worked so diligently to train will fail to heal fully. Each workout thereafter will only promote further fatigue, and eventually overtraining will result in a loss of strength and performance. Therefore, you should be equally concerned with the amount and type of food that you are providing your body. Recovery is the key to success in any workout plan—nutrition and rest constitute a plan of recovery. Remember that working out causes microscopic damage in the cells of the muscles. Failing to sleep and eat properly will result in an inability to build this muscle back up.

- **Mental preparation.** Another important factor to consider is the mental training that parallels physical training. Physical success is virtually impossible unless the mental desire to succeed accompanies your physical efforts. Almost every athlete believes that he can perform a physical task until he fails the first time. Each failure thereafter only solidifies the athlete's doubt in his ability to succeed. Therefore, you must create planned workouts that promote achievement rather than failure. Structured achievement is linked to constructive goal setting.

- **Goal setting.** Setting a goal can be motivational. Setting an objective that you can realistically reach can act as a stimulus to prove yourself. Goals can be simple, like getting out of bed in the morning when the alarm rings. Goals can be difficult too, such as rushing for 1,000 yards or making 80 solo tackles in a season. Whatever you choose as your goals, make plans to obtain them realistically and systematically.

In a physical-conditioning program, you should set specific goals that you can divide into smaller steps. These steps are small goals within themselves that lead to the ultimate goal. Using this step-by-step approach may require you to spend months or even years to reach the ultimate goal, but by planning a series of small steps and then gaining confidence by completing each one, you can more easily obtain your ultimate or long-range goal. You can do this a number of ways; it depends on you, your trainers, and your coaches how you approach that goal. Coaches and trainers need to adopt a plan that an athlete is comfortable with and has taken some part in designing. In this way, an athlete will approach the goal with more enthusiasm. Confidence is an athlete's biggest weapon against defeat. With successful goal setting, an athlete can gain that all-so-important confidence, making the goal more easily obtainable.

With this book it is important to observe the format and order in which I have arranged the exercises, but at the foundation of the workout are three rules:

1. Be consistent and train on a regular basis. For your body to respond maximally, you must continually challenge it.

2. Work hard and smart. Hard work with intelligent regard for recovery during the postexercise period will produce greater results.

3. Rest thoroughly when it is time to rest. Workouts break you down; resting builds you back up.

The biggest obstacle between you and success is yourself. Only through consistent, structured training and an unflinching desire to be the best will you meet your goals. So what are you waiting for? Let's go train.

Drill Finder   Resistance Training

Exercise name	1	2	3	4	5	6	Part II p. #
Ab-ad	x	x				x	185
Alternating dumbbell press		x		x	x	x	160
Alternating dumbbell curl	x	x	x	x	x	x	176
Alternating leg lunge		x			x	x	185
Backward lunge		x		x	x	x	186
Ballistic push-up					x		152
Bar shrug		x				x	172
Bar triceps extension		x			x	x	178
Behind neck press	x	x		x	x	x	159
Bench press	x	x		x	x	x	148
Bent dumbbell raise	x	x		x		x	173
Box squat		x		x		x	186
BW one-leg calf				x			193
Cable shrug	x						172
Cable upright row	x					x	171
Calf raise/leg press						x	193
Close high lat			x		x	x	155
Close incline press				x		x	150
Close low lat	x	x	x	x	x	x	156
Close-grip bench		x		x		x	182
Close-grip lat	x	x		x	x	x	153
Close-grip push-up						x	182
Combo exercises			x	x	x	x	194-196
Crabbing			x				196
Cylinder circuit	x	x	x	x	x	x	188-192
Dead lift		x		x	x		187
Dip	x	x	x	x	x	x	149
Dumbbell French press		x	x	x		x	179
Dumbbell pull press			x	x	x	x	166-167
Dumbbell push press			x	x	x	x	161
Dumbbell shrug	x	x		x		x	172
Dumbbell snatch			x	x	x	x	162
Dumbbell stroll			x	x	x	x	173
EZ-bar curl	x					x	177
EZ-bar pullover	x			x			157
Flat dumbbell fly				x		x	151
Flat dumbbell press	x	x	x	x		x	149
Fourth-quarter tour			x				196
Free-weight upright row	x	x		x		x	170
Front dumbbell raise	x			x			164
Glute-ham raise			x				189
Ham 10 chest			x			x	151
Ham decline					x	x	150
Hammer curl				x		x	178
Hang clean			x	x		x	171
High lat front	x	x		x	x	x	154
High lat rear		x	x	x	x	x	155
Incline bench press	x	x	x	x	x	x	148
Incline curl			x			x	177

Drill Finder — Resistance Training (continued)

Exercise name	Phase 1	2	3	4	5	6	Part II p. #
Incline dumbbell fly	X			X		X	151
Incline dumbbell press	X	X	X	X	X	X	149
Jump rope		X	X	X		X	196
Kickback	X		X	X	X	X	180-181
One- or two-leg curl	X	X	X	X		X	185
Leg dragging			X		X		196
One- or two-leg extension	X	X	X			X	184
One- or two-leg press	X	X		X	X	X	184
Lunge—3 pumps	X	X					185
Manual front deltoid	X						165
Manual neck		X	X	X	X	X	194
Manual rear deltoid	X			X		X	174
Manual side raise	X						165
Manual upright row						X	171
Medicine ball circuit			X		X	X	166
Military press	X	X		X		X	158
Moon push-up				X			152
Musketeer lunge		X		X		X	186
Nautilus multicalf	X						192
One stiff leg dead	X	X		X		X	186
One-arm dumbbell row		X	X	X	X		154
One-arm dumbbell triceps extension						X	181
Power clean		X			X	X	169
Power pull		X					168
Power row		X			X	X	170
Preacher curl	X	X			X	X	176
Pull-up		X	X		X	X	155
Push press		X	X		X	X	161
Rear deltoid swim			X	X		X	175
Reverse dip			X			X	182
Roll-out			X		X	X	158
Smith behind neck						X	159
Shoulder fly			X		X		164
Side dumbbell raise	X	X		X	X	X	163
Side lunge		X	X	X		X	188
Slideboard		X	X		X	X	188
Snatch squat with stick						X	187
Split dumbbell pullover					X	X	157
Squat	X	X	X	X	X	X	183
Standing calf raise	X	X		X		X	193
Step-up		X	X	X	X		188
Straight dumbbell pullover		X		X	X		156
Straight-bar curl	X	X		X	X	X	176
Triceps push-down	X	X	X	X	X	X	180
Two-arm dumbbell press	X	X		X		X	160
Two-arm dumbbell row				X		X	153
Two-arm dumbbell triceps extension				X			179
Wall explosion					X		182
Wrist flex				X			196

Drill Finder   Conditioning and Skill Training

Exercise name	| Phase 1	2	3	4	5	6	Part II p. #
Agility drills (four-station)		x			x		233-236
Agility over bags		x		x	x		237
Alternate leg bound		x			x		215
Bags		x		x	x		237
Balance drill #1		x		x			227
Balance drill #2		x		x			227
Balance drill #3		x		x			228
Balance drill #4		x		x	x		228
Ball-drop reaction drill		x		x	x		243
Basic reaction drill		x			x		242
Crosses		x		x	x		202
Cutting inside and outside legs		x			x		238
Dodge ball		x		x	x		243
Downhill running		x					224
Fartlek		x		x		x	203-204
Foot-speed workout #1		x		x			229
Foot-speed workout #2		x		x			230-231
Foot-speed workout #3		x		x			231-232
Game simulation sprints		x		x	x		199-201
Gassers						x	203
Hash and back				x			203
Hill training		x					204
Indian running				x		x	204
Intervals	x	x		x		x	201-202
Lateral quick run, sprint out		x					236
Lateral shuffle over low hurdle		x			x		238
Lateral two in, two out, sprint out		x			x		237
Medicine ball chest pass			x	x			217
Movement course #1		x		x			238-239
Movement course #2		x		x	x		240
Movement course #3		x		x			241-242
One in, three out, sprint out		x			x		237
Plyometrics—jumps		x	x		x		211-217
Plyometrics—upper body			x		x		217-219
Power skip		x			x		216
Quick feet drills		x			x		233
Quick run, sprint out		x					236
Reaction drills		x		x	x		242
Shuttles		x		x	x	x	202
Sideline ladders				x		x	203
Skate bound			x		x		213
Sprint-stride-sprint					x		220-221
Stadium runs				x		x	204
Standing long jump		x			x		214
Standing triple jump		x			x		214-215
Starts (thrusts)		x		x	x		222-223
Strides		x					220-221
Tag games		x		x	x		243-244
Three cone reaction drill		x		x	x		242
Three-sided square drills			x	x	x	x	230-231
Timed run (endurance training)		x		x		x	204-205
Towing				x	x		223-224
Transitional carioca		x			x		232
Underhand backward throw			x		x		219
Uphill sprints		x					223-224

PART

I

Year-Round Training for Football

The 52-week football-conditioning plan presented in this book is one example of how to set up a solid, complete, and constructive exercise plan. The purpose of the program is to show you—whether you're an athlete or a coach—how to incorporate all the aspects of your daily workouts into a consolidated working exercise plan. Consider this program one of many methods of exercise planning. Some methods produce better results for specific athletes and teams because of the construction of the program and the times of the year when it applies certain training elements. I have constructed this workout plan with consideration for the football player and his team, with particular attention to the stresses the player might confront on and off the football field.

Program Structure

I designed the following program—a 52-week macrocycle—around a typical collegiate football athletic and academic calendar. The macrocycle is a method of structuring and viewing a complete workout plan based on a long-term observation and goal-setting period. An Olympic athlete may choose to structure his macrocycle on a four-year observation period; the football player should structure the macrocycle on one full year of training. This is a realistic program for a collegiate schedule, but it can be easily adapted for high school student-athletes whose athletic and academic calendars and busy schedules are similar to those of collegiate players. The timing of each peak in intensity during the training year is affected by the academic schedule as well as the athlete's sport seasons; this 52-week training plan accommodates those considerations.

The macrocycle is divided into in-season, postseason, and preseason periods. The program emphasizes different exercise elements within each of the periods. For example, as the in-season period approaches, the training becomes increasingly specific to football. In this way you can convert the basic strength you acquired in the weight room during the postseason period to more functional strength that you can apply to your skills on the football field.

The number of days per week of training (frequency) and the length of the training session (duration) are determined by these three primary training periods, which are further broken down into phases called mesocycles. Each mesocycle is covered separately in chapters 1 through 6: postseason (chapter 1), winter (chapter 2), spring ball (chapter 3), early summer (chapter 4), preseason (chapter 5), and in-season (chapter 6). Each mesocycle is further broken down into 8 to 12 microcycles—each microcycle is one week of training. In this program we have 52 separate microcycles in one macrocycle (fig I.1).

The in-season, postseason, and preseason phase divisions mark the route to the upcoming football season, providing points to observe whether progress has been made during that portion of the training. Some phases flow into the next with little, if any, break in the workout. Other phases are separated by a planned week off.

This 52-week plan also considers breaks in the academic calendar that occur in the in-season, postseason, and preseason periods. Academic breaks

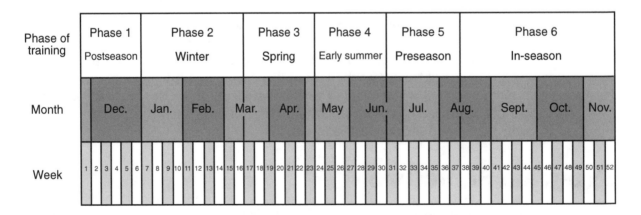

Figure I.1 Each 52-week macrocycle is broken into six phases.

create periods when you may be away from the training environment. Planning these breaks into the training program helps you maintain consistency in your fitness while away from school. The plan can use academic breaks as time off for recovery, or it can provide workouts for you to take home. Take-home workouts can prevent a loss in the physical improvements already achieved.

Program Components

Each workout outlined in part I (chapters 1 through 6) is made up of four main components:

1. *Warming up and flexibility exercises* to prepare your muscles for the workout, increase your range of motion, and reduce risk of injury (chapter 7)
2. *Resistance training* for increased muscle stability to protect you from injury as well as for increased muscular endurance, size, and power (chapter 8)
3. *Running and conditioning* for aerobic fitness as well as speed, power, and agility training (chapters 9 and 10)
4. *Skill training* for transferring your fitness into excellent on-the-field football play (chapters 10 and 11)

Before beginning the workout you should understand several points that can accelerate your progress. This book provides the structure of the workout, the types and order of exercises, the number of sets and repetitions for each exercise, and the amount of rest between each exercise. Each chapter in part I provides weekly workout programs for each week within that mesocycle. Each week in the mesocycle divides the workouts into three parts—resistance training, conditioning, and applied-skill training. Part II of this text explains and illustrates the specific exercises you will use throughout the 52-week program.

At some point you may want to create your own workout. Understanding the structural components of a workout will help you in your endeavors.

Warming Up

Warming up briefly before a workout is beneficial in several ways.

1. It warms and prepares the muscle tissue for more intense activity. By gradually warming up the muscle, you ensure that your muscles are adapting to more intense exercise. This ability to sustain muscular activity can therefore benefit endurance activities like running and biking.
2. Warming up before exercise has been shown to increase nerve activity in the working muscles, resulting in both increased contraction speed of the muscle fiber cells and greater power output of the muscle. This type of response is especially beneficial for power and strength athletes.

3. Warming up before exercise may reduce the potential for injury by increasing muscle flexibility. This can help reduce the occurrence of strains and tears in muscles and connective tissues.

4. Your blood pressure naturally rises at the beginning of exercise. Warming up before exercise can lessen this rise in blood pressure and thus place less stress on the heart. This can be important to an athlete who might already have high blood pressure, as well as to all athletes who are concerned about their personal health.

5. Overall, research has shown that athletes who warm up before exercise can increase their performance.

So what constitutes an adequate warm-up period? I recommend first doing a 5- to 10-minute overall body warm-up at a submaximal effort. Try activities such as calisthenics, form running, cariocas, and jumping rope. This overall body activity will increase your heart rate and the flow of blood to your muscles. Then do one or two sets or spend a few minutes doing a more specific warm-up for the activity that you are about to perform, such as a warm-up set on the bench press if weight training. This more specific warm-up will increase your body temperature in the specific area of the body that you will be exercising.

I address warming up in the workout primarily before the conditioning workouts. The flexibility portion of the workout is composed of a prepractice static stretching routine. Before resistance training, you can achieve an adequate warm-up by doing light calisthenics and light sets of the exercises you are about to perform (see table I.1). You may include light stretching, but understand that overstretching the muscle before a resistance-training session can result in muscle instability, reducing your ability to stabilize the weight.

Table I.1 Sample Warm-Up Exercises

Specific	Overall body
Push-ups (for arm work)	Jogging in place
Pull-ups	Jumping jacks
Deep knee bends	Jumping rope
Stretching	Stationary cycling
Very light single set of the exercise to be performed	

Resistance Training

Resistance training is an integral part of the football athlete's workout plan; it ensures constructive gains in body weight and builds the strength and power necessary for success on the football field. After you have built strength and power in the weight room, you can fine-tune it through work on the practice field and through the conditioning and applied-skills sections of the workout. You will thus become a stronger and more powerful football athlete.

Normally, I create two separate resistance-training workouts: one addresses the strength needs of the linemen—offensive line (OL), defensive line (DL), tight ends (TE), outside linebackers (OLB), inside linebackers (ILB)—while the other workout is for the backs—running backs (RB) defensive backs (DB), quarterbacks (QB), wide receivers (WR), punters (P), kickers (K). This division addresses both the specific needs of the individual player positions and meets the needs of weight-room flow and management. During a four-day routine, for example, the backs perform Monday's workout plan while the linemen perform Thursday's workout plan. Each group does a workout in different parts of the room. This keeps you and your teammates from running into one another or wasting time waiting to get on a bench or machine. Student-athletes are students first and don't want to be in the weight room all day or night. Players have classes to attend, papers to write, and tests to study for. The workout should work with this in mind.

How to Read the Resistance-Training Workout

Each week of the program notes the amount of rest to take between basic exercises (b), supporting exercises (s), and, where applicable, circuit exercises (c) as well as the amount of rest between the actual exercises in minutes and seconds. To the right of each exercise name, you'll see the number of repetitions to be performed for each set and the amount of weight given in percentage of one repetition maximum (1 RM) for that exercise:

Bench press   8 × 70 percent, 8 × 75 percent, and 8 × 80 percent

means you are doing three sets of 8 repetitions of the bench press at 70 percent, 75 percent, and 80 percent of your 1 RM. If your 1 RM on the bench press is 200, you would lift

70 percent of 200 (.70 × 200) or 140 pounds on the first set,

75 percent of 200 (.75 × 200) or 150 pounds on the second set, and

80 percent of 200 (.80 × 200) or 160 pounds on the third set.

These percentages are approximate levels of resistance that athletes should use. This means that 60 percent is lighter than 90 percent; on a day when you see 60 percent, you should consider that day a lighter resistance workout. That is not to say that the workout is easy, just that the resistance is less. The lighter resistance will allow you to concentrate more on the style of repetition, to allow for higher repetitions or combination sets. Therefore, even the light workouts can be difficult.

Determining Your One-Repetition Maximum

To determine your one repetition maximum (1 RM)—the most weight you can lift for an exercise for one repetition—gather 1 RMs for selected exercises to use as the basis for your resistance-training program. You need not test every exercise for maximal ability. By using several core-lift maximums, you can estimate other exercise maximums. You should determine 1 RMs for the following exercises:

- Bench press—as the basis for all upper body push exercises
- Close-grip lat—as the basis for all upper body pull exercises
- Leg press or squat—as the basis for all lower body exercises

Then, by using or observing week-to-week workout sheets or logbooks for the number of repetitions, you can fine-tune your resistance levels and make adjustments as you become stronger. If you are a younger or inexperienced athlete, especially if you are a high school freshman, I advise you not to attempt 1 RM lifts. Instead, choose a manageable weight and perform as many repetitions as you can just short of complete muscular failure.

Use the percentages indicated on the workouts as guidelines, but don't be afraid to adjust your 1 RM on a lift as your strength improves. For example, perhaps Bob has improved on the bench press, and he's ready to increase his last set of the exercise by 5 pounds on the next workout. But when he looks at the exercise plan, he sees that his last set of bench press is to be 80 percent. In fact, he's scheduled to lift 80 percent on the last set for the next four weeks. The weight Bob is currently using is too easy for him, but he needs to continue progressing. Just because the workout plan says to use 80 percent for the next four weeks, should Bob lift the same weight all four weeks? I hope not.

Let's say Bob's previous 1 RM for the bench press was 300 pounds (80 percent of 300 pounds is 240). The workout suggests using 240 pounds for the next four weeks regardless of whether Bob has improved. The way to address strength improvement using the workout plan is to increase the 1 RM by about 5 pounds (when using free weights the most common increase is to add a 2 1/2-pound plate to each side of the bar). This adjustment will make Bob's new 1 RM 305 pounds and bump his workout weight to 244 pounds (80 percent of 305). Rounded to the next 5 pounds, Bob's new workout weight is 245 pounds.

This method of increasing the 1 RM is useful because it projects your training and improvement upward through the end of the training cycle. If this method of increasing weight is too difficult, you can simply keep records of your weekly progress in each lift. Keeping your own records can lead to poorly kept data and lost record sheets, but this may be the only method you can use. You may be asking why even keep records? Why not simply go in, work hard in the weight room, and kick butt? That's all that matters, right? You may choose to work out this way, but the gains you make will be minimal, and you may burn out or develop fatigue-related injuries.

Breathing During Resistance Training

When doing resistance training, you must breathe correctly for both the success of the lift and your long-term health. If you can breathe normally during a lift—breathing in when lowering the resistance and breathing out during the exertion of the lift—do so. As the resistance you lift increases, you wil be tempted to hold your breath to create a sense of stability and control over the weight. If you are tempted to hold your breath, I suggest this method for breathing during the course of a resistance exercise:

1. Remove the bar from the resting position and stabilize.
2. Take a deep breath.
3. Hold the breath and begin the exercise movement.
4. Begin to return the weight to the starting point.
5. Release the breath during the last one-half or two-thirds of the movement.
6. Repeat the cycle.

This method of breathing in and then holding your breath can contribute to the success of the movement. Holding your breath can increase the pressure in the abdominal area. This pressure increase can help stabilize the spine, which in turn can stabilize the shoulders and rib cage.

If you hold the breath too long during the lift, however, the pressure may become excessive, resulting in some potentially harmful side effects:

1. Holding the breath can cause the muscles to become tense. These tense muscles and interabdominal pressure can press on veins, thus reducing the amount of blood flowing back to the heart.
2. Your exercising body still needs blood to deliver oxygen to the muscles. Because returning blood flow is reduced to the heart, the heart must beat faster to deliver a similar quantity of blood to those needy muscles. This is known as the Valsalva effect.
3. During heavy lifting, systolic blood pressure can rise to 200 mmHg as a result of the heart rapidly trying to drive blood through narrowed arteries. This stresses the cardiac muscle. As the body senses the increase in blood pressure, it attempts to reduce the stress by dilating vascular pathways to allow blood to flow more freely.
4. However, upon releasing the breath, interabdominal pressure rapidly falls. This reduction in pressure against dilated arteries and veins results in a momentary drop in blood pressure and blood returning to the heart and other organs. If blood pressure is not rapidly restored, the heart may not be able to eject enough blood to the brain and fainting can occur.
5. Fainting is not a major concern, but should still be safe-guarded against. The body is very adaptive and this is rarely a problem in the mature

athlete who has trained his body under breath-holding conditions. However, the increased pressure and stress placed on the heart during repeated breath holding can cause the heart to enlarge which can lead to potential blood flow problems and electrical disturbances as the athlete ages.

A healthy athlete's vascular system should not be over-burdened by such breath-holding techniques, but to minimize risk, remember to breathe normally whenever possible and if you must hold your breath for stability, release the breath during the last one-half to two-thirds of the exercise movement.

Running and Conditioning

Running and conditioning in this training plan refer to anaerobic and aerobic training through wind sprints, combination running (sprint and jog), or other running workouts that place a constructive demand on the cardiorespiratory system.

Perform cardiorespiratory conditioning three to four times per week. You can do your cardiorespiratory training before or after the resistance-training portion of the workout. If you perform it first, however, note that fatigue induced through cardiorespiratory training will adversely affect weight-room performance. The reverse holds true as well. Arrange ample recovery time between these types of workouts to ensure the effectiveness of both. For example, schedule your running in the morning and your resistance training in the afternoon to effect full recovery.

Running and conditioning workouts consist of a 10-minute flexibility and warm-up session followed by the scheduled workout. Flexibility training (see chapter 7) consists of a warm-up stretch and a combination of form runs, step slides, and low-level plyometrics. The approximate total workout time appears in the conditioning workout plan, but you can extend or reduce it depending on how you are feeling and performing.

For each running and conditioning workout, I've provided interval times for three groups: the wide receivers, defensive backs, and running backs (WR, DB, RB); the linebackers, tight ends, and fullbacks (LB, TE, FB); and the offensive and defensive linemen (LINE). Perform all repetitions of the exercise within the times noted for your position. Dividing the times between groups in this way makes the workout more personalized while still accommodating a large group. Even though the time may be easy on the first couple of sprints or runs, these first bouts can serve as moderately intense warm-ups leading to the more exhausting bouts near the end of the workout as fatigue sets in. Chapter 9 details the benefits and specific drills included in the phase 1 through phase 6 workouts.

Skill Training

Skill training is also an essential part of the athlete's workout plan. Foot speed, agility, balance, and position-specific skills are what differentiate the football athlete from other athletes. The resistance-training program produces explosive, powerful, and quick muscular ability. Raw muscular ability, however, is useless in a controlled athletic environment. Skill training refines and shapes the athlete with raw muscular ability into a football player.

Skill training is blended into the workout plan on various days during the week. You work on some skills "on your own," others with teammates "by position." These drills act as bridges that connect the newly acquired weight-room strength to a more functional and athletic activity, thus focusing the strength and conditioning exercises on the common goal of producing highly conditioned football players, not simply highly conditioned individuals. Your position coach may also suggest some drills to assist you with your position. I've suggested days and times to include these drills in your workout and to coordinate positions together for combined workouts. You'll see the details about how to perform the on-your-own drills in chapters 10 and 11.

Athlete Evaluation

Evaluate your performance each week to see if you made progress in physical conditioning within the microcycle:

1. Did you achieve all the assigned repetitions for a particular exercise?
2. Was it easy or hard to complete all the repetitions assigned?

If you achieved all the work, then it's time to increase your workout resistance for the next microcycle. At the end of each week note any decrease or increase in the workout resistance or running times. A decrease in performance in one exercise, or during one day of training, should not necessarily raise a warning flag; any number of variables may have caused it. If an entire week of exercises shows declines, however, then you need to assess why. It could be anything from a common cold coming on to a fatigue or overtraining problem. If warranted, you may require three days off from the training routine for constructive recovery.

At the end of each week, you may need to make subtle adjustments to the resistance exercises. Reducing or increasing the resistance can promote gradual increases along the entire course of the training plan. If you don't keep track of the weight you lift, you may prematurely burn out from having worked too heavy, too soon, thus dowsing any hopes of reaching your full potential. Working out with too light a load, on the other hand, will insufficiently challenge your muscles, reducing the effectiveness of the workout. In evaluating the microcycle this way, you maintain a personal, interactive approach to the training. By having an interactive training plan, you can avoid overestimating or underestimating your potential. This, in turn, will produce the best results by the time the in-season portion of the exercise plan arrives.

I recommend that coaches perform tests at the end of phases 2 and 5 as a means of determining the effectiveness of the program. Phase 2 test results can be provided to the head coach if desired. Test results taken during this time of the year, however, should not be considered too strongly. If coaches wish to compare scores from phase 2 testing, it is best to compare scores of an athlete to his previous phase 2 test scores. If your team has the good fortune to play in a game beyond the regular season, you will delay starting your postseason program while you continue working out under the in-season format until the bowl or championship game. This delay will shorten the postseason routine and minimize the significance of test results in the first test period.

Phase 5 ends with a test evaluation just before the in-season period, about the second week of August. These tests measure more accurately the level of the athlete's improvement and the effectiveness of the workout program. The head coach may be interested in these test results because they are the primary indicator of increased performance, especially when compared with previous phase 5 test scores.

Coaches can evaluate improvements during any phase of the training year using observational analysis rather than a physical test. Before analyzing the workout or the athletes, however, remember that too much analysis or testing can reduce performance. Too much pressure placed on the athlete can promote failure rather than success. By benignly observing an athlete's workout log from one month to the next, coaches can determine if resistance exercises and running times are improving. Of course, the ultimate test is whether the team wins ball games.

Coaches perform testing to determine the effectiveness of the training program in producing power and endurance. The tests consist of lifts to determine the gain in raw power and functional activities to determine how effectively the athlete has made the transition from resistance exercises to athletic movements.

Evaluation Test

Resistance exercises, used to determine raw power
- Bench press—performed for 1 RM
- Bench press—225 pounds performed for maximal repetitions
- Squat—performed for 1 RM (Leg press can be substituted for squat. The athlete chooses a weight and performs as many repetitions as possible.)

Speed and quickness
- 40-yard sprint
- 20-yard shuttle

Athletic power
- In-place vertical jump
- Long jump

Conditioning
- 8 × 200-yard sprints with the following goal times: 32 seconds for wide receivers (WR), defensive backs (DB), and running backs (RB); 34 seconds for linebackers (LB), tight ends(TE), and full backs (FB); and 36 seconds for linemen (Line). Each athlete must complete all

eight sprints in less than the allotted time or perform extra work until he makes the time.

Keeping a Training Log

This book provides you with a foundation for a training log, the 52-week program itself. Record your daily workout weights and times and jot down notes about how you feel during the workout session.

Consistency is crucial to successful training. Working out regularly in a planned fashion creates the foundation for continuous improvement. Keeping records will serve as a map—reminding you what you accomplished in previous workouts and keeping you on track with your goals. Keeping this information in a training log helps you and your coach examine the training program to determine if you are achieving the desired results.

The training log shown in table I.2 records the following items:

1. Date of workout
2. Order in which you performed the exercises
3. How much weight or resistance you used
4. Number of sets and repetitions of each exercise
5. How much time you took for rest between sets of an exercise
6. How you felt during the workout
7. Whether you performed conditioning before or after weight training
8. Any other item that seems pertinent to your success

© Anthony Neste

Table I.2 Sample Workout Log

Name _____

Date: _____   Date: _____

Exercise	Weight reps	Weight reps	Weight reps	Weight reps	Rest	Exercise	Weight reps	Weight reps	Weight reps	Weight reps	Rest

Comments:

Conditioning:

CHAPTER 1

PHASE 1:
Postseason Workouts

GOAL *To develop basic strength by frequently experiencing momentary muscular fatigue during the first three weeks of the workout.*

Phase 1, the postseason phase, begins after your last football game of the season and lasts for six weeks. Regrettably, if you're doing this particular phase in November, you're sitting at home rather than playing in a January bowl game or a December championship game. This is the time, however, to lay the foundation for the next season. If an extra game is your team's reward, you could just continue phase 6 (the in-season phase) for two to three weeks after the regular season. You would then start training with the first two to three weeks of the postseason phase immediately after the bowl or championship game.

If you are playing a bowl or championship game in December or January, you could also consider starting phase 1 after the regular season for two to three weeks. Scale back practice immediately following the season, allowing more time for resistance training and conditioning. Beginning phase 1 at this time would help you build muscle size through the hypertrophy training scheduled early in the phase. After bowl practice begins, resume an in-season workout format (see chapter 6) to conserve your energy for the game. After the bowl you can more easily begin phase 2 training, without having to move too quickly into the heavy-set schemes.

Weeks 1 through 3 of this phase are conducted as a team, on campus. Week 4 allows an off week for the holiday break, and weeks 5 and 6 include take-home workouts. The first three weeks of this phase are intense. You will become tired and sore, so use precaution to avoid injury.

Resistance Training

The purpose of resistance training during this phase is to create a muscular base (muscle hypertrophy). Following this phase, a gradual increase in intensity continues toward a peak in power output some weeks ahead. If you consider the periodization model, this phase is the hypertrophy stage and the beginning of the basic strength stage.

Types of Exercises

The exercises during phase 1 consist of core lifts and supporting and assisting exercises. You will use the core lifts throughout the macrocycle to maintain or build a power base. The purpose of the supporting and assisting exercises in this phase is to place higher levels of stress on individual muscles. This, in turn, promotes greater potential for hypertrophy in those muscles. By increasing muscle size, you achieve more joint stability. Thus, as the resistance increases in the latter stages of the training year, there is less potential for injury.

You perform many exercises manually (for example, the manual side raise) by having a coach or training partner apply resistance to your arms or legs, using the force or strength of his arms or body. If you perform these exercises correctly, they are strenuous and thus excellent for inducing extreme fatigue or momentary muscular failure (MMF). You perform other exercises using a cable device, which reduces worry about getting the weight up and allows you to focus on using the designated muscle group to perform the work.

The exercise sequence addresses the larger muscle groups first in the workout and then the smaller muscle groups. Unique to this phase is the use of preexhaustion sets and supersets to produce greater muscular fatigue.

Rest, Volume, and Special Sets

The amount of rest between the sets of phase 1 exercises is relatively low—1:00 between sets of basic (b) exercises and 0:45 between sets of supporting (s) exercises. The reduced amount of rest ensures that you will efficiently fatigue the muscle. The amount of rest between exercises is 1:30.

The number of sets and repetitions in phase 1 workouts is high. This high volume is another method of increasing overall fatigue during the workout.

I've mentioned supersets and manual exercises as a unique aspect of this phase. Also I've included decreasing resistance sets as a means of increasing the fatigue factor. Notice that the bench press, two-arm dumbbell press, and EZ bar curl begin with a warm-up set of 10×60 percent and then continue to a set of 8×80 percent, 8×75 percent, and finally down to a set of 8×70 percent. These weight percentages may appear low, but you can induce fatigue by maintaining a constant movement tempo.

Repetition Style and Speed

During this phase the style of repetition is strict. Perform each repetition deliberately and slowly. Imagine yourself squeezing the muscle. When doing the bench press, for example, imagine a coin sitting on the center of your chest (don't put the coin there, however; injury could occur). Then imagine each pectoral muscle squeezing together in the center and folding the coin in half. You can apply this imagery technique to any area of the body. Another method of accomplishing proper flexion of the muscle in this phase is to push the hands isometrically toward one another during a pushing exercise and pull the hands isometrically apart during a pulling exercise. (The hands will not actually move on the apparatus or bar; they are simply squeezing.) Be sure to breathe correctly while using these techniques (see part I, page 7).

Keep the tempo or cadence of the repetitions constant during this phase of the exercise plan. You should not interrupt the repetition at the bottom or top of the movement. During this phase the only reason to stop the movement is to flex the muscle more intensely.

Running and Conditioning

The first four weeks of this phase include no planned running or conditioning. Even so, you should stay active on your own, perhaps participating in activities like basketball, volleyball, tennis, or swimming. These activities serve as an active rest period away from football and require slightly different muscle motor patterns. The development of these motor patterns can provide a stronger muscle motor unit base. At the same time, participation in these sports doesn't involve the mental stress of having to reach a certain level as you would if training for football. In this way, you stay physically active but perceive the activity to be less stressful. During weeks 5 and 6, most athletes are off from school for the holiday break; I've planned a mild distance run as well as an easy interval run for each week. This scheduled running helps reinitiate you to more controlled activity.

Phase 1 ■ Week 1

Resistance training

MONDAY

Exercise		Repetitions × % 1 RM			
Bench press	b	10 × 60	8 × 80	8 × 75	8 × 70
Incline dumbbell fly (superset)	s	12 × 70	12 × 70	12 × 70	
Incline dumbbell press (superset)	s	8 × 45	8 × 45	8 × 45	
Military press	b	8 × 75	8 × 75	8 × 75	
Side dumbbell raise	s	12 × 55	12 × 55	12 × 55	
Preacher curl (push-pull)	s	8 × 75	8 × 75	10 × 70	
Kickback (push-pull)	s	10 × 70	10 × 70	10 × 70	
Cylinder circuit #1					

Resistance training

TUESDAY

Exercise		Repetitions × % 1 RM			
High lat front	s	8 × 75	8 × 75	8 × 75	
Close low lat	s	8 × 75	8 × 75	8 × 75	
Manual rear deltoid	s	12 reps	12 reps	12 reps	
EZ-bar pullover	s	12 × 60	12 × 60	12 × 60	
Squat	b	12 × 55	12 × 55	12 × 55	
Two-leg extension	s	15 × 60	15 × 60	15 × 60	
Two-leg curl	s	10 × 70	10 × 70	10 × 70	10 × 70
Nautilus multicalf		100 reps			

Rest: b (basic)—1:00 between sets
        s (supporting)—0:45 between sets
        Take 1:30 between exercises

Resistance training					
Exercise		*Repetitions × % 1 RM*			
Flat dumbbell press	s	8 × 75	8 × 75	8 × 75	
Incline bench press	b	8 × 75	8 × 75	8 × 75	
Dip	b	max reps	max reps	max reps	
Manual side raise (superset)	s	10 reps	10 reps		
Manual front deltoid (superset)	s	10 reps	10 reps		
Manual rear deltoid (superset)	s	10 reps	10 reps		
Two-arm dumbbell press	s	10 × 60	8 × 80	8 × 75	8 × 70
EZ-bar curl (push-pull)	b	10 × 60	8 × 80	8 × 75	8 × 70
Triceps push-down (push-pull)	s	10 × 55	10 × 55	10 × 55	
Cylinder circuit #1					

THURSDAY

Resistance training				
Exercise		*Repetitions × % 1 RM*		
High lat front	s	8 × 75	8 × 75	8 × 75
Cable shrug (superset)	s	15 × 55	15 × 55	15 × 55
Cable upright row (superset)	s	8 × 75	8 × 75	8 × 75
Leg press	s	10 × 55	10 × 55	10 × 55
Lunge—3 pumps	s	6 reps	6 reps	6 reps
Ab-ad	s	15 × 60	15 × 60	
Standing calf raise		100 reps		

FRIDAY

December

Resistance training				
Exercise		**Repetitions × % 1 RM**		
Bench press	b	10 × 60 8 × 80 8 × 75 8 × 70		
Incline dumbbell fly (superset)	s	12 × 70 12 × 70 12 × 70		
Incline dumbbell press (superset)	s	8 × 45 8 × 45 8 × 45		
Military press	b	8 × 75 8 × 75 8 × 75		
Side dumbbell raise	s	12 × 55 12 × 55 12 × 55		
Preacher curl (push-pull)	s	8 × 75 8 × 75 10 × 70		
Kickback (push-pull)	s	10 × 70 10 × 70 10 × 70		
Cylinder circuit #1				

MONDAY

Resistance training				
Exercise		**Repetitions × % 1 RM**		
High lat front	s	8 × 75 8 × 75 8 × 75		
Close low lat	s	8 × 75 8 × 75 8 × 75		
Manual rear deltoid	s	12 reps 12 reps 12 reps		
EZ-bar pullover	s	12 × 60 12 × 60 12 × 60		
Squat	b	12 × 55 12 × 55 12 × 55		
Two-leg extension	s	15 × 60 15 × 60 15 × 60		
Two-leg curl	s	10 × 70 10 × 70 10 × 70 10 × 70		
Nautilus multicalf		100 reps		

TUESDAY

Rest: b (basic)—1:00 between sets
s (supporting)—0:45 between sets
Take 1:30 between exercises

Resistance training

Exercise		Repetitions × % 1 RM			
Flat dumbbell press	s	8 × 75	8 × 75	8 × 75	
Incline bench press	b	8 × 75	8 × 75	8 × 75	
Dip	b	max reps	max reps	max reps	
Manual side raise (superset)	s	10 reps	10 reps		
Manual front deltoid (superset)	s	10 reps	10 reps		
Manual rear deltoid (superset)	s	10 reps	10 reps		
Two-arm dumbbell press	s	10 × 60	8 × 80	8 × 75	8 × 70
EZ-bar curl (push-pull)	b	10 × 60	8 × 80	8 × 75	8 × 70
Triceps push-down (push-pull)	s	10 × 55	10 × 55	10 × 55	
Cylinder circuit #1					

THURSDAY

Resistance training

Exercise		Repetitions × % 1 RM		
High lat front	s	8 × 75	8 × 75	8 × 75
Cable shrug (superset)	s	15 × 55	15 × 55	15 × 55
Cable upright row (superset)	s	8 × 75	8 × 75	8 × 75
Leg press	s	10 × 55	10 × 55	10 × 55
Lunge—3 pumps	s	6 reps	6 reps	6 reps
Ab-ad	s	15 × 60	15 × 60	
Standing calf raise	s	100 reps		

FRIDAY

December

Resistance training

Exercise		Repetitions × % 1 RM			
MONDAY Bench press	b	10 × 60	8 × 80	8 × 75	8 × 70
Incline dumbbell fly (superset)	s	12 × 70	12 × 70	12 × 70	
Incline dumbbell press (superset)	s	8 × 45	8 × 45	8 × 45	
Military press	b	8 × 75	8 × 75	8 × 75	
Side dumbbell raise	s	12 × 55	12 × 55	12 × 55	
Preacher curl (push-pull)	s	8 × 75	8 × 75	10 × 70	
Kickback (push-pull)	s	10 × 70	10 × 70	10 × 70	
Cylinder circuit #1					

Resistance training

Exercise					
TUESDAY High lat front	s	8 × 75	8 × 75	8 × 75	
Close low lat	s	8 × 75	8 × 75	8 × 75	
Manual rear deltoid	s	12 reps	12 reps	12 reps	
EZ-bar pullover	s	12 × 60	12 × 60	12 × 60	
Squat	b	12 × 55	12 × 55	12 × 55	
Two-leg extension	s	15 × 60	15 × 60	15 × 60	
Two-leg curl	s	10 × 70	10 × 70	10 × 70	10 × 70
Nautilus multicalf		100 reps			

Resistance training

Exercise					
THURSDAY Flat dumbbell press	s	8 × 75	8 × 75	8 × 75	
Incline bench press	b	8 × 75	8 × 75	8 × 75	
Dip	b	max reps	max reps	max reps	
Manual side raise (superset)	s	10 reps	10 reps		
Manual front deltoid (superset)	s	10 reps	10 reps		
Manual rear deltoid (superset)	s	10 reps	10 reps		
Two-arm dumbbell press	s	10 × 60	8 × 80	8 × 75	8 × 70
EZ-bar curl (push-pull)	b	10 × 60	8 × 80	8 × 75	8 × 70
Triceps push-down (push-pull)	s	10 × 55	10 × 55	10 × 55	
Cylinder circuit #1					

Resistance training

Exercise					
FRIDAY High lat front	s	8 × 75	8 × 75	8 × 75	
Cable shrug (superset)	s	15 × 55	15 × 55	15 × 55	
Cable upright row (superset)	s	8 × 75	8 × 75	8 × 75	
Leg press	s	10 × 55	10 × 55	10 × 55	
Lunge—3 pumps	s	6 reps	6 reps	6 reps	
Ab-ad	s	15 × 60	15 × 60		
Standing calf raise		100 reps			

Rest: b (basic)—1:00 between sets   s (supporting)—0:45 between sets   Take 1:30 between exercises

Week off—winter holiday

December

Resistance training

Exercise		Repetitions × % 1 RM			
Bench press	b	8 × 60	8 × 65	8 × 70	8 × 75
Incline dumbbell press	b	8 × 75	8 × 75	8 × 75	8 × 75
Incline dumbbell fly	s	10 × 70	10 × 70	10 × 70	10 × 70
Military press	b	8 × 65	8 × 70	8 × 75	
Side dumbbell raise	s	10 × 55	10 × 55	10 × 55	
Straight-bar curl	b	8 × 60	8 × 65	8 × 75	
Preacher curl (cable)	s	8 × 60	8 × 65	8 × 75	
Triceps push-down	s	10 × 70	10 × 70	10 × 70	
Standing calf raise	s	50 × 30	50 × 30		

MONDAY

Conditioning training

		WR, DB, RB	LB, TE, FB	Line
Flexibility and warm-up: 10:00				
Total workout time: 37:00	Mile	8:30	9:00	11:00
Intervals	Rest	5:00	5:00	5:00
	Mile	8:30	9:00	11:00

Resistance training

Exercise		Repetitions × % 1 RM			
High lat front	s	8 × 65	8 × 70	8 × 75	
Close low lat	s	8 × 65	8 × 70	8 × 75	
Dumbbell shrug	s	15 × 60	15 × 60	15 × 60	
Free-weight upright row	b	8 × 65	8 × 70	8 × 75	
Front dumbbell raise	s	15 × 60	15 × 60	15 × 60	
Squat	b	8 × 55	8 × 60	8 × 65	8 × 70
Two-leg extension	s	12 × 65	12 × 65	12 × 65	12 × 65
Two-leg curl	s	10 × 70	10 × 70	10 × 70	10 × 70
Cylinder circuit #1					

TUESDAY

Rest: b (basic)—1:00 between sets
s (supporting)—0:45 between sets
Take 1:30 between exercises

Resistance training

Exercise		Repetitions × % 1 RM			
Flat dumbbell press	s	8 × 75	8 × 75	8 × 75	8 × 75
Incline bench press	b	8 × 75	8 × 75	8 × 75	8 × 75
Dip	b	max reps	max reps	max reps	
Behind neck press	s	8 × 65	8 × 70	8 × 75	
Two-arm dumbbell press	s	8 × 70	8 × 70	8 × 70	
Side dumbbell raise	s	10 × 55	10 × 55	10 × 55	
Alternating dumbbell curl	b	8 × 70	8 × 70	8 × 70	
Kickback	s	10 × 70	10 × 70	10 × 70	
Triceps push-down	s	8 × 75	8 × 75	8 × 75	
Standing calf raise	s	50 × 30	50 × 30		

Conditioning training

Flexibility and warm-up: 10:00
Workout time: 36:00
Rest between sets: 1:10, 1:12, 1:14
Intervals

	WR, DB, RB	LB, TE, FB	Line
1 × 880	3:30	3:40	4:00
Rest	4:00	4:00	4:00
2 × 440	1:30	1:35	1:45
Rest	3:00	3:00	3:00
2 × 220	:30	:32	:34

THURSDAY

Resistance training

Exercise		Repetitions × % 1 RM			
Close-grip lat	b	8 × 60	8 × 65	8 × 70	8 × 75
High lat front	s	8 × 60	8 × 65	8 × 70	8 × 75
Bent dumbbell raise	s	15 × 60	15 × 60	15 × 60	
Leg press	s	8 × 55	8 × 60	8 × 65	8 × 70
Lunge—3 pumps	s	6 × 70	6 × 70	6 × 70	
One stiff leg dead	s	10 reps	10 reps	10 reps	
Cylinder circuit #2					

FRIDAY

January

Resistance training

Exercise		Repetitions × % 1 RM			
Bench press	b	8 × 60	8 × 65	8 × 70	8 × 75
Incline dumbbell press	b	8 × 75	8 × 75	8 × 75	8 × 75
Incline dumbbell fly	s	10 × 70	10 × 70	10 × 70	10 × 70
Military press	b	8 × 65	8 × 70	8 × 75	
Side dumbbell raise	s	10 × 55	10 × 55	10 × 55	
Straight-bar curl	b	8 × 60	8 × 65	8 × 75	
Preacher curl (cable)	s	8 × 60	8 × 65	8 × 75	
Triceps push-down	s	10 × 70	10 × 70	10 × 70	
Standing calf raise	s	50 × 30	50 × 30		

MONDAY

Conditioning training

		WR, DB, RB	LB, TE, FB	Line
Flexibility and warm-up: 10:00				
Total workout time: 30:30	Mile	7:30	8:00	10:30
Intervals	Rest	4:00	4:00	4:00
	2 × 880	3:30	3:40	4:00

Resistance training

Exercise		Repetitions × % 1 RM			
High lat front	s	8 × 65	8 × 70	8 × 75	
Close low lat	s	8 × 65	8 × 70	8 × 75	
Dumbbell shrug	s	15 × 60	15 × 60	15 × 60	
Free-weight upright row	b	8 × 65	8 × 70	8 × 75	
Front dumbbell raise	s	15 × 60	15 × 60	15 × 60	
Squat	b	8 × 55	8 × 60	8 × 65	8 × 70
Two-leg extension	s	12 × 65	12 × 65	12 × 65	12 × 65
Two-leg curl	s	10 × 70	10 × 70	10 × 70	10 × 70
Cylinder circuit #1					

TUESDAY

Rest: b (basic)—1:00 between sets
s (supporting)—0:45 between sets
Take 1:30 between exercises

Resistance training

Exercise		Repetitions × % 1 RM			
Flat dumbbell press	s	8 × 75	8 × 75	8 × 75	8 × 75
Incline bench press	b	8 × 75	8 × 75	8 × 75	8 × 75
Dip	b	max reps	max reps	max reps	
Behind neck press	s	8 × 65	8 × 70	8 × 75	
Two-arm dumbbell press	s	8 × 70	8 × 70	8 × 70	
Side dumbbell raise	s	10 × 55	10 × 55	10 × 55	
Alternating dumbbell curl	b	8 × 70	8 × 70	8 × 70	
Kickback	s	10 × 70	10 × 70	10 × 70	
Triceps push-down	s	8 × 75	8 × 75	8 × 75	
Standing calf raise	s	50 × 30	50 × 30		

THURSDAY

Conditioning training

	WR, DB, RB	LB, TE, FB	Line
Flexibility and warm-up: 10:00			
Workout time: 36:00			
Intervals			
2 × 440	1:15	1:20	1:30
Rest	2:50	2:50	2:50
3 × 220	:30	:32	:34
Rest	1:10	1:12	1:14
3 × 110	:13	:15	:17
Rest	2:00	2:00	2:00
3 × 110	:13	:15	:17

Resistance training

Exercise		Repetitions × % 1 RM			
Close-grip lat	b	8 × 60	8 × 65	8 × 70	8 × 75
High lat front	s	8 × 60	8 × 65	8 × 70	8 × 75
Bent dumbbell raise	s	15 × 60	15 × 60	15 × 60	
Leg press	s	8 × 55	8 × 60	8 × 65	8 × 70
Lunge—3 pumps	s	6 × 70	6 × 70	6 × 70	
One stiff leg dead	s	10 reps	10 reps	10 reps	
Cylinder circuit #2					

FRIDAY

CHAPTER 2

PHASE 2:
Winter Workouts

GOAL *To increase nerve activity and excitability by gradually increasing the intensity of the resistance on each core and supercore exercise. The result should be optimal power and explosive potential for football.*

Phase 2 begins during the second week of January (week 7) and continues through the third week in March (week 16), when spring ball practice begins. The progression of this phase gradually carries you from the hypertrophy stage of the periodization model toward a power stage. At the end of this 10-week phase, you perform tests to measure physical improvements. The battery of tests is similar to those administered by pro scouts during their scouting visits.

Resistance Training

The basic purpose of this phase is to increase gradually, over a period of weeks, your level of nerve activity and excitability. Muscle mass will continue to increase, but less from a fatigue-related response than from the load increases planned during the exercises.

During this phase, the progression toward power is subtle; the decrease in the number of repetitions moves from eight to six to five to four, and finally to a single repetition near test time. Some may argue that this approach provides less of a shock to the neuromuscular unit, thus resulting in less power potential. My athletes, however, have gained the best results performing with this stair-step descent in repetitions. I feel that the success of the program depends on close supervision by the strength coach. The strength coach must persuade athletes to avoid working to momentary muscular failure after the phase 1 period. The stress must increase gradually toward all-out intensity at week 16. If you progress too rapidly, then you will not perform well when test time arrives.

Types of Exercises

The exercises during this phase consist of core, supporting, and assisting exercises. The supporting exercises include more multijoint exercises (for example, flat dumbbell fly rather than flat dumbbell press) than in phase 1. This swings the emphasis from individual muscle fatigue desired in phase 1 to the promotion of intermuscular cooperation, in which several muscular groups work together to produce a powerful movement. You will use fewer cable and machine-resistance exercises. Also you make a progression toward using primarily free-weight resistance and more power-producing techniques. As is phase 1, you work the larger muscle groups first in the workout and the smaller muscle groups later. You will no longer do the supersets and decreasing-resistance sets.

Rest, Volume, and Special Sets

The amount of rest between the sets of an exercise increases as the phase progresses. As phase 2 begins, rest between sets is 1:00 for supporting (s) exercises and 1:30 for basic (b) exercises. By week 16 rest is 2:30 for (b) exercises. The increased rest as the phase progresses is an adjustment that compensates for the ever increasing load of the resistance during the workout. This added recovery between sets ensures that with each repetition you will efficiently excite the nerve pathways that activate the muscle. The amount of rest between exercises remains at 1:30.

The number of sets and repetitions in phase 2 workouts begins to decrease gradually over the 10-week period. This lowered volume is another method of heightening the overall level of nerve activity and excitability, which will result in greater power output.

This phase includes no special sets. I used some transitional set schemes on weeks 10 and 11. For example, increases such as 6 × 70 percent, 6 × 75 percent, 4 × 80 percent, 4 × 85 percent assist you in making the transition from straight sets of 6 repetitions to straight sets of 4 repetitions.

Repetition Style and Speed

During this phase the style of repetition is less strict. Perform each repetition intelligently. Use good form to avoid injury. By incorporating more speed into the movement, you can use greater resistance. By week 16, you should be pushing with everything you have to move the resistance while retaining good exercise form.

Execute the repetitions in the phase with a pausing tempo. You can perform some repetitions without pause; however, as the resistance begins to cause fatigue, pause for an instant in a locked-out position to recover for a moment. This helps ensure that each repetition is a powerful one.

Running and Conditioning

Conditioning during this phase is highly diversified and addresses many of your physiological needs. At the same time you must remember the physical requirements of football; don't try to put too much stuff in the workout. Time limitations may prevent you from doing so anyway. In the first weeks of this phase, weeks 7 through 10, the plan includes four running conditioning sessions per week with these emphases:

Monday—Interval sprint work (chapter 9)

Tuesday—Active recovery with short distance or longer intervals (chapter 9)

Thursday—Speed work (practical strength for sprint form and starts; chapters 10 and 11)

Friday—Combination work (shuttles, fartleks, Indian runs, and so on; chapter 9)

By week 10 the workouts incorporate more agility work, eventually replacing interval sprints entirely with agility drills. You can perform these drills at high speeds with little rest, thus producing good cardiorespiratory benefits. The workload is reduced from four days per week to three.

Monday—Agility drills (chapter 11)

Tuesday—Game simulation sprints (chapter 10)

Thursday—Speed work (practical strength for sprint form and starts; chapter 10)

This reduction in days per week boosts recovery from workout to workout and helps to enhance power production that coincides with work performed in the weight room. You complete the conditioning phase by week 13. On week 14, Monday and Tuesday are void of conditioning to allow you to regain your legs before sprint testing on Thursday of that week.

Note that the academic spring break usually occurs during the second week in March. This break allows added recovery before testing.

Phase 2 ▪ Week 7

MONDAY

Resistance training

Exercise		Repetitions × % 1 RM			
Bench press	b	6 × 65	6 × 70	6 × 75	6 × 80
Incline dumbbell press	b	8 × 65	8 × 70	8 × 75	
Close-grip bench	b	6 × 65	6 × 75	6 × 80	
Military press	s	6 × 65	6 × 70	6 × 75	6 × 80
Side dumbbell raise	s	8 × 60	8 × 60	8 × 60	
Straight-bar curl	b	8 × 65	8 × 70	8 × 75	
Preacher curl (cable)	s	8 × 60	8 × 65	8 × 75	
Triceps push-down	s	8 × 60	8 × 65	8 × 75	
Standing calf raise	s	30 × 40	30 × 40		

Skill training

On your own: Balance drill #1

Conditioning training

Flexibility and warm-up: 10:00
Total workout time: 37:00
Intervals: Perform on a track.

	WR, DB, RB	LB, TE, FB	Line
1 × 440	1:15	1:20	1:30
2 × 220	:30	:32	:34
Rest between reps	1:10	1:12	1:14
8 × 110	:13	:15	:17
Rest break	1:30 after every 4 sprints		
4 × 55	:08	:08	:09
Rest between reps	:20	:20	:20

TUESDAY

Resistance training

Exercise		Repetitions × % 1 RM			
High lat rear	s	8 × 65	8 × 70	8 × 75	
Close low lat	s	8 × 65	8 × 70	8 × 75	
Dumbbell shrug	s	12 × 65	12 × 65		
Free-weight upright row	b	8 × 70	8 × 75	8 × 80	
Squat	b	6 × 65	6 × 70	6 × 80	6 × 85
One-leg extension	s	10 × 70	10 × 70	10 × 70	
One stiff leg dead	s	10 reps	10 reps	10 reps	
Cylinder circuit #2					
Manual neck					

Skill training

Work on these skills according to your position.

DB: Pass coverage against WRs
WR: Pass routes against DBs
QB: Passing game
LB: Pass drops and covering flats
OL: Pass protection against a DL
DL: Pass rush against an OL
RB: Work with #2 QB on pass receiving
KICK: Kick
PUNT: Punt

Conditioning training

Flexibility and warm-up: 10:00
Total workout time: 33:00
Intervals

	WR, DB, RB	LB, TE, FB	Line
3 × 880	2:20	2:30	2:40
Rest between reps	5:00	5:00	5:00

Rest: b (basic)—1:30 between sets   s (supporting)—1:00 between sets   Take 1:30 between exercises

THURSDAY

Resistance training

Exercise		Repetitions × % 1 RM			
Flat dumbbell press	s	8 × 60	8 × 65	8 × 75	
Incline bench press	b	6 × 80	6 × 80	6 × 80	6 × 80
Dip	b	max reps	max reps	max reps	
Behind neck press	s	6 × 65	6 × 70	6 × 75	6 × 80
Two-arm dumbbell press	s	8 × 65	8 × 70	8 × 75	
Alternating dumbbell curl	b	8 × 65	8 × 70	8 × 75	
Dumbbell French press	b	8 × 75	8 × 75	8 × 75	
Standing calf raise	s	30 × 40	30 × 40		
Manual neck					

Skill training

On your own: Foot-speed drill #1

Conditioning training

Flexibility and warm-up: 10:00
Total workout time: 35:00
Linear speed work

Uphill sprints; run to the top and jog back, three groups running one after the other.

2 × 40 yd strides
6 × 40 yd sprints
4 × 40 yd alternate leg bounding (see chapter 10)

Flat surface work

8 × 40 yd; run straight line; 4 at 75% speed, 4 at full speed.

FRIDAY

Resistance training

Exercise		Repetitions × % 1 RM			
Close-grip lat	b	8 × 65	8 × 70	8 × 75	
High lat front	s	8 × 65	8 × 70	8 × 75	
Bent dumbbell raise	s	12 × 60	12 × 60	12 × 60	
Straight dumbbell pullover	s	10 × 70	10 × 70	10 × 70	
Leg press	s	6 × 65	6 × 70	6 × 80	6 × 85
Two-leg curl	s	10 × 70	10 × 70	10 × 70	10 × 70
Ab-ad	s	15 × 60	15 × 60		
Cylinder circuit #3					
Manual neck					

Skill training

On your own: Movement course #1

Conditioning training

Flexibility and warm-up: 10:00
Total workout time: 23:00
Shuttle

	WR, DB, RB	LB, TE, FB	Line
1 × 1,000 yd shuttle	3:30	3:45	4:00

January

MONDAY

Resistance training					Skill training
Exercise		**Repetitions × % 1 RM**			On your own: Balance drill #2
Bench press	b	6 × 65 6 × 70 6 × 75 6 × 80			
Incline dumbbell press	b	8 × 65 8 × 70 8 × 75			
Close-grip bench	b	6 × 65 6 × 75 6 × 80			
Military press	b	6 × 65 6 × 70 6 × 75 6 × 80			
Side dumbbell raise	s	8 × 60 8 × 60 8 × 60			
Straight-bar curl	b	8 × 65 8 × 70 8 × 75			
Preacher curl (cable)	s	8 × 60 8 × 65 8 × 75			
Triceps push-down	s	8 × 60 8 × 65 8 × 75			
Standing calf raise	s	30 × 40 30 × 40			
Manual neck					

Conditioning training

		WR, DB, RB	LB, TE, FB	Line
Flexibility and warm-up: 10:00				
Total workout time: 37:00	1 × 440	1:15	1:20	1:30
Intervals: Perform on a track.	1 × 220	:30	:32	:34
	Rest between reps	1:10	1:12	1:14
	8 × 110	:13	:15	:17
	Rest break	1:30 after every 4 sprints		
	6 × 55	:08	:08	:09
	Rest between reps	:20	:20	:20

TUESDAY

Resistance training					Skill training
Exercise		**Repetitions × % 1 RM**			Work on these skills according to your position.
High lat rear	s	8 × 65 8 × 70 8 × 75			**DB:** Pass catching (JUGS machine)
Close low lat	s	8 × 65 8 × 70 8 × 75			**WR:** Blocks using a sled
Dumbbell shrug	s	12 × 65 12 × 65			**QB:** Play dodge ball
Free-weight upright row	b	8 × 70 8 × 75 8 × 80			**LB:** Pass catching (JUGS machine)
Squat	b	6 × 65 6 × 70 6 × 80 6 × 85			**OL:** Sled work
Two-leg extension	s	10 × 70 10 × 70 10 × 70 10 × 70			**DL:** RIPS and SWIMS (tackle dummy)
One stiff leg dead	s	10 reps 10 reps 10 reps			**RB:** Play tag games
Cylinder circuit #2					**KICK:** Kick
Manual neck					**PUNT:** Play tag games, punt

Conditioning training

		WR, DB, RB	LB, TE, FB	Line
Flexibility and warm-up: 10:00				
Total workout time: 21:00	1 × 2,100 yd	8:00	8:30	9:00
Timed run				

Rest: b (basic)—1:30 between sets

s (supporting)—1:00 between sets

Take 1:30 between exercises

Resistance training		Repetitions × % 1 RM				Skill training
Exercise						On your own: Foot-speed drill #2
Flat dumbbell press	s	8 × 60	8 × 65	8 × 75		
Incline bench press	b	6 × 80	6 × 80	6 × 80	6 × 80	
Dip	b	max reps	max reps	max reps		
Behind neck press	s	6 × 65	6 × 70	6 × 75	6 × 80	
Two-arm dumbbell press	s	8 × 65	8 × 70	8 × 75		
Alternating dumbbell curl	b	8 × 65	8 × 70	8 × 75		
Dumbbell French press	b	8 × 75	8 × 75	8 × 75		
Standing calf raise	s	30 × 40	30 × 40			
Manual neck						

THURSDAY

Conditioning training

Flexibility and warm-up: 10:00
Total workout time: 36:00
Linear speedwork

Uphill sprints; run to the top and jog back, three groups running one after the other.

- 2 × 40 yd strides
- 6 × 40 yd sprints
- 4 × 40 yd standing triple jumps (chapter 10)

Flat surface work

- 4 × low hurdle run (each leg)
- 4 × low hurdle (two-step)
- 8 × 40 yd; run straight line; 4 at 75% speed, 4 at full speed.

Resistance training		Repetitions × % 1 RM				Skill training
Exercise						On your own: Movement course #2
Close-grip lat	b	8 × 65	8 × 70	8 × 75		
High lat front	s	8 × 65	8 × 70	8 × 75		
Bent dumbbell raise	s	12 × 60	12 × 60	12 × 60		
Straight dumbbell pullover	s	10 × 70	10 × 70	10 × 70		
Leg press	s	6 × 65	6 × 70	6 × 80	6 × 85	
Two-leg curl	s	10 × 70	10 × 70	10 × 70	10 × 70	
Ab-ad	s	15 × 60	15 × 60			
Cylinder circuit #3						
Manual neck						

FRIDAY

Conditioning training

Flexibility and warm-up: 10:00
Total workout time: 23:00
Shuttle

	WR, DB, RB	LB, TE, FB	Line
3 × long 300 yd shuttle	:58	1:02	1:04
Rest between reps	2:10	2:10	2:10

A shuttle is performed by running back and forth between yard lines on the football field (3 × 100 yd sprints = one 300 yd shuttle).

January

MONDAY

Resistance training					Skill training

Exercise		Repetitions × % 1 RM			
Bench press	b	6 × 70	6 × 75	4 × 80	4 × 85
Incline dumbbell press	b	8 × 65	8 × 70	8 × 75	
Close-grip bench	b	6 × 70	6 × 80	6 × 85	
Military press	b	6 × 70	6 × 75	6 × 80	6 × 85
Side dumbbell raise	s	8 × 60	8 × 60	8 × 60	
Straight-bar curl	b	8 × 65	8 × 75	8 × 80	
Dumbbell French press	b	6 × 80 ·	6 × 80	6 × 80	
Standing calf raise	s	25 × 45	25 × 45		
Manual neck					

Skill training: On your own: Balance drill #3

Conditioning training

Flexibility and warm-up: 10:00
Total workout time: 28:36
Intervals: Perform on football field.

	WR, DB, RB	LB, TE, FB	Line
2 × 200	:30	:32	:34
Rest between reps	1:10	1:10	1:12
8 × 100	:13	:15	:17
Rest break	1:00 after every 4 sprints		
10 × 50	All-out effort		
Rest break	2:00 after every 5 sprints		

TUESDAY

Resistance training					Skill training

Exercise		Repetitions × 1 RM			
One-arm dumbbell row	b	8 × 65	8 × 70	8 × 75	
High lat rear	s	8 × 65	8 × 70	8 × 75	
Power pull	b	8 × 60	8 × 65	8 × 75	
Squat	b	6 × 65	6 × 70	4 × 80	4 × 85
Leg press	s	8 × 75	8 × 75	8 × 75	8 × 75
One stiff leg dead	s	10 reps	10 reps	10 reps	
Cylinder circuit #3					
Manual neck					

Skill training: Work on these skills according to your position.
DB: Pass coverage against WRs
WR: Pass routes against DBs
QB: Passing game
LB: Agility over bags
OL: Play tag games
DL: Agility over bags
RB: Balance drill #4
KICK: Kick
PUNT: Balance drill #4, punt

Conditioning training

Flexibility and warm-up: 10:00
Total workout time: 36:00
Shuttle

	WR, DB, RB	LB, TE, FB	Line
2 × 1,000 yd shuttle	3:45	4:00	4:15
Rest between reps	8:00	8:00	8:00

Rest: b (basic)—1:45 between sets   s (supporting)—1:00 between sets   Take 1:30 between exercises

THURSDAY

Resistance training					Skill training
Exercise		**Repetitions × % 1 RM**			On your own: Foot-speed drill #3
Incline bench press	b	6 × 65 6 × 70 6 × 75 6 × 80			
Dip	b	max reps max reps max reps			
Behind neck press	s	6 × 70 6 × 75 4 × 80 4 × 85			
Alternating dumbbell press	s	6 × 65 6 × 75 6 × 80			
Alternating dumbbell curl	b	6 × 65 6 × 75 6 × 80			
Triceps push-down	s	8 × 65 8 × 70 8 × 75			
Standing calf raise	s	25 × 45 25 × 45			
Manual neck					

Conditioning training

Flexibility and warm-up: 10:00
Total workout time: 35:00
Strides and starts

4 × 60 yd strides
4 × 40 yd strides
6 × 20 yd starts
Ball-drop reaction drill × 6 drops each player (partners)

FRIDAY

Resistance training				Skill training
Exercise		**Repetitions × % 1 RM**		On your own: Movement course #3
Close-grip lat	b	8 × 65 8 × 70 8 × 75		
High lat front	s	8 × 65 8 × 70 8 × 75		
Dead lift	b	8 × 60 8 × 65 8 × 75		
Free-weight upright row	b	6 × 70 6 × 80 6 × 85		
One-leg press	s	6 × 65 6 × 70 4 × 80 4 × 85		
Two-leg curl	s	10 × 70 10 × 70 10 × 70 10 × 70		
Side lunge	s	12 reps 12 reps		
Cylinder circuit #3				
Manual neck				

Conditioning training

Flexibility and warm-up: 10:00
Total workout time: 25:00
Shuttle

	WR, DB, RB	**LB, TE, FB**	**Line**
2 × short 300 yd shuttle	:58	1:02	1:05
Rest between reps	2:00	2:00	2:00
1 × short 150 yd shuttle	:58	1:02	1:05

January

Resistance training						Skill training
MONDAY						On your own: Balance drill #1

Exercise		*Repetitions × % 1 RM*			
Bench press	b	6 × 70	6 × 75	4 × 80	4 × 85
Incline dumbbell press	b	8 × 65	8 × 70	8 × 75	
Military press	b	6 × 70	6 × 75	6 × 80	6 × 85
Side dumbbell raise	s	8 × 65	8 × 65	8 × 65	
Straight-bar curl	b	8 × 65	8 × 75	8 × 80	
Dumbbell French press	b	6 × 80	6 × 80	6 × 80	
Standing calf raise	s	25 × 45	25 × 45		
Manual neck					

Conditioning training

Flexibility and warm-up: 10:00
Total workout time: 38:00

Four-station agility drill: Run to each station listed at right, break down, and line up (5:00 at each station; see chapter 11 for full diagrams of each station).

T drill   Snake   S drill   Bags

8 × 60 all-out effort; rest 1:00 after every 4 sprints

Resistance training						Skill training
TUESDAY						Work on these skills according to your position.

Exercise		*Repetitions × 1 RM*			
One-arm dumbbell row	b	8 × 65	8 × 70	8 × 75	
High lat rear	s	8 × 65	8 × 70	8 × 75	
Power pull	b	8 × 60	8 × 65	8 × 75	
Squat	b	6 × 65	6 × 70	4 × 80	4 × 85
One-leg press	s	8 × 75	8 × 75	8 × 75	8 × 75
One stiff leg dead	s	10 reps	10 reps	10 reps	
Cylinder circuit #3					
Manual neck					

Skill training (TUESDAY):
Work on these skills according to your position.
DB: Play tag games
WR: Balance drill #4
QB: Play tag games
LB: Play dodge ball
OL: Pass protection against a DL
DL: Pass rush against an OL
RB: Block practice using a sled
KICK: Kick
PUNT: Pass football, punt

Conditioning training

Flexibility and warm-up: 10:00
Total workout time: 35:00

Game simulation sprints: 1st quarter (see chapter 9)

Rest: b (basic)—1:45 between sets   s (supporting)—1:00 between sets   Take 1:30 between exercises

THURSDAY

Resistance training					Skill training
Exercise		**Repetitions × % 1 RM**			On your own: Foot-speed drill #1
Incline bench press	b	6 × 65 6 × 70	6 × 75	6 × 80	
Dip	b	max reps max reps	max reps		
Behind neck press	s	6 × 70 6 × 75	4 × 80	4 × 85	
Alternating dumbbell press	s	6 × 65 6 × 75	6 × 80		
Alternating dumbbell curl	b	6 × 65 6 × 75	6 × 80		
Triceps push-down	s	8 × 65 8 × 70	8 × 75		
Standing calf raise	s	25 × 45 25 × 45			
Manual neck					

Conditioning training

Flexibility and warm-up: 10:00
Total workout time: 35:00

5% grade downhill running. For each repetition to the right, build speed first 20 yd; sprint last 40 yd; jog uphill after each. If no hill is available repeat Thursday of week 9.

4 × 60 yd
Rest: 2:00
4 × 60 yd
Rest: 2:00
3 × 60 yd
Rest: 2:00
3 × 60 yd

FRIDAY

Resistance training					Skill training
Exercise		**Repetitions × % 1 RM**			On your own: Movement course #1
Close-grip lat	b	8 × 70 8 × 75	8 × 80		
High lat front	s	8 × 65 8 × 70	8 × 75		
Dead lift	b	8 × 65 8 × 75	8 × 80		
Free-weight upright row	b	6 × 70 6 × 80	6 × 85		
Leg press	s	6 × 65 6 × 70	4 × 80	4 × 85	
Two-leg curl	s	10 × 70 10 × 70	10 × 70	10 × 70	
Side lunge	s	12 reps 12 reps			
Cylinder circuit #3					
Manual neck					

Conditioning training

Flexibility and warm-up: 10:00   Four-section fartlek: 12:00
Total workout time: 24:00

MONDAY

Resistance training

Exercise		Repetitions × % 1 RM			
Bench press	b	5 × 70	5 × 75	4 × 80	4 × 85
Incline dumbbell press	b	6 × 65	6 × 70	6 × 75	6 × 80
Military press	b	5 × 70	5 × 75	4 × 80	4 × 85
Side dumbbell raise	s	8 × 65	8 × 65	8 × 65	
Straight-bar curl	b	8 × 65	8 × 75	8 × 80	
Bar triceps extension	b	6 × 65	6 × 75	6 × 80	
Manual neck					

Skill training

On your own: Balance drill #2

Conditioning training

Flexibility and warm-up: 10:00
Total workout time: 40:00

In groups of five players, perform the following exercises:

1. 10 × 10 yd crosses (a series of 10 yd sprints in which you alternate your foot plant each time both directions)
2. Jump rope 2 × 100
3. Transitional carioca (changing directions on command)
4. **Linemen:** Lateral shuffle over low hurdles, sprint out forward
   Backs: Cutting inside and outside legs from cone to cone
5. Tag games: Your choice

TUESDAY

Resistance training

Exercise		Repetitions × % 1 RM			
One-arm dumbbell row	b	6 × 65	6 × 75	6 × 80	
High lat rear	s	8 × 65	8 × 70	8 × 75	
Power clean or power row	b	6 × 60	6 × 70	6 × 75	
Bar shrug	s	12 × 65	12 × 65		
Squat	b	6 × 65	6 × 70	4 × 80	4 × 85
Step-up	s	10 reps	10 reps	10 reps	
Backward lunge	s	10 reps	10 reps	10 reps	
Cylinder circuit #3					
Manual neck					

Skill training

Work on these skills according to your position.

DB: Play dodge ball
WR: Work on pass catching (JUGS machine)
QB: Balance drill #4
LB: Work on pass drops and covering flats
OL: Agility over bags
DL: Work on RIPS and SWIMS (tackle dummy)
RB: Work on pass catching (JUGS machine)
KICK: Kick
PUNT: Play dodge ball, punt

Conditioning training

Flexibility and warm-up: 10:00
Total workout time: 35:00

Game simulation sprints: 1st and 2nd quarters

Rest: b (basic)—2:00 between sets   s (supporting)—1:00 between sets   Take 1:30 between exercises

Resistance training

Exercise		Repetitions × % 1 RM			
Incline bench press	b	5 × 70	5 × 75	4 × 80	4 × 85
Dip	b	max reps	max reps	max reps	
Behind neck press	s	5 × 70	5 × 75	4 × 80	4 × 85
Alternating dumbbell press	s	6 × 65	6 × 75	6 × 80	
Alternating dumbbell curl	b	6 × 65	6 × 75	6 × 80	
Triceps push-down	s	8 × 65	8 × 70	8 × 75	
Jump rope	b	100 reps	100 reps		
Manual neck					

Skill training

On your own: Foot-speed drill #2

THURSDAY

Conditioning training

Flexibility and warm-up: 10:00
Total workout time: 35:00
Speed work for sprint acceleration

Plyometrics (see chapter 10)
   4 × 20 yd alternate leg bounding
   4 × 20 yd horizontal power skip
   4 × 30 yd standing triple jump
   4 × 40 yd standing long jump
   5 × 20 yd shuttles. Create as many stations as you need to
      divide team; this is practice for the skills test to be administered later.

Resistance training

Exercise		Repetitions × % 1 RM			
Close-grip lat	b	8 × 70	8 × 75	8 × 80	
High lat front	s	8 × 65	8 × 70	8 × 75	
Dead lift	b	8 × 65	8 × 75	8 × 80	
Free-weight upright row	b	6 × 70	6 × 80	6 × 85	
Leg press	b	5 × 65	5 × 70	4 × 80	4 × 90
Alternating leg lunge	s	10 reps	10 reps		
Slideboard	s	30 crosses		30 crosses	
Cylinder circuit #4					
Manual neck					

Skill training

On your own: Movement course #2

FRIDAY

February

MONDAY

Resistance training							Skill training
Exercise		*Repetitions × % 1 RM*					On your own: Balance drill #3
Bench press	b	4 × 70	4 × 75	4 × 80	4 × 90		
Incline dumbbell press	b	6 × 65	6 × 70	6 × 75	6 × 80		
Push press	b	4 × 70	4 × 75	4 × 80	4 × 90		
Two-arm dumbbell press	s	6 × 80	6 × 80	6 × 80	6 × 80		
Bar triceps extension	b	6 × 80	6 × 80	6 × 80			
Jump rope	s	100 reps	100 reps				
Manual neck							

Conditioning training

Flexibility and warm-up: 10:00
Total workout time: 40:00

Four-station agility drill: Run to each station listed at right, break down, and line up (4 × 5:00 stations).

Bags   Cones   Triangle   Reaction drills

12 × 40 all-out effort; rest 1:00 after every 6 sprints.

TUESDAY

Resistance training							Skill training
Exercise		*Repetitions × % 1 RM*					Work on these skills according to your position.
One-arm dumbbell row	b	6 × 65	6 × 75	6 × 80			**DB:** Pass coverage against WRs
Power clean or power row	b	4 × 65	4 × 75	4 × 80			**WR:** Pass routes against DBs
Bar shrug	s	12 × 65	12 × 65				**QB:** Passing game
Straight-bar curl	b	6 × 70	6 × 80	6 × 85			**LB:** Balance drill #4
Squat	b	4 × 65	4 × 70	4 × 80	4 × 90		**OL:** Play dodge ball
Step-up	s	10 reps	10 reps	10 reps			**DL:** Play tag games
Backward lunge	s	10 reps	10 reps	10 reps			**RB:** Work with #1 QB on pass receiving
Cylinder circuit #4							**KICK:** Kick
Manual neck							**PUNT:** Pass football, punt

Conditioning training

Flexibility and warm-up: 10:00
Total workout time: 35:00
Speed work for cutting speed and acceleration

Agility ladder (see chapter 11)
  4 × quick run and sprint out
  4 × lateral two in, two out, sprint out
  4 × lateral run and sprint out
  4 × one in, three out, sprint out

Starts: 10 × 10 yd thrusts (see chapter 10)

Resistance training

Exercise		Repetitions × % 1 RM			
Incline bench press	b	4 × 70	4 × 75	4 × 80	4 × 85
Ballistic push-up	b	10 reps	10 reps	10 reps	
Behind neck press	s	4 × 70	4 × 75	4 × 80	4 × 90
Alternating dumbbell press	s	6 × 65	6 × 75	6 × 80	
Triceps push-down	s	8 × 65	8 × 70	8 × 75	
Jump rope	s	100 reps	100 reps		
Manual neck					

Skill training

On your own: Foot-speed drill #3

THURSDAY

Resistance training

Exercise		Repetitions × % 1 RM			
Pull-up	b	max reps	max reps	max reps	
Dead lift	b	6 × 65	6 × 75	6 × 80	
Free-weight upright row	b	6 × 70	6 × 80	6 × 85	
Alternating dumbbell curl	b	6 × 65	6 × 75	6 × 80	
Leg press	b	4 × 65	4 × 70	4 × 80	4 × 90
Alternating leg lunge	s	10 reps	10 reps	10 reps	
Slideboard	s	30 crosses		30 crosses	
Cylinder circuit #4					
Manual neck					

Skill training

On your own: Movement course #3

FRIDAY

Phase 2 ▪ Week 12

Rest: b (basic)—2:30 between sets
s (supporting)—1:00 between sets
Take 1:30 between exercises

Phase 2 ▪ Week 13

MONDAY

Resistance training						Skill training
Exercise		*Repetitions* × *% 1 RM*				On your own: Balance drill #1
Bench press	b	10 × 65 4 × 75 2 × 80 1 × 90				
		1 × 95 1 ×100*				
Incline dumbbell press	b	6 × 65	6 × 70	6 × 75	6 × 80	
Push press	b	4 × 70	4 × 75	4 × 80	4 × 90	
Two-arm dumbbell press	s	6 × 80	6 × 80	6 × 80	6 × 80	
Bar triceps extension	b	6 × 80	6 × 80	6 × 80		
Jump rope	s	100 reps 100 reps				
Manual neck						
		* 1 RM or complete muscular failure is not advised for athletes under age 16. Use estimated repetition instead.				

Conditioning training

Flexibility and warm-up: 10:00
Total workout time: 40:00

1. 4 × 25 yd shuttle (alternate foot plant each time both directions)
2. Three-cone reaction drill
3. **Line:** Lateral shuffle over bags, sprint out forward
   Backs: Ball-drop reaction drills
4. Dodge ball: Groups

TUESDAY

Resistance training					Skill training
Exercise		*Repetitions* × *% 1 RM*			Work on these skills according to your position.
One-arm dumbbell row	b	6 × 65	6 × 75	6 × 80	**DB:** Balance drill #4
Power clean or power row	b	4 × 65	4 × 75	4 × 80	**WR:** Blocking using sleds
Bar shrug	s	12 × 65	12 × 65		**QB:** Review plays (prep for spring ball)
Straight-bar curl	b	6 × 70	6 × 80	6 × 85	**LB:** Pass catching (JUGS machine)
Step-up (20 lb added)	s	8 reps	8 reps	8 reps	**OL:** Pass protection against a DL
Musketeer lunge	s	10 reps	10 reps	10 reps	**DL:** Pass rush against an OL
Cylinder circuit #4					**RB:** Balance drill #4
Manual neck					**KICK:** Kick
					PUNT: Punt

Conditioning training

Flexibility and warm-up: 10:00
Total workout time: 35:00

Game simulation sprints: 1st, 2nd, 3rd, and 4th quarters

Resistance training						Skill training
Exercise		*Repetitions × % 1 RM*				On your own: Foot-speed drill #1
Incline bench press	b	5 × 70	5 × 75	4 × 80	4 × 85	
Ballistic push-up	b	10 reps	10 reps	10 reps		
Behind neck press	b	4 × 70	4 × 75	4 × 80	4 × 90	
Alternating dumbbell press	s	6 × 70	6 × 80	6 × 85		
Jump rope	s	100 reps	100 reps			
Manual neck						

THURSDAY

Conditioning training	
Flexibility and warm-up: 10:00 Total workout time: 35:00	Speed work for sprint acceleration and starts Sprint-stride-sprint 12 × 60 yd 5 × 20 yd shuttles. Create as many stations as needed to divide team.

Resistance training						Skill training
Exercise		*Repetitions × 1 RM*				On your own: Movement course #1
Pull-up	b	max reps	max reps	max reps		
Dead lift	b	8 × 70	8 × 80	8 × 90		
Free-weight upright row	b	6 × 70	6 × 80	6 × 85		
Leg press	b	4 × 70	4 × 75	4 × 80	4 × 90	
Box squat	s	10 reps	10 reps	10 reps		
Slideboard	s	30 crosses		30 crosses		
Cylinder circuit #5						
Manual neck						

FRIDAY

Rest: b (basic)—2:30 between sets
s (supporting)—1:00 between sets
Take 1:30 between exercises

February

	Resistance training							
MONDAY	*Exercise*		*Repetitions* × *% 1 RM*					
	Bench press	b	10 × 65	4 × 75	2 × 80	1 × 90	1 × 95	1 × 100*
	Bench press		max reps × 225 lb*					
	Push press	b	6 × 80	6 × 80	6 × 80	6 × 80		
	Two-arm dumbbell press	s	6 × 80	6 × 80	6 × 80	6 × 80		
	Jump rope	b	100 reps	100 reps				
	Manual neck							
			* 1 RM or complete muscular failure and weights of 225 lb are not advised for athletes under age 16. Use an estimated 1 RM instead.					

	Resistance training				
TUESDAY	*Exercise*		*Repetitions* × *% 1 RM*		
	One-arm dumbbell row	b	6 × 65	6 × 75	6 × 80
	Power clean or power row	b	4 × 65	4 × 75	4 × 80
	Bar shrug	s	12 × 65	12 × 65	
	Straight-bar curl	b	6 × 70	6 × 80	6 × 85
	Box squat	s	10 reps	10 reps	10 reps
	One stiff leg dead	s	10 reps	10 reps	10 reps
	Cylinder circuit #5				
	Manual neck				

	Resistance training							
THURSDAY	*Exercise*		*Repetitions* × *% 1 RM*					
	Bench press		max reps × 225 lb*					
	Squat	b	10 × 65	4 × 75	2 × 80	1 × 90	1 × 95	1 × 100*
			* 1 RM or complete muscular failure and weights of 225 lb are not advised for athletes under age 16. Use an estimated 1 RM instead.					

Conditioning training	
Flexibility and warm-up: 10:00	Test 40 yd timing

	Conditioning training	
FRIDAY	Flexibility and warm-up: 10:00	Vertical jump test 20-yd shuttle test Long jump test Conditioning test (8 × 200 yd sprints :32, :34, :36)

Rest: b (basic)—2:30 between sets   Take 1:30 between exercises
s (supporting)—1:00 between sets

Week off—spring break

March

MONDAY

Resistance training

Exercise		Repetitions × % 1 RM
Bench press		max reps × 225 lb
Squat	b	10 × 65 4 × 75 2 × 80 1 × 90 1 × 95 1 × 100*

* 1 RM or complete muscular failure and weights of 225 lb are not advised for athletes under age 16. Use an estimated 1 RM instead.

Conditioning training

Flexibility and warm-up: 10:00   Test 40-yd timing
20-yd shuttle test

TUESDAY

Resistance training

Exercise		Repetitions × % 1 RM
Bench press	b	8 × 70 8 × 70 8 × 70
Incline dumbbell press	s	10 × 70 10 × 70 10 × 70
Close-grip lat	b	10 × 75 10 × 75 10 × 75
Close low lat	s	10 × 70 10 × 70 10 × 70
Behind neck press	b	8 × 70 8 × 70 8 × 70
Side dumbbell raise	s	15 × 55 15 × 55
Preacher curl (push-pull)	s	12 × 65 12 × 65
Kickback (push-pull)	s	12 × 65 12 × 65
Cylinder circuit #5		
Manual neck	s	

Conditioning training

Flexibility and warm-up: 10:00   Vertical jump test
Long jump test
Conditioning test: 8 × 200 yd sprints :32, :34, :36

Rest: b (basic)—2:30 between sets
s (supporting)—1:00 between sets
Take 1:30 between exercises

CHAPTER 3

PHASE 3:
Spring Workouts

GOAL *To increase resistance slowly on the core lifts each week when possible and induce momentary muscle fatigue (MMF) on the last set of all supporting exercises.*

Phase 3 is a maintenance phase that typically begins around the end of March and ends about early-May—weeks 17 through 23. This maintenance phase can correspond to a collegiate player's spring football practice or to a high school athlete's involvement in another spring sport. The last week of this phase provides a week off from training, planned to correspond to the collegiate academic break that usually occurs between the spring semester and the start of the first session of summer school. This planned break can also work to the advantage of high school athletes involved in other sports or as a recovery week before starting phase 4. Phase 3 requires three workout days per week.

Resistance Training

The purpose of this phase is to maintain the levels of power and endurance you gained during phase 2. This phase is an extension of phase 2, a bridge that leads to the summer months when you can again build power and endurance to their peak.

Types of Exercises

The exercises during this phase consist of core lifts and supporting and assisting exercises. I have included some additional exercises that may seem unusual at first. These exercises include leg dragging, crabbing, roll-outs, dumbbell strolls, and dumbbell combo exercises. Implement these exercises to break the boredom of the routine and to provide an element of functional training. As in phases 1 and 2, do exercises for the larger muscle groups first in the workout before you address the smaller muscle groups.

Rest, Volume, and Special Sets

The amount of rest between exercise sets remains the same as the phase progresses—1:30 between the sets of (b) exercises and 1:00 between the sets of (s) exercises. The amount of rest between exercises remains at 1:30. You can reduce these times by 15 to 30 seconds if your position or team meetings limit the time you can spend in the weight room. As you balance your time between study, sport conditioning, and personal time, burnout is most apt to occur during this phase, so keep the workouts short but challenging.

Phase 3 workouts maintain the number of repetitions at six for bench press and dumbbell press exercises. This repetition pattern ensures maintenance of power. Eight repetitions are prescribed for supporting exercises to help address muscular endurance and fatigue levels. To be sure that you accomplish this, perform the last set of the supporting exercises to failure.

This phase includes no special sets or reps. But during this phase you'll perform many drills at high speed. Even though the overall resistance is not extreme, the exercise intensity as a result of movement speed will be increased. As a result of spring football practice, conditioning drills, and activities, the legs are often fatigued; thus, there is less need to compound the fatigue with excessive off-field legwork.

Repetition Style and Speed

Execute the repetitions in this phase with a pausing tempo on the core lifts and a more constant tempo on the supporting lifts. This combination of movement tempo ensures that you maintain both power and endurance.

Running and Conditioning

Conditioning during this phase is incorporated into practice with drills and games. Some players will be at a disadvantage because of their reserved playing status, either as a result of injury or because they are low on the depth chart. As a result, their physical conditioning will undoubtedly suffer. For this reason, I urge all athletes to run on their own. The conditioning or position coach can determine the quantity and frequency of the runs. If you are having problems controlling your body weight or are rehabilitating from an injury, you may want to set special times with your coach to come by and perform assigned running, treadmill, stair-climber, or bike work. If you are injured and not needed at practice, then reserve the practice time for reconditioning toward playing status. Near the end of the spring season the head coach and the strength and conditioning coach may collaborate and include a postpractice conditioning session that can meet conditioning needs.

© Active Images

Phase 3 ▪ Week 17

Resistance training

MONDAY

Exercise		Repetitions × % 1 RM		
Flat dumbbell press	b	8 × 75	8 × 75	8 × 75
Medicine ball chest pass	b	15 reps	15 reps	15 reps
Dumbbell pull press	b	8 × 75	8 × 75	8 × 75
Shoulder fly	s	8 × 75	8 × 75	8 × 75
Alternating dumbbell curl	b	8 × 70	8 × 70	8 × 70
Dumbbell French press	b	8 × 75	8 × 75	8 × 75
Cylinder circuit #2				
Manual neck				

Resistance training

TUESDAY

Exercise		Repetitions × % 1 RM		
Pull-up	b	max reps	max reps	max reps
Dumbbell stroll	b	walk for 1 min	walk for 1 min	
One arm-dumbbell row	b	8 × 80	8 × 80	
Squat	b	8 × 75	8 × 75	8 × 75
Glute-ham raise	b	10 reps	10 reps	10 reps
Skate bound		10 reps	10 reps	10 reps
Cylinder circuit #1				
Manual neck				

Resistance training

THURSDAY

Exercise		Repetitions × % 1 RM		
One-leg extension	s	15 × 60	15 × 60	
One-leg curl	s	12 × 70	12 × 70	12 × 70
Slideboard	s	30 crosses		30 crosses
Incline bench press	b	8 × 70	8 × 70	8 × 70
Medicine ball underhand backward throw	b	15 reps	15 reps	
High lat rear	s	8 × 75	8 × 75	8 × 75
Push press	b	8 × 75	8 × 75	8 × 75
Kickback	s	10 × 70	10 × 70	10 × 75
Cylinder circuit #2				
Manual neck				

Rest: b (basic)—1:30 between sets
s (supporting)—1:00 between sets
Take 1:30 between exercises

Phase 3 ■ Week 18

Resistance training				
Exercise		**Repetitions × % 1 RM**		
Flat dumbbell press	b	8 × 75	8 × 75	8 × 75
Medicine ball chest pass	b	15 reps	15 reps	15 reps
Dumbbell pull press	b	8 × 75	8 × 75	8 × 75
Shoulder fly	s	8 × 75	8 × 75	8 × 75
Alternating dumbbell curl	b	8 × 70	8 × 70	8 × 70
Dumbbell French press	b	8 × 75	8 × 75	8 × 75
Cylinder circuit #2				
Manual neck				

MONDAY

Resistance training				
Exercise		**Repetitions × % 1 RM**		
Pull-up	b	max reps	max reps	max reps
Dumbbell stroll	b	walk for 1 min	walk for 1 min	
One-arm dumbbell row	b	8 × 80	8 × 80	
Squat	b	8 × 75	8 × 75	8 × 75
Glute-ham raise	s	10 reps	10 reps	10 reps
Skate bound		10 reps	10 reps	10 reps
Cylinder circuit #1				
Manual neck				

TUESDAY

Resistance training				
Exercise		**Repetitions × % 1 RM**		
One-leg extension	s	15 × 60	15 × 60	
One-leg curl	s	12 × 70	12 × 70	12 × 70
Slideboard	s	30 crosses		30 crosses
Incline bench press	b	8 × 75	8 × 75	8 × 75
Medicine ball underhand backward throw	b	15 reps	15 reps	
High lat rear	s	8 × 75	8 × 75	8 × 75
Push press	b	8 × 75	8 × 75	8 × 75
Kickback	s	10 × 70	10 × 70	10 × 75
Cylinder circuit #3				
Manual neck				

THURSDAY

Rest: b (basic)—1:30 between sets
s (supporting)—1:00 between sets
Take 1:30 between exercises

Phase 3 ▪ Week 19

Resistance training

MONDAY

Exercise		Repetitions × % 1 RM		
Flat dumbbell press	b	8 × 75	8 × 75	8 × 75
Medicine ball chest pass	b	15 reps	15 reps	15 reps
Dumbbell pull press	b	8 × 75	8 × 75	8 × 75
Shoulder fly	s	8 × 75	8 × 75	8 × 75
Alternating dumbbell curl	b	8 × 70	8 × 70	8 × 70
Dumbbell French press	b	8 × 75	8 × 75	8 × 75
Cylinder circuit #3				
Manual neck				

Resistance training

TUESDAY

Exercise		Repetitions × % 1 RM		
Pull-up	b	max reps	max reps	max reps
Dumbbell squat, two-arm dumbbell press	b	10 × 65	10 × 65	10 × 65
Dumbbell lunge, upright row	b	10 × 65	10 × 65	10 × 65
Skate bound		10 reps	10 reps	10 reps
Cylinder circuit #2				
Manual neck				

Resistance training

THURSDAY

Exercise		Repetitions × % 1 RM			
Step-up (alternating legs, 25-lb dumbbell)	s	20 reps	20 reps		
Crabbing	s	30 yd	30 yd	30 yd	30 yd
Slideboard	s	30 crosses		30 crosses	
Incline bench press	b	8 × 75	8 × 75	8 × 75	
Medicine ball underhand backward throw	b	15 reps	15 reps		
Close high lat	s	8 × 75	8 × 75	8 × 75	
Push press	b	8 × 75	8 × 75	8 × 75	
Kickback	s	10 × 70	10 × 70	10 × 75	
Cylinder circuit #3					
Manual neck					

Rest: b (basic)—1:30 between sets
s (supporting)—1:00 between sets
Take 1:30 between exercises

Resistance training

Exercise		Repetitions × % 1 RM			
Flat dumbbell press	b	6 × 80	6 × 80	6 × 80	
Dip	b	max reps	max reps	max reps	
Dumbbell snatch	b	8 × 75	8 × 75	8 × 75	
Rear deltoid swim	s	20 reps	20 reps		
Incline curl	b	8 × 70	8 × 70	8 × 70	
Triceps push-down	b	8 × 75	8 × 75	8 × 75	
Medicine ball circuit	b	20 reps	20 reps		
Cylinder circuit #4					
Manual neck					

MONDAY

Resistance training

Exercise		Repetitions × % 1 RM			
Pull-ups	b	max reps	max reps	max reps	
Dumbbell squat, two-arm dumbbell press	b	10 × 65	10 × 65	10 × 65	
Dumbbell lunge, upright row	b	10 × 65	10 × 65	10 × 65	
Skate bound		10 reps	10 reps	10 reps	
Cylinder circuit #1					
Three-sided square drills		30 sec	30 sec	30 sec	
Manual neck					

TUESDAY

Resistance training

Exercise		Repetitions × % 1 RM			
Step-up (alternating legs, 25-lb dumbbell)	s	20 reps	20 reps		
Crabbing	s	30 yd	30 yd	30 yd	30 yd
Fourth quarter tour					
Incline bench press	b	6 × 80	6 × 80	6 × 80	
Hang clean	b	8 × 70	8 × 70	8 × 70	
Close high lat	s	8 × 75	8 × 75	8 × 75	
Dumbbell push press	b	6 × 80	6 × 80	6 × 80	
Reverse dip	s	12 reps	12 reps	12 reps	
Cylinder circuit #4					
Manual neck					

THURSDAY

Phase 3 ■ Week 20

Rest: b (basic)—1:30 between sets
s (supporting)—1:00 between sets
Take 1:30 between exercises

Phase 3 ▪ Week 21

Resistance training

MONDAY

Exercise		Repetitions × % 1 RM		
Bench press	b	6 × 80	6 × 80	6 × 80
Dip	b	max reps	max reps	max reps
Dumbbell snatch	b	8 × 75	8 × 75	8 × 75
Rear deltoid swim	s	20 reps	20 reps	20 reps
Incline curl	b	8 × 70	8 × 70	8 × 70
Triceps push-down	b	8 × 75	8 × 75	8 × 75
Medicine ball circuit	b	20 reps	20 reps	20 reps
Cylinder circuit #2				
Manual neck				

Resistance training

TUESDAY

Exercise		Repetitions × % 1 RM			
Pull-ups	b	max reps	max reps	max reps	
Dumbbell squat, two-arm dumbbell press	b	10 × 65	10 × 65	10 × 65	
Dumbbell lunge, upright row	b	10 × 65	10 × 65	10 × 65	
Roll-out	s	10 reps	10 reps	10 reps	
Cylinder circuit #1					
Three-sided square drills		30 sec	30 sec	30 sec	30 sec
Manual neck					

Resistance training

THURSDAY

Exercise		Repetitions × % 1 RM			
Box squat	b	15 reps	15 reps		
Leg dragging	s	15 yd	15 yd	15 yd	15 yd
Side lunge	s	10 reps	10 reps		
Incline dumbbell press	b	6 × 80	6 × 80	6 × 80	
Hang clean	b	8 × 70	8 × 70	8 × 70	
Close low lat	s	8 × 75	8 × 75	8 × 75	
Dumbbell push press	b	6 × 80	6 × 80	6 × 80	
Reverse dip	s	12 reps	12 reps	12 reps	
Cylinder circuit #5					
Manual neck					

Rest: b (basic)—1:30 between sets
s (supporting)—1:00 between sets
Take 1:30 between exercises

Resistance training

Exercise		Repetitions × % 1 RM			
Bench press	b	6 × 80	6 × 80	6 × 80	
Dip	b	max reps	max reps	max reps	
Dumbbell snatch	b	8 × 75	8 × 75	8 × 75	
Rear deltoid swim	s	20 reps	20 reps		
Incline curl	b	8 × 70	8 × 70	8 × 70	
Triceps push-down	b	8 × 75	8 × 75	8 × 75	
Medicine ball circuit	b	20 reps	20 reps		
Manual neck					

MONDAY

Resistance training

Exercise		Repetitions × % 1 RM			
Pull-up	b	max reps	max reps	max reps	
Dumbbell squat, two-arm dumbbell press	b	10 × 65	10 × 65	10 × 65	
Dumbbell side lunge, shoulder fly	b	10 × 65	10 × 65	10 × 65	
Roll-out	s	10 reps	10 reps	10 reps	
Cylinder circuit #1					
Jump rope	b	3 min	3 min	3 min	3 min
Manual neck					

TUESDAY

Resistance training

Exercise		Repetitions × % 1 RM			
Box squat	b	15 reps	15 reps		
Leg dragging	s	15 yd	15 yd	15 yd	15 yd
Side lunge	s	10 reps	10 reps		
Incline dumbbell press	b	6 × 80	6 × 80	6 × 80	
Hang clean	b	8 × 70	8 × 70	8 × 70	
Close low lat	s	8 × 75	8 × 75	8 × 75	
Dumbbell push press	b	6 × 80	6 × 80	6 × 80	
Reverse dip	s	12 reps	12 reps	12 reps	
Cylinder circuit #5					
Manual neck					

THURSDAY

Rest: b (basic)—1:30 between sets
s (supporting)—1:00 between sets
Take 1:30 between exercises

Week off

CHAPTER 4

PHASE 4:
Early Summer Workouts

GOAL *To increase nerve activity and excitability by gradually increasing the level of resistance on each core and supercore exercise. The result should be optimal power and explosive potential for football.*

After taking a week off early in May, we begin phase 4. Depending on the college or high school you attend, your break may occur during a different week. The break in the workout schedule should correspond to your particular academic calendar. This eliminates the possibility of having to miss too many days of working out. Phase 4 returns to what was initiated in phase 2—a gradual increase in intensity with an eventual decrease in exercise volume. This phase of the program produces the highest potential for athletic power. This 7-week phase flows into phase 5 with no break, creating a 14-week period of structured work before the in-season period.

Resistance Training

This phase, like phase 2, will increase nerve activity and excitability. Muscle mass will increase during this phase, but less from a fatigue-related response and more from the load increases planned during the exercises.

Types of Exercises

The exercises during this phase consist of core lifts and supporting and assisting exercises. We change the supporting exercises in this phase from single-joint exercises to more multijoint exercise. You will use less cable and machine resistance. You will also make a progression to primarily free-weighted resistance and more power-producing techniques. The order of exercises works the larger muscle groups first followed by the smaller muscle groups.

Rest, Volume, and Special Sets

The amount of rest between the sets of basic exercise increases as the phase progresses. You'll start at 1:30 between the sets of basic exercises; by week 30 you will take 1:45. Take 1:00 between the sets of all supporting exercises throughout this phase. The increased rest as the phase progresses compensates for the ever increasing load of the resistance during the workout. This added recovery between sets ensures that with each repetition you will effectively excite the nerve pathways that activate the muscle. Rest between exercises remains at 1:30.

The number of sets and repetitions in the workouts begins to decrease gradually over the seven-week period. This lowered volume is another method of increasing the overall level of nerve activity and excitability, which in turn results in greater power output. There are no special sets in this phase.

Repetition Style and Speed

During this phase the style of repetition is less strict. Perform each repetition with good form to avoid injury. You can incorporate more speed into the movement so that you can use higher resistance. As you move from phase 4 to phase 5 you are pushing with everything you have to move the resistance while maintaining good form.

Execute the repetitions in this phase with a pausing tempo. Although you can perform some repetitions without pause, as the resistance begins to cause fatigue pause for an instant in a locked-out position to allow momentary recuperation. This will help ensure that each repetition is powerful.

Running and Conditioning

Conditioning during this phase is much the same as the conditioning in phase 2—you can choose additional running and conditioning activities to provide more movement information for your sports skills. The progression of running workouts during phases 4 and 5 is more subtle than in phase 2.

In weeks 24 to 30, do your running and conditioning four times per week with these emphases:

Monday—Interval sprint work (chapter 9)

Tuesday—Active recovery with a short distance or longer interval run (chapter 9)

Thursday—Speedwork (practical strength for sprint form and starts; chapter 10)

Friday—Combination work (shuttles, fartleks, Indian runs, and so forth; chapter 9)

As in phase 2, I begin to incorporate more agility work in phase 4, eventually replacing interval sprints altogether with agility drills in phase 5. You can perform these drills at high speeds with little rest to produce good cardiorespiratory benefit. I reduce the workload from four days per week to three at week 30 to help boost recovery from workout to workout. This also helps to enhance power production, which coincides with work performed in the weight room. Thus, the plan for week 30 (and into phase 5) includes the following:

Monday—Agility drills (chapter 11)

Tuesday—Game-simulation sprints (chapter 10)

Thursday—Speed work (practical strength for sprint form and starts; chapter 10)

© Active Images

MONDAY

Resistance training

Exercise		Repetitions × % 1 RM			
Bench press	b	8 × 60	8 × 65	8 × 70	8 × 75
Incline dumbbell press	b	8 × 75	8 × 75	8 × 75	8 × 75
Incline dumbbell fly	s	10 × 70	10 × 70	10 × 70	
Military press	b	8 × 65	8 × 70	8 × 75	
Side dumbbell raise	s	10 × 55	10 × 55	10 × 55	
Triceps push-down	s	10 × 70	10 × 70	10 × 70	
Standing calf raise	s	50 × 30	50 × 30		

Conditioning training

Flexibility and warm-up: 10:00

Total workout time: 36:00

Intervals: Perform on a track.

	WR, DB, RB	**LB, TE, FB**	**Line**
2 × 440	1:15	1:20	1:30
Rest	2:50	2:50	2:50
3 × 220	:30	:32	:34
Rest	1:10	1:12	1:14
6 × 110	:13	:15	:17
Rest	2:00 after every three reps		

TUESDAY

Resistance training

Exercise		Repetitions × % 1 RM			
High lat rear	s	8 × 65	8 × 70	8 × 75	
Close low lat	s	8 × 65	8 × 70	8 × 75	
Dumbbell shrug	s	5 × 60	15 × 60	15 × 60	
Free-weight upright row	b	8 × 65	8 × 70	8 × 75	
Front dumbbell raise	s	15 × 60	15 × 60	15 × 60	
Squat	b	8 × 55	8 × 60	8 × 65	8 × 70
Step-up (alternating legs)	s	20 reps	20 reps		
One stiff leg dead	s	10 reps	10 reps	10 reps	
Cylinder circuit #3					

Rest: b (basic)—1:30 between sets
s (supporting)—1:00 between sets
Take 1:30 between exercises

Resistance training

Exercise		Repetitions × % 1 RM			
Flat dumbbell press	s	8 × 75	8 × 75	8 × 75	8 × 75
Incline bench press	b	8 × 75	8 × 75	8 × 75	8 × 75
Dip	b	max reps	max reps	max reps	
Two-arm dumbbell press	s	8 × 70	8 × 70	8 × 70	
Side dumbbell raise	s	10 × 55	10 × 55	10 × 55	
Alternating dumbbell curl	b	8 × 70	8 × 70	8 × 70	
Kickback	s	10 × 70	10 × 70	10 × 70	
Calf raise/leg press	s	30 × 80	30 × 80		

Conditioning training

Flexibility and warm-up: 10:00

Total work time: 26:00

Shuttle

	WR, DB, RB	LB, TE, FB	Line
3 × long 300 yd shuttle	:58	1:02	1:04
Rest between reps	:20	:20	:20

Resistance training

Exercise		Repetitions × % 1 RM			
Close-grip lat	b	8 × 60	8 × 65	8 × 70	8 × 75
High lat front	s	8 × 60	8 × 65	8 × 70	8 × 75
Manual rear deltoid	s	15 reps	15 reps	15 reps	
Leg press	s	8 × 55	8 × 60	8 × 65	8 × 70
Side lunge	s	6 × 70	6 × 70	6 × 70	
Two-leg curl	s	10 × 70	10 × 70	10 × 70	10 × 70
Cylinder circuit #5					

THURSDAY

FRIDAY

Phase 4 ■ Week 24

MONDAY

Resistance training						Skill training
Exercise		**Repetitions × % 1 RM**				On your own: Balance drill #1
Bench press	b	6 × 65	6 × 70	6 × 75	6 × 80	
Incline dumbbell press	b	8 × 65	8 × 70	8 × 75		
Incline dumbbell fly	s	10 × 70	10 × 70	10 × 70		
Military press	b	6 × 65	6 × 70	6 × 75	6 × 80	
Side dumbbell raise	s	8 × 60	8 × 60	8 × 60		
Triceps push down	s	8 × 60	8 × 65	8 × 75		
Standing calf raise	s	30 × 40	30 × 40			
Manual neck						

Conditioning training

Flexibility and warm-up: 10:00
Total workout time: 37:00
Intervals: Perform on a track.

	WR, DB, RB	**LB, TE, FB**	**Line**
1 × 440	1:15	1:20	1:30
2 × 220	:30	:32	:34
Rest	1:10	1:12	1:14
8 × 110	:13	:15	:17
Rest	1:30 after every 4 reps		
4 × 55	:08	:08	:09
Rest	:20	:20	:20

TUESDAY

Resistance training						Skill training
Exercise		**Repetitions × % 1 RM**				**DB:** Pass coverage against WRs **WR:** Pass routes against DBs **QB:** Passing game **LB:** Pass drops and covering flats **OL:** Pass protection against a DL **DL:** Pass rush against an OL **RB:** Work with #2 QB on pass receiving **KICK:** Kick **PUNT:** Punt
High lat rear	s	8 × 65	8 × 70	8 × 75		
Close low lat	s	8 × 65	8 × 70	8 × 75		
Dumbbell shrug	s	12 × 65	12 × 65			
Free-weight upright row	b	8 × 70	8 × 75	8 × 80		
Squat	b	6 × 65	6 × 70	6 × 80	6 × 85	
Step-up (alternating legs)	s	20 reps	20 reps			
One stiff leg dead	s	10 reps	10 reps	10 reps		
Cylinder circuit #3						
Manual neck						

Conditioning training

Flexibility and warm-up: 10:00
Total workout time: 23:00
Shuttle

	WR, DB, RB	**LB, TE, FB**	**Line**
1 × 1,000 yd shuttle	3:30	3:45	4:00
Rest	5:00	5:00	5:00

Rest: b (basic)—1:30 between sets
s (supporting)—1:00 between sets
Take 1:30 between exercises

Resistance training

Exercise		Repetitions × % 1 RM			
Flat dumbbell press	s	8 × 60	8 × 65	8 × 75	
Incline bench press	b	6 × 80	6 × 80	6 × 80	6 × 80
Dip	b	max reps	max reps	max reps	
Two-arm dumbbell press	s	8 × 65	8 × 70	8 × 75	
Alternating dumbbell curl	b	8 × 65	8 × 70	8 × 75	
Dumbbell French press	b	8 × 75	8 × 75	8 × 75	
Calf raise/leg press	s	30 × 80	30 × 80		
Manual neck					

Skill training

On your own:

Foot-speed drill #1

Conditioning training

Flexibility and warm-up: 10:00

Total workout time: 30:00

Stadium run: 20:00

THURSDAY

Resistance training

Exercise		Repetitions × % 1 RM			
Close-grip lat	b	8 × 65	8 × 70	8 × 75	
High lat front	s	8 × 65	8 × 70	8 × 75	
Manual rear deltoid	s	15 reps	15 reps	15 reps	
Straight dumbbell pullover	s	10 × 70	10 × 70	10 × 70	
Leg press	s	6 × 65	6 × 70	6 × 80	6 × 85
Side lunge	s	6 × 70	6 × 70	6 × 70	
Two-leg curl	s	10 × 70	10 × 70	10 × 70	10 × 70
Cylinder circuit #4					
Manual neck					

Skill training

On your own:

Movement course #1

Conditioning training

		WR, DB, RB	**LB, TE, FB**	**Line**
Flexibility and warm-up: 10:00				
Total workout time: 25:00	2-mile run	14:00	14:30	15:00

FRIDAY

Phase 4 ■ Week 26

MONDAY

Resistance training						Skill training
Exercise		*Repetitions × % 1 RM*				On your own: Balance drill #2
Bench press	b	6 × 65	6 × 70	6 × 75	6 × 80	
Close incline press	b	8 × 65	8 × 70	8 × 75		
Flat dumbbell fly	b	6 × 65	6 × 75	6 × 80		
Alternating dumbbell press	b	6 × 65	6 × 70	6 × 75		
Push-up	s	20 reps	20 reps			
Triceps push-down	s	8 × 60	8 × 65	8 × 75		
Standing calf raise	s	30 × 40	30 × 40			
Manual neck						

Conditioning training

	WR, DB, RB	LB, TE, FB	Line
Flexibility and warm-up: 10:00			
Total workout time: 31:00			
3 × 6 crosses	:58	1:02	1:05
Rest between	2:00	2:00	2:00
Intervals 3 × sideline ladders	:34	:35	:36
2 × 10 hash and back	:58	1:00	1:02
Rest between sets	Time required for next two groups to run		

TUESDAY

Resistance training						Skill training
Exercise		*Repetitions × % 1 RM*				**DB:** Pass catching (JUGS machine) **WR:** Blocking with sleds **QB:** Play dodge ball **LB:** Pass catching (JUGS machine) **OL:** Sled work **DL:** Work on RIPS and SWIMS (tackle dummy) **RB:** Play tag games **KICK:** Kick **PUNT:** Play tag games/punt
High lat rear	s	8 × 65	8 × 70	8 × 75		
Close low lat	s	8 × 65	8 × 70	8 × 75		
Dumbbell shrug	s	12 × 65	12 × 65			
Free-weight upright row	b	8 × 70	8 × 75	8 × 80		
Squat	b	6 × 65	6 × 70	6 × 80	6 × 85	
Musketeer lunge	s	10 reps	10 reps	10 reps		
Box squat	s	10 reps	10 reps	10 reps		
Cylinder circuit #3						
Manual neck						

Conditioning training

	WR, DB, RB	LB, TE, FB	Line
Flexibility and warm-up: 10:00			
Total workout time: 21:00			
1 × 2,100 yd shuttle	8:00	8:30	9:00

Rest: b (basic)—1:30 between sets
s (supporting)—1:00 between sets
Take 1:30 between exercises

Resistance training						Skill training
Exercise		*Repetitions* × *% 1 RM*				On your own:
Flat dumbbell press	s	8 × 60	8 × 65	8 × 75		Foot-speed drill #2
Incline bench press	b	6 × 80	6 × 80	6 × 80	6 × 80	
Dip	b	max reps	max reps	max reps		
Behind neck press	s	6 × 65	6 × 70	6 × 75	6 × 80	
Two-arm dumbbell press	s	8 × 65	8 × 70	8 × 75		
Alternating dumbbell curl	b	8 × 65	8 × 70	8 × 75		
Dumbbell French press	b	8 × 75	8 × 75	8 × 75		
Standing calf raise	s	30 × 40	30 × 40			
Manual neck						

Conditioning training

Flexibility and warm-up: 10:00   Sharks in the tank (tag game): 20:00

Total workout time: 30:00

THURSDAY

Resistance training						Skill training
Exercise		*Repetitions* × *% 1 RM*				On your own:
Close-grip lat	b	8 × 65	8 × 70	8 × 75		Movement course #2
Straight dumbbell pullover	s	8 × 65	8 × 70	8 × 75		
Bent dumbbell raise	s	12 × 60	12 × 60	12 × 60		
Straight dumbbell pullover	s	10 × 70	10 × 70	10 × 70		
Leg press	s	6 × 65	6 × 70	6 × 80	6 × 85	
One stiff leg dead (10-lb dumbbell)	s	12 reps	12 reps	12 reps		
Cylinder circuit #5						
Manual neck						

Conditioning training

Flexibility and warm-up: 10:00

Total workout time: 26:00

	WR, DB, RB	LB, TE, FB	Line
2-mile run	14:00	14:30	15:00

FRIDAY

Phase 4 ▪ Week 26

Phase 4 ■ Week 27

MONDAY

Resistance training						Skill training
Exercise		**Repetitions × % 1 RM**				On your own: Balance drill #3
Bench press	b	6 × 70	6 × 75	4 × 80	4 × 85	
Close incline press	b	8 × 65	8 × 70	8 × 75		
Flat dumbbell fly	b	6 × 65	6 × 75	6 × 80		
Alternating dumbbell press	b	6 × 65	6 × 70	6 × 75		
Push-up	s	20 reps	20 reps			
Straight-bar curl	b	8 × 65	8 × 75	8 × 80		
Dumbbell French press	b	6 × 80	6 × 80	6 × 80		
BW one-leg calf	s	25 reps	25 reps			
Manual neck						

Conditioning training

Flexibility and warm-up: 10:00

Total workout time: 30:00

Intervals: Perform on football field.

	WR, DB, RB	LB, TE, FB	Line
3 × 220 yd	:30	:32	:34
Rest between reps	1:10	1:10	1:12
8 × 110 yd	:13	:15	:17
Rest	1:00 after every 4 sprints		
10 × 55 yd	All-out effort		
Rest	2:00 after every 5 sprints		

TUESDAY

Resistance training						Skill training
Exercise		**Repetitions × % 1 RM**				**DB:** Pass coverage against WRs **WR:** Pass routes against DBs **QB:** Review plays (preparation for season) **LB:** Agility over bags **OL:** Play tag games **DL:** Agility over bags **RB:** Balance drill #4 **KICK:** Kick **PUNT:** Balance drill #4, punt
Two-arm dumbbell row	b	8 × 65	8 × 70	8 × 75		
High lat rear	s	8 × 65	8 × 70	8 × 75		
Dumbbell stroll (70+ lb dumbbells)	s	40 yd and back	40 yd and back			
Squat	b	6 × 65	6 × 70	4 × 80	4 × 85	
Musketeer lunge	s	15 reps	15 reps			
Box squat	s	12 reps	12 reps			
Cylinder circuit #3						
Manual neck						

Conditioning training

Flexibility and warm-up: 10:00

Total workout time: 36:00

Shuttle

	WR, DB, RB	LB, TE, FB	Line
2 × 1,000 yd shuttle	3:45	4:00	4:15
Rest between reps	8:00	8:00	8:00

Rest: b (basic)—1:45 between sets

s (supporting)—1:00 between sets

Take 1:30 between exercises

Resistance training | Skill training

Exercise		Repetitions × % 1 RM			
Incline bench press	b	6 × 65	6 × 70	6 × 75	6 × 80
Moon push-up	b	10 reps	10 reps		
Behind neck press	s	6 × 70	6 × 75	4 × 80	4 × 85
Alternating dumbbell press	s	6 × 65	6 × 75	6 × 80	
Hammer curl	b	8 × 80	8 × 80	8 × 80	
Two-arm dumbbell triceps extension	b	8 × 65	8 × 70	8 × 75	
Jump rope		100 reps	100 reps		
Manual neck					

Skill training — On your own: Foot-speed drill #3

THURSDAY

Conditioning training

Flexibility and warm-up: 10:00

Total workout time: 30:00

8 × through movement course #1

Resistance training | Skill training

Exercise		Repetitions × % 1 RM			
Close-grip lat	b	8 × 65	8 × 70	8 × 75	
Straight dumbbell pullover	s	8 × 65	8 × 70	8 × 75	
Free-weight upright row	b	6 × 70	6 × 80	6 × 85	
Bent dumbbell raise	s	12 × 60	12 × 60	12 × 60	
Leg press	s	6 × 65	6 × 70	4 × 80	4 × 85
One stiff leg dead (10 lb)	s	12 reps	12 reps	12 reps	
Cylinder circuit #2					
Manual neck					

Skill training — On your own: Movement course #3

FRIDAY

Conditioning training

Flexibility and warm-up: 10:00

Total workout time: 24:00

Shuttle

	WR, DB, RB	LB, TE, FB	Line
2 × short 300 yd shuttle	:58	1:02	1:05
Rest between reps	2:00	2:00	2:00
1 × short 150 yd shuttle	:24	:26	:28

Phase 4 ■ Week 27

Phase 4 ■ Week 28

MONDAY

Resistance training

Exercise		Repetitions × % 1 RM			
Bench press	b	6 × 70	6 × 75	4 × 80	4 × 85
Incline dumbbell press	b	8 × 65	8 × 70	8 × 75	
Close-grip bench	b	6 × 70	6 × 80	6 × 85	
Dumbbell push press	b	6 × 70	6 × 75	6 × 80	6 × 85
Side dumbbell raise	s	8 × 60	8 × 60	8 × 60	
Hammer curl	b	8 × 80	8 × 80	8 × 80	
Dumbbell French press	b	6 × 80	6 × 80	6 × 80	
BW one-leg calf	s	25 reps	25 reps		
Manual neck					

Skill training

On your own:

Balance drill #1

Conditioning training

	WR, DB, RB	LB, TE, FB	Line
4 × 6 crosses	:58	1:02	1:05
Rest between sets	2:00	2:00	2:00
3 × sideline ladders	:34	:35	:36
Rest between sets	1:10	1:10	1:10
2 × 10 hash and back	:58	1:00	1:02
Rest between sets	Time required for next two groups to run		

Flexibility and warm-up: 10:00

Total workout time: 29:00

Intervals: Perform on a football field.

TUESDAY

Resistance training

Exercise		Repetitions × % 1 RM			
Two-arm dumbbell row	b	8 × 65	8 × 70	8 × 75	
High lat rear	s	8 × 65	8 × 70	8 × 75	
Dumbbell stroll (70+ lb dumbbells)	s	40 yd and back	40 yd and back		
Squat	b	6 × 65	6 × 70	4 × 80	4 × 85
One-leg press	s	8 × 80	8 × 80		
Backward lunge	s	10 reps	10 reps	10 reps	
Cylinder circuit #3					
Manual neck					

Skill training

DB: Play tag games

WR: Pass catching (JUGS machine)

QB: Passing game

LB: Play dodge ball

DL: Balance drill #4

OL: Play dodge ball

RB: Pass catching (JUGS machine)

KICK: Kick

PUNT: Balance drill #4, Punt

Conditioning training

Flexibility and warm-up: 10:00   8 × through movement course #2

Total workout time: 36:00

Rest: b (basic)—1:45 between sets
s (supporting)—1:00 between sets
Take 1:30 between exercises

Resistance training / Skill training

Exercise		Repetitions × % 1 RM				Skill training
						On your own:
Incline bench press	b	6 × 65	6 × 70	6 × 75	6 × 80	Foot-speed drill #1
Medicine ball chest pass	b	10 reps	10 reps			
Military press	s	6 × 70	6 × 75	4 × 80	4 × 85	
Alternating dumbbell press	s	6 × 65	6 × 75	6 × 80		
Wrist flex (each hand)	s	100 reps	100 reps			
Two-arm dumbbell triceps extension	b	8 × 65	8 × 70	8 × 75		
Jump rope	b	100 reps	100 reps			
Manual neck						

Conditioning training

Flexibility and warm-up: 10:00

Total workout time: 32:00

Two-section fartlek: 20:00

THURSDAY

Resistance training / Skill training

Exercise		Repetitions × % 1 RM				Skill training
						On your own:
Close-grip lat	b	8 × 65	8 × 70	8 × 75		Work on starts and starting stances
EZ-bar pullover	s	8 × 65	8 × 70	8 × 75		
Rear deltoid swim	s	20 reps	20 reps			
Free-weight upright row	b	6 × 70	6 × 80	6 × 85		
Leg press	s	6 × 65	6 × 70	4 × 80	4 × 85	
One stiff leg dead (15 lb)	s	10 reps	10 reps	10 reps		
Cylinder circuit #4						
Manual neck						

Conditioning training

Flexibility and warm-up: 10:00

Total workout time: 24:00

Agility ladder drills

   4 × quick run and sprint out

   4 × lateral two in, two out, sprint out

   4 × lateral run and sprint out

   4 × one in, three out, sprint out

Sprint-stride-sprint

12 × 60 yd

FRIDAY

Phase 4 ■ Week 28

June

MONDAY

Resistance training						Skill training
Exercise		*Repetitions × % 1 RM*				On your own:
Bench press	b	6 × 70	6 × 75	4 × 80	4 × 85	Balance drill #2
Incline dumbbell press	b	8 × 65	8 × 70	8 × 75		
Close-grip bench	b	6 × 70	6 × 80	6 × 85		
Military press	b	6 × 70	6 × 75	6 × 80	6 × 85	
Side dumbbell raise	s	8 × 60	8 × 60	8 × 60		
Straight-bar curl	b	8 × 65	8 × 75	8 × 80		
Dumbbell French press	b	6 × 80	6 × 80	6 × 80		
Standing calf raise	s	25 × 45	25 × 45			
Manual neck						

Conditioning training

Flexibility and warm-up: 10:00

		WR, DB, RB	LB, TE, FB	Line
Total workout time: 29:00				
Intervals	2 × 200	:32	:34	:36
	Rest	1:10	1:10	1:12

TUESDAY

Resistance training					Skill training
Exercise		*Repetitions × % 1 RM*			**DB:** Pass coverage against WRs
One-arm dumbbell row	b	8 × 65	8 × 70	8 × 75	**WR:** Blocking with sleds
Close high lat	s	8 × 65	8 × 70	8 × 75	**QB:** Play tag games
Dumbbell pull press	b	8 × 70	8 × 70	8 × 70	**LB:** Play tag games
Dumbbell side lunge, shoulder fly	b	8 × 70	8 × 70	8 × 70	**OL:** Balance drill #4
Dumbbell lunge, upright row	b	8 × 70	8 × 70	8 × 70	**DL:** Agility over bags
Cylinder circuit #3					**RB:** Balance drill #4
Manual neck					**KICK:** Kick
					PUNT: Balance drill #4, punt

Conditioning training

Flexibility and warm-up: 10:00   8 × through movement course #3

Total workout time: 36:00

Rest: b (basic)—1:45 between sets
s (supporting)—1:00 between sets
Take 1:30 between exercises

THURSDAY

Resistance training						Skill training
Exercise		**Repetitions × % 1 RM**				On your own:
Incline bench press	b	6 × 65	6 × 70	6 × 75	6 × 80	Foot-speed drill #2
Medicine ball chest pass	b	10 reps	10 reps			
Military press	s	6 × 70	6 × 75	4 × 80	4 × 85	
Dumbbell push press	s	6 × 65	6 × 75	6 × 80		
Wrist flex (each hand)	s	100 reps	100 reps			
Triceps push-down	s	8 × 65	8 × 70	8 × 75		
Jump rope	b	100 reps	100 reps			
Manual neck						

Conditioning training

Flexibility and warm-up: 10:00

Total workout time: 35:00

Indian run: 20:00

FRIDAY

Resistance training						Skill training
Exercise		**Repetitions × % 1 RM**				On your own:
Close-grip lat	b	8 × 65	8 × 70	8 × 75		Ball-drop reaction drill and starts
EZ-bar pullover	s	8 × 65	8 × 70	8 × 75		
Rear deltoid swim	s	20 reps	20 reps			
Hang clean (light)	b	8 × 70	8 × 70	8 × 70		
Leg press	s	6 × 65	6 × 70	4 × 80	4 × 85	
Two-leg curl	s	10 × 70	10 × 70	10 × 70	10 × 70	
Backward lunge	s	10 reps	10 reps	10 reps		
Cylinder circuit #4						
Manual neck						

Conditioning training

Flexibility and warm-up: 10:00

Total workout time: 25:00

Three-cone reaction drill

8 × 60 yd parachute, sled pulling, or partner-resisted run with a release of the resistance at 30 yd

Phase 4 ■ Week 29

Resistance training						Skill training

MONDAY

Exercise		Repetitions × % 1 RM			
Bench press	b	6 × 70	6 × 75	4 × 80	4 × 85
Incline dumbbell press	b	8 × 65	8 × 70	8 × 75	
Military press	b	6 × 70	6 × 75	6 × 80	6 × 85
Side dumbbell raise	s	8 × 65	8 × 65	8 × 65	
Straight-bar curl	b	8 × 65	8 × 75	8 × 80	
Dumbbell French press	b	6 × 80	6 × 80	6 × 80	
Standing calf raise	s	25 × 45	25 × 45		
Manual neck					

Skill training — On your own: Balance drill #3

Conditioning training

Flexibility and warm-up: 10:00

Total workout time: 38:00

Four-station agility: Run to each station (4 × 5:00 stations).

T drill Snake S drill Bags

Sprints: 8 × 60 all-out effort; rest 1:00 after every 4 sprints

Resistance training					Skill training

TUESDAY

Exercise		Repetitions × % 1 RM		
One-arm dumbbell row	b	8 × 65	8 × 70	8 × 75
Close high lat	s	8 × 65	8 × 70	8 × 75
Dumbbell snatch, push press	b	8 × 70	8 × 70	8 × 70
Dumbbell step-up, shoulder fly	b	8 × 70	8 × 70	8 × 70
Backward lunge, dumbbell upright row	b	8 × 70	8 × 70	8 × 70
Cylinder circuit #3				
Manual neck				

Skill training:
DB: Play tag games
WR: Play dodge ball
QB: Agility over bags
LB: Review defensive signal calls
OL: Work on pass protection against a DL
DL: Work on pass rush against an OL
RB: Work on blocking (sled)
KICK: Kick
PUNT: Work on passing football, punt

Conditioning training

Flexibility and warm-up: 10:00

Total workout time: 35:00

Game simulation sprints: 1st quarter

Rest: b (basic)—1:45 between sets
s (supporting)—1:00 between sets
Take 1:30 between exercises

Phase 4 ■ Week 30

Resistance training | Skill training

Exercise		Repetitions × % 1 RM			
Incline bench press	b	6 × 65	6 × 70	6 × 75	6 × 80
Dip	b	max reps	max reps	max reps	
Behind neck press	s	6 × 70	6 × 75	4 × 80	4 × 85
Dumbbell push press	s	6 × 65	6 × 75	6 × 80	
Alternating dumbbell curl	s	6 × 65	6 × 75	6 × 80	
Triceps push-down	s	8 × 65	8 × 70	8 × 75	
Three-sided square drills		30 sec	30 sec	30 sec	30 sec
Manual neck					

Skill training

On your own:

Foot-speed drill #3

THURSDAY

Conditioning training

Flexibility and warm-up: 10:00

Total workout time: 35:00

5% grade downhill running. Build speed first 20 yd, sprint last 40 yd. Jog back up hill after each. If no hill is available, do the same Thursday workout as week 31.

4 × 60 yd

Rest: 2:00

4 × 60 yd

Rest: 2:00

3 × 60 yd

Rest: 2:00

3 × 60 yd

Resistance training | Skill training

Exercise		Repetitions × % 1 RM			
Close-grip lat	b	8 × 70	8 × 75	8 × 80	
High lat front	s	8 × 65	8 × 70	8 × 75	
Dumbbell dead lift	b	8 × 65	8 × 75	8 × 80	
Hang clean (light)	b	8 × 70	8 × 70	8 × 70	
Leg press	s	6 × 65	6 × 70	4 × 80	4 × 85
Two-leg curl	s	10 × 70	10 × 70	10 × 70	10 × 70
Slideboard	s	30 crosses		30 crosses	
Cylinder circuit #2					
Manual neck					

Skill training

On your own:

Movement course #3

FRIDAY

Phase 4 ■ Week 30

73

CHAPTER 5

PHASE 5:
Preseason Workouts

GOAL *To increase nerve activity and excitability by gradually increasing the level of resistance on each core and supercore exercise. The result is optimal power and explosive potential for football.*

Phase 5 continues the exercise plan through early August, when the second session of summer school ends for many collegiate players. During the second week in August, collegiate athletes return for fall camp, and high school athletes are getting into their practice season. This is a good time for coaches to test players for the year. Players should be reaching a peak in their power output and performance in agility and speed activities.

Resistance Training

The basic purpose of this phase is again to increase gradually your level of nerve activity and excitability. Muscle mass continues to increase but less from a fatigue-related response and more from the load increases planned during the exercises.

Types of Exercises

The exercises during this phase consist of basic lifts and multijoint supporting and assisting exercises. You will use less cable and machine resistance in favor of free-weight resistance and power-producing techniques. As in all phases of the plan, you exercise the larger muscle groups first in the workout, working smaller muscle groups last.

Rest, Volume, and Special Sets

Rest 2:00 between the sets of basic exercises and 1:00 between the sets of all supporting exercises throughout this phase. This added recovery between sets of basic exercises ensures that with each repetition you will effectively excite the nerve pathways that activate the muscle. Rest between exercises remains at 1:30.

The number of sets and repetitions in the workouts gradually decreases over the seven-week period. This lowered volume is another method of increasing the overall level of nerve activity and excitability, which, in turn, increases power output. This phase includes no special sets.

Repetition Style and Speed

During this phase the style of repetition is less strict. Perform each repetition with good form to avoid injury. Incorporate more speed or force into the movement to compensate for the higher resistance that you are using. Even though the speed of the arms and legs may seem slower because of the heavier weight, the muscles will be working at a higher speed or force at the cellular level. By week 35, you should be pushing with everything you have to move the resistance while maintaining good form.

Speed means power. This simply means that the faster you can move a heavy resistance, the more powerful you are. This also means that the faster you can move your body against a resistance, or against gravity, the more powerful you are.

The objective during power-type resistance training is not overall muscular fatigue or momentary muscular failure, as in hypertrophy resistance training (phase 1). In fact, failure of the muscle to perform may be detrimental during a power-producing phase of training.

Power training produces its result at the level of the nervous system. Proper power training can result in improvements in motor unit recruitment, increased firing rate of the motor units, synchronization of motor units, and clearer, faster nerve information arriving to the muscle (disinhibition). In short, power training trains your nervous system to send a fast and clear signal from the brain to a more readily accepting muscle. As a result, you can call more muscle fibers into play and therefore produce a more powerful movement.

To prompt the nervous system to produce a more powerful impulse, I recommend doing some movements, such as medicine ball throws or jumping exercises, with a moderate level of resistance (60 percent of 1 RM). This will produce higher movement speeds. You can perform other movements, such as weight-training exercises, with heavy resistance (80 percent or greater of 1 RM), which will result in slower movement speeds. Some strength coaches feel it is necessary to perform traditional weight-training workouts with low resistance at high speeds to optimize speed or power output. What is occurring inside the muscle, however, is independent of the external speed of the arm or leg. The speed of muscle-fiber contraction determines the power output. Some athletes may seem to move slowly, but they still might be generating high muscular force.

Execute the repetitions in this phase with a pausing tempo. You can perform some repetitions without pause. But as the resistance begins to cause fatigue, pause for an instant in a locked-out position to allow momentary recuperation. This will help insure that each repetition is powerful.

Running and Conditioning

Conditioning during this phase is much the same as the conditioning in phase 2. If you would like to create a different plan for this time of the year, be sure to emphasize a gradual increase in sprint training yardage over the phase. Usually yardage begins around 700 to 900 yards and increases over the weeks, to somewhat less than 2,000 yards per sprint workout session. After a heavy sprint workout, customarily conducted near the first day of the week, a reduction in exercise intensity can provide a form of active recovery. The second exercise session of the week can therefore consist of combination runs or short distance work. The final session of the week can return to sprint training or agility work, foot-speed drills, and plyometric activities. A second sprint workout should include fewer yards and a slower time than the first workout of the week. Using different exercises and exercise formats provides you with more movement information for your sports skills.

When scanning the program you may wonder where the plyometric drills are. I use plyometric drills on the speed days of week 31. But other plyometric movements are subtly incorporated into the conditioning plan, in the applied-skills section of the workout page. Remember that most athletic movement is somewhat plyometric. Unlike track, football consists of a variety of events meshed together rather than one event performed in one direction. With that in mind, plyometrics should probably be incorporated into related football movement drills. Do not overuse plyometric techniques by performing them too often. One plyometric workout per week should provide benefits while minimizing potential harm. Also keep the number of sets and repetitions of a plyometric workout in the low to moderate range. One or two sets of 10 repetitions conducted over five exercises should provide a safe and sufficient plyometric workout. More is not better with this type of exercise.

Weeks 31 to 37 include three conditioning workouts each with these emphases:

Monday—Agility drills (chapter 11)

Tuesday—Game simulation sprints (chapter 10)

Thursday—Speedwork (practical strength for sprint form and starts; chapter 10)

By the end of phase 5 agility work has replaced interval sprints altogether. You can perform these drills at high speed with little rest, thus producing good cardiorespiratory benefits. The conditioning training workload is reduced from four days per week to three to boost recovery, in turn furthering power output.

© Active Images

MONDAY

Resistance training						Skill training
Exercise		**Repetitions × % 1 RM**				On your own:
Bench press	b	5 × 70	5 × 75	4 × 80	4 × 85	10 quality vertical jumps (Jump to measured height; attempt to better previous jump.)
Ham decline	b	6 × 65	6 × 70	6 × 75	6 × 80	
Dumbbell snatch	b	8 × 75	8 × 80	6 × 85		
Shoulder fly	s	8 × 65	8 × 65	8 × 65		
Straight-bar curl	b	8 × 65	8 × 75	8 × 80		
Bar triceps extension	b	6 × 65	6 × 75	6 × 80		
Three-sided square drills		30 sec	30 sec	30 sec		
Manual neck						

Conditioning training

Flexibility and warm-up: 10:00

Total workout time: 40:00

Cutting quickness (four stations with groups of five)

1. 10 × 10 yd crosses (alternate plant foot each time both directions)
2. Transitional carioca (changing directions on command)
3. **Line:** Lateral shuffle over low hurdles, sprint out forward
   Backs: Cutting inside and outside legs from cone to cone
4. Tag games: Your choice

TUESDAY

Resistance training					Skill training
Exercise		**Repetitions × % 1 RM**			**WR:** Work on pass catching (JUGS machine)
Close high lat	b	6 × 65	6 × 75	6 × 80	**DB:** Play dodge ball
High lat rear	s	8 × 65	8 × 70	8 × 75	**QB:** Balance drill #4
Dumbbell pull press	b	8 × 70	8 × 70	8 × 70	**LB:** Work on pass drops and covering flats
Dumbbell step-up, shoulder fly	b	8 × 70	8 × 70	8 × 70	**OL:** Agility over bags
Backward lunge, dumbbell upright row	b	8 × 70	8 × 70	8 × 70	**DL:** Work on RIPS and SWIMS (tackle dummy)
Cylinder circuit #3					**RB:** Review offensive plays (prep for season)
Manual neck					**KICK:** Kick
					PUNT: Play dodge ball, punt

Conditioning training

Flexibility and warm-up: 10:00

Total workout time: 35:00

Game simulation spring: 1st and 2nd quarters

78

Resistance training

Exercise		Repetitions × % 1 RM			
Incline bench press	b	5 × 70	5 × 75	4 × 80	4 × 85
Dip	b	max reps	max reps	max reps	
Behind neck press	s	5 × 70	5 × 75	4 × 80	4 × 85
Alternating dumbbell press (hard)	s	6 × 65	6 × 75	6 × 80	
Alternating dumbbell curl	b	6 × 65	6 × 75	6 × 80	
Triceps push-down	s	8 × 65	8 × 70	8 × 75	
Medicine ball circuit	b	10 reps	10 reps		
Manual neck					

On your own:

10 quality long jumps (Jump to measured length; attempt to better previous jump.)

THURSDAY

Conditioning training

Flexibility and warm-up: 10:00	4 × 30 yd standing triple jump
Total workout time: 35:00	4 × 40 yd standing long jump
Sprint and acceleration	5 × 20 yd shuttles (as many stations as needed to divide team)

Plyometrics (chapter 9)

4 × 20 yd alternate leg bounding

4 × 20 yd horizontal power skip

Resistance training

Exercise		Repetitions × % 1 RM			
Close-grip lat	b	8 × 70	8 × 75	8 × 80	
High lat front	s	8 × 65	8 × 70	8 × 75	
Dumbbell dead lift	b	8 × 65	8 × 75	8 × 80	
Roll-out	b	10 reps	10 reps	10 reps	
Leg press	b	5 × 65	5 × 70	4 × 80	4 × 90
Alternating leg lunge	s	10 reps	10 reps	10 reps	
Slideboard	s	30 crosses		30 crosses	
Cylinder circuit #5					
Manual neck					

On your own:

Movement course #1

FRIDAY

Phase 5 ■ Week 31

Rest: b (basic)—2:00 between sets

s (supporting)—1:00 between sets

Take 1:30 between exercises

MONDAY

Resistance training

Exercise		Repetitions × % 1 RM			
Bench press	b	4 × 70	4 × 75	4 × 80	4 × 90
Ham decline	b	6 × 65	6 × 70	6 × 75	6 × 80
Push press	b	4 × 70	4 × 75	4 × 80	4 × 90
Straight dumbbell pullover	b	15 × 75	15 × 75		
Bar triceps extension	b	6 × 80	6 × 80	6 × 80	
Three-sided square drills		30 sec	30 sec	30 sec	30 sec
Manual neck					

Skill training

On your own:

10 quality vertical jumps

Conditioning training

Flexibility and warm-up: 10:00

Total workout time: 40:00

Four-station agility drill: Run to each station.

Bags   Cones   Triangle   Reaction drills

Sprints 12 × 40 all-out effort; rest 1:00 after every 6 sprints

TUESDAY

Resistance training

Exercise		Repetitions × % 1 RM			
High lat rear	b	8 × 75	8 × 80	8 × 85	
Power clean or power row	b	4 × 65	4 × 75	4 × 80	
Dumbbell stroll (70+ lb dumbbells)	s	40 yd and back 40 yd and back			
Straight-bar curl	b	6 × 70	6 × 80	6 × 85	
Squat	b	4 × 65	4 × 70	4 × 80	4 × 90
Step-up (alternating legs, 15 lb dumbbell)	s	20 reps	20 reps		
Cylinder circuit #3					
Manual neck					

Skill training

DB: Pass coverage against WRs

QB: Passing game

WR: Pass routes against DBs

LB: Balance drill #4

OL: Review blocking assignments

DL: Play tag games

RB: Work with #1 QB on pass receiving

KICK: Kick

PUNT: Pass, punt

Conditioning training

Flexibility and warm-up: 10:00

Total workout time: 35:00

Game simulation sprints: 1st, 2nd, and 3rd quarters

Resistance training — Skill training

Exercise		Repetitions × % 1 RM			
Incline bench press	b	4 × 70	4 × 75	4 × 80	4 × 85
Ballistic push-up	b	10 reps	10 reps	10 reps	
Dumbbell push press	s	4 × 70	4 × 75	4 × 80	4 × 90
Alternating dumbbell press (hard)	s	6 × 65	6 × 75	6 × 80	
Triceps push-down	s	8 × 65	8 × 70	8 × 75	
Medicine ball circuit	b	10 reps	10 reps		
Manual neck					

Skill training

On your own:

10 quality long jumps

THURSDAY

Conditioning training

Flexibility and warm-up: 10:00

Total workout time: 35:00

Three-cone reaction drill

8 × 60 yd parachute, sled, or partner-resisted run with a release of resistance at 30 yd

Resistance training — Skill training

Exercise		Repetitions × % 1 RM			
Pull-up	b	max reps	max reps	max reps	
Dead lift	b	6 × 65	6 × 75	6 × 80	
Roll-out	b	10 reps	10 reps	10 reps	
Alternating dumbbell curl	b	6 × 65	6 × 75	6 × 80	
Leg press	b	4 × 65	4 × 70	4 × 80	4 × 90
Alternating leg lunge	s	10 reps	10 reps	10 reps	
Skate bound		10 reps	10 reps	10 reps	
Cylinder circuit #4					
Manual neck					

Skill training

On your own:

Movement course #2

FRIDAY

Phase 5 ■ Week 32

Rest: b (basic)—2:00 between sets

s (supporting)—1:00 between sets

Take 1:30 between exercises

MONDAY

Resistance training

Exercise		Repetitions × % 1 RM			
Bench press	b	10 × 65 4 × 75 2 × 80 1 × 90			
		1 × 95 1 × 100			
Incline dumbbell press	b	6 × 65	6 × 70	6 × 75	6 × 80
Push press	b	4 × 70	4 × 75	4 × 80	4 × 90
Straight dumbbell pullover	b	15 × 75	15 × 75		
Slideboard, wall explosion		10 reps	10 reps	10 reps	
Manual neck					

Skill training

On your own:

10 quality vertical jumps

Conditioning training

Flexibility and warm-up: 10:00

Total workout time: 40:00

1. Quick feet drills: 3 × 30 sec
2. 4 × 20 yd shuttle: Alternate foot plant each time for both directions; this drill strengthens the ability to cut to the side from either leg.
3. **Line:** Lateral shuffle over bags, sprint out forward
   Backs: Ball-drop reaction drills
4. Dodge ball: Groups

TUESDAY

Resistance training

Exercise		Repetitions × % 1 RM			
Close low lat	b	8 × 75	8 × 80	8 × 85	
Power clean or power row	b	4 × 65	4 × 75	4 × 80	
Medicine ball underhand backward throw	b	15 reps	15 reps	15 reps	
Straight-bar curl	b	6 × 70	6 × 80	6 × 85	
Squat	b	4 × 65	4 × 70	4 × 80	4 × 90
Step-up (alternating legs, 20 lb dumbbells)	s	20 reps	20 reps		
Vertical jump (for max height)		10 reps			
Cylinder circuit #3					
Manual neck					

Skill training

DB: Balance drill #4

WR: Balance drill #4

QB: Review plays (prep for season)

LB: Pass catching (JUGS machine)

OL: Pass protection against a DL

DL: Pass rush against an OL

RB: Blocking with sled

KICK: Kick

PUNT: Punt

Conditioning training

Flexibility and warm-up: 10:00

Total workout time: 35:00

Game simulation sprints: 1st, 2nd, 3rd, and 4th quarters

Resistance training

Exercise		Repetitions × % 1 RM			
Incline bench press	b	5 × 70	5 × 75	4 × 80	4 × 85
Ballistic push-up	b	10 reps	10 reps	10 reps	
Dumbbell push press	b	4 × 70	4 × 75	4 × 80	4 × 90
Alternating dumbbell press	s	6 × 70	6 × 80	6 × 85	
Medicine ball circuit	b	10 reps	10 reps		
Manual neck					

Skill training

On your own:

10 quality long jumps

THURSDAY

Conditioning training

Flexibility and warm-up: 10:00

Total workout time: 35:00

Sprint-stride-sprint: 12 × 60 yd

Starts: 10 × 10 yd thrusts (These assist in speed coming out of the blocks on the start of the 40 yd dash test.)

Resistance training

Exercise		Repetitions × % 1 RM			
Pull-up	b	max reps	max reps	max reps	
Dead lift	b	8 × 70	8 × 80	8 × 90	
Leg dragging	s	15 yd	15 yd	15 yd	15 yd
Leg press	b	4 × 70	4 × 75	4 × 80	4 × 90
Alternating leg lunge	s	10 reps	10 reps	10 reps	
Skate bound		10 reps	10 reps	10 reps	
Cylinder circuit #2					
Manual neck					

Skill training

On your own:

10 quality vertical jumps

FRIDAY

Phase 5 ■ Week 33

Rest: b (basic)—2:00 between sets
s (supporting)—1:00 between sets
Take 1:30 between exercises

Phase 5 ▪ Week 34

MONDAY

Resistance training

Exercise		Repetitions × % 1 RM			
Bench press	b	10 × 65	4 × 75	2 × 80	1 × 90
		1 × 95	1 × 100*		
Incline dumbbell press	b	6 × 65	6 × 70	6 × 75	6 × 80
Push press	b	4 × 70	4 × 75	4 × 80	4 × 90
Split dumbbell pullover	b	15 × 60	15 × 60		
Slideboard, wall explosion		10 reps	10 reps	10 reps	
Manual neck					

*1 RM or complete muscular failure is not advised for athletes under age 16. Use estimated repetition instead.

Skill training

On your own:

10 quality vertical jumps

Conditioning training

Flexibility and warm-up: 10:00

Total workout time: 40:00

Cutting speed (groups of three)

1. Quick feet drills 3 × 30 sec
2. 4 × 20 yd shuttle (alternate foot plant each time both directions)
3. **Line:** Lateral shuffle over bags, sprint out forward
   Backs: Ball-drop reaction drills
4. Dodge ball: Groups

TUESDAY

Resistance training

Exercise		Repetitions × % 1 RM			
Close low lat	b	8 × 75	8 × 80	8 × 85	
Power clean or power row	b	4 × 65	4 × 75	4 × 80	
Medicine ball underhand backward throw	b	15 reps	15 reps		
Straight-bar curl	b	6 × 70	6 × 80	6 × 85	
Squat	b	4 × 65	4 × 70	4 × 80	4 × 90
Step-up (alternating legs, 25-lb dumbbells)	b	20 reps	20 reps		
Vertical jump (for max height)		10 reps			
Cylinder circuit #3					
Manual neck					

Skill training

DB: Balance drill #4

WR: Blocking with sled

QB: Agility over bags

LB: Review defensive signal calls

OL: Pass protection against a DL

DL: Pass rush against an OL

RB: Review offensive plays (prep for season)

KICK: Kick

PUNT: Punt

Conditioning training

Flexibility and warm-up: 10:00

Total workout time: 35:00

Sprints

	WR, DB, RB	LB, TE, FB	Line
8 × 200 yd	:32	:34	:36

Resistance training

Exercise		Repetitions × % 1 RM			
Incline bench press	b	5 × 70	5 × 75	4 × 80	4 × 85
Ballistic push-up	b	10 reps	10 reps	10 reps	
Dumbbell push press	b	4 × 70	4 × 75	4 × 80	4 × 90
Alternating dumbbell press	s	6 × 70	6 × 80	6 × 85	
Medicine ball circuit	b	10 reps	10 reps		
Manual neck					

Skill training

On your own:

10 quality long jumps

Conditioning training

Flexibility and warm-up: 10:00

Total workout time: 35:00

5 × 20 yd shuttles. Create as many stations as needed to divide team efficiently.

Starts: 10 × 10 yd thrusts

THURSDAY

Resistance training

Exercise		Repetitions × % 1 RM			
Pull-up	b	max reps	max reps	max reps	
Dead lift	b	8 × 70	8 × 80	8 × 90	
Leg dragging	s	15 yd	15 yd	15 yd	15 yd
Leg press	b	4 × 70	4 × 75	4 × 80	4 × 90
Alternating leg lunge	s	10 reps	10 reps	10 reps	
Skate bound		10 reps	10 reps	10 reps	
Cylinder circuit #5					
Manual neck					

Skill training

On your own:

10 quality vertical jumps

FRIDAY

Rest: b (basic)—2:00 between sets
s (supporting)—1:00 between sets
Take 1:30 between exercises

Phase 5 ■ Week 34

MONDAY

Resistance training

Exercise		Repetitions × % 1 RM
Bench press	b	10 × 65 4 × 75 2 × 80 1 × 90 1 × 95 1 × 100*
Bench press		max reps × 225 lb
Push press	b	6 × 80 6 × 80 6 × 80 6 × 80
Split dumbbell pullover	b	15 × 60 15 × 60
Quick feet drills		30 sec 30 sec 30 sec
Manual neck		
		* 1 RM or complete muscular failure is not advised for athletes under age 16. Use estimated repetition instead.

TUESDAY

Resistance training

Exercise		Repetitions × % 1 RM
Pull-up	b	max reps max reps max reps
Power clean or power row	b	4 × 65 4 × 75 4 × 80
Medicine ball underhand backward throw	b	15 reps 15 reps 15 reps
Straight-bar curl	b	6 × 70 6 × 80 6 × 85
Step-up (alternating legs, 25 lb dumbbells)	s	20 reps 20 reps
Vertical jump (for max height)		10 reps
Cylinder circuit #3		
Manual neck		

THURSDAY

Resistance training

Exercise		Repetitions × % 1 RM
Bench press		max reps × 225 lb
Squat	b	10 × 65 4 × 75 2 × 80 1 × 90 1 × 95 1 × 100*

Conditioning training

Flexibility and warm-up: 10:00

Test: 40 yd timing

FRIDAY

Conditioning training

Flexibility and warm-up: 10:00   20 yd shuttle test

Vertical jump test   Long jump test

Conditioning test (8 × 200 yd sprints :32, :34, :36)

Rest: b (basic)—2:00 between sets   Take 1:30 between exercises

s (supporting)—1:00 between sets

Week off

MONDAY

Resistance training

Exercise		Repetitions × % 1 RM
Bench press		max reps × 225 lb
Squat	b	10 × 65 4 × 75 2 × 80 1 × 90 1 × 95 1 × 100*
		*1 RM or complete muscular failure is not advised for athletes under age 16. Use estimated repetition instead.

Conditioning training

Flexibility and warm-up: 10:00	Test 40 yd timing
	20 yd shuttle test

TUESDAY

Conditioning training

Flexibility and warm-up: 10:00	Vertical jump test
	Long jump test
	Conditioning test (8 × 200 yd sprints :32, :34, :36)

THURSDAY

Resistance training

Exercise		Repetitions × % 1 RM		
Bench press	b	8 × 70	8 × 70	8 × 70
Incline dumbbell press	s	10 × 70	10 × 70	10 × 70
Close-grip lat	b	10 × 75	10 × 75	10 × 75
Close low lat	s	10 × 70	10 × 70	10 × 70
Behind neck press	b	8 × 70	8 × 70	8 × 70
Side dumbbell raise	s	15 × 55	15 × 55	
Preacher curl (push-pull)	s	12 × 65	12 × 65	
Kickback (push-pull)	s	12 × 65	12 × 65	
Cylinder circuit #4				
Manual neck				

Rest: b (basic)—2:00 between sets
      s (supporting)—1:00 between sets
      Take 1:30 between exercises

CHAPTER 6

PHASE 6:
In-Season Workouts

GOAL *To increase resistance slowly on the core lifts each week when possible and induce momentary muscle fatigue (MMF) on the last set of all supporting exercises.*

Phase 6 begins with football season. This plan details week 38 through the end of the training year, week 52, but may last longer in the event of a bowl bid or championship game (see chapter 1, page 13). The last week of the in-season workout can be repeated as needed to complete the bowl-season extension, or you can repeat the last three weeks of the in-season workouts in order. This will not impede fitness because the in-season portion of the workout plan is a maintenance period. Shifting this period will not reduce your yearly workout effort.

This maintenance phase considers the participation status of both starters (travel squad—**T**) and nonstarters (nontravel squad—**N**). The nontravel group works out more days per week than the travel squad. More work allows these players more opportunity to enhance their strength, even during the in-season period. **E** marks workouts designed for the entire team.

Resistance Training

The purpose of this phase for the travel squad is to maintain the power and endurance gained during phases 4 and 5. For the nontravel athlete, workout frequency is higher, workout volume is lower, but the workout is still relatively high in intensity.

Types of Exercises

The exercises during this phase consist of basic lifts and multijoint supporting exercises. Push-pull techniques (described in "Rest, Volume, and Special Sets" below) are applied to every workout in each of these weeks. On week 40, the travel squad begins working out twice a week, while the nontravel squad works out three times per week. The nontravel squad performs traditional straight sets on their exercises, while the travel squad applies the push-pull techniques on the second workout day. These push-pull lifts speed up the workout and increase its intensity.

Rest, Volume, and Special Sets

The rest between the sets of an exercise remains the same as the phase progresses—1:30 between sets of basic exercises and 1:00 between sets of supporting exercises. You can reduce this time proportionately if your position or team meetings limit the time available for your workout. During in-season training, you have a high risk of experiencing burnout or overload, so keep your workout short but challenging. You can complete these workouts in 30 minutes. The amount of rest between exercises remains at 1:30.

The in-season also provides the opportunity for circuit resistance training. In circuit training, take only enough time between each set for your partner to complete all his reps, then move onto the next exercise.

Phase 6 workouts maintain the number of repetitions at 6 for basic exercises. This ensures power maintenance. Perform 8 repetitions of supporting exercises to address muscular endurance and fatigue levels. To make sure that you accomplish this, perform the last set of the supporting exercises to failure. Perform 12 repetitions of light-weight leg work. Light weight and high reps increase blood flow to the muscle without inducing extreme fatigue. The particular leg exercises highlighted during this phase are just a suggestion. It is fine to use squats and leg presses in your routine during the in-season phase if you wish, but keep the repetitions high and the weight light.

Along with the push-pull workouts, the travel squad uses some supersets to save time during the workout and to heighten intensity. Push-pull workouts involve alternating each set of a push-pull pair. For example, you'll follow a set of incline bench press with a set of high lat front and then repeat the cycle until you complete all sets of both exercises. Perform these supersets through week 45. At week 45 stop both the supersets and the push-pull sets. Even though the exercises are set up so that a pull exercise follows a push exercise, complete all sets of each exercise type before moving to the next type. This change in exercise format will begin a subtle swing toward the style of lifting you will perform in the hypertrophy stage in the upcoming off-season.

Repetition Style and Speed

During this phase the style of repetition is less strict on the basic lifts but more strict on the supporting lifts. This ensures that you meet both power and endurance needs. Execute the repetitions in this phase with a pausing tempo on the basic lifts and a more constant tempo on the supporting lifts. This way you will maintain both power and endurance.

Running and Conditioning

The majority of conditioning in this phase is incorporated into football practice, during drills and play. You may, however, want to do some postpractice conditioning to help you acclimatize to the August heat. Up to now, you have been training in the heat but not with football apparel, which presents a new conditioning element. You can adjust to the increased heat by wearing your gear for 4 to 14 days of hot-weather training.

Coaches may collaborate and include a postpractice conditioning session that can meet your conditioning needs. If postpractice conditioning is not part of the practice plan, some players will undoubtedly be at a disadvantage. Because of their second or third playing status, their physical conditioning may suffer. For this reason, I encourage all athletes to run on their own. The strength and conditioning staff may administer these runs, which might not be mandatory, during the early morning before classes begin. If you choose to run on your own during the in-season, the runs should primarily address your sprint conditioning needs. The sprint workouts should not exceed 800 total yards per session, and you should perform them no more than twice per week. You can perform a light sprint workout or combination running on another day later in the week.

Anthony Neste ©

MONDAY

Resistance training   Ⓔ

Exercise		Repetitions × % 1 RM		
Bench press	b	8 × 75	8 × 75	8 × 75
Close-grip lat	b	8 × 75	8 × 75	8 × 75
Military press	b	10 × 65	10 × 65	
Free-weight upright row	b	10 × 65	10 × 65	
Close-grip bench	b	8 × 75	8 × 75	
Straight-bar curl	b	8 × 75	8 × 75	
Two-leg extension	s	15 × 60	15 × 60	
Two-leg curl	s	12 × 75	12 × 75	12 × 75
Slideboard	s	30 crosses	30 crosses	
Cylinder circuit #1				
Manual neck				

Conditioning training   Ⓔ

Camp, except for those players who did not pass the conditioning test.

TUESDAY

Resistance training   Ⓔ

Exercise		Repetitions × % 1 RM		
Bench press	b	8 × 75	8 × 75	8 × 75
Close-grip lat	b	8 × 75	8 × 75	8 × 75
Military press	b	10 × 65	10 × 65	
Free-weight upright row	b	10 × 65	10 × 65	
Close-grip bench	b	8 × 75	8 × 75	
Straight-bar curl	b	8 × 75	8 × 75	
Two-leg extension	s	15 × 60	15 × 60	
Two-leg curl	s	12 × 75	12 × 75	12 × 75
Slideboard	s	30 crosses	30 crosses	
Cylinder circuit #1				
Manual neck				

Conditioning training   Ⓔ

Camp, except for those players who did not pass the conditioning test.

Rest: b (basic)—1:30 between sets
      s (supporting)—1:00 between sets
      Take 1:30 between exercises

Resistance training ⒠

Exercise		Repetitions × % 1 RM		
Incline bench press	b	10 × 65	10 × 65	10 × 65
One-arm dumbbell row	b	8 × 75	8 × 75	8 × 75
Alternating dumbbell press	s	10 × 65	10 × 65	10 × 65
Bar shrug	s	20 × 50	20 × 50	
Preacher curl (cable)	s	10 × 65	10 × 65	
Triceps push-down	s	10 × 65	10 × 65	
Alternating leg lunge	b	15 reps	15 reps	
Two-leg curl	s	12 × 70	12 × 70	12 × 70
Ab-ad	s	25 × 45		
Cylinder circuit #2				
Manual neck				

Conditioning training ⒠

Camp, except for those players who did not pass the conditioning test.

THURSDAY

Resistance training ⒠

Exercise		Repetitions × % 1 RM		
Incline bench press	b	10 × 65	10 × 65	10 × 65
One-arm dumbbell row	b	8 × 75	8 × 75	8 × 75
Alternating dumbbell press	b	10 × 65	10 × 65	
Bar shrug	s	20 × 50	20 × 50	
Preacher curl (cable)	s	10 × 65	10 × 65	
Triceps push-down	s	10 × 65	10 × 65	
Alternating leg lunge	b	15 reps	15 reps	
Two-leg curl	s	12 × 70	12 × 70	12 × 70
Ab-ad	s	25 × 45		
Cylinder circuit #2				
Manual neck				

Conditioning training ⒠

Camp, except for those players who did not pass the conditioning test.

FRIDAY

Phase 6 ■ Week 38

Resistance training · E

MONDAY

Exercise		Repetitions × % 1 RM		
Bench press	b	8 × 75	8 × 75	8 × 75
Close-grip lat	b	8 × 75	8 × 75	
Military press	b	10 × 65	10 × 65	8 × 75
Free-weight upright row	b	10 × 65	10 × 65	
Close-grip bench	b	8 × 75	8 × 75	
Straight-bar curl	b	8 × 75	8 × 75	
Two-leg extension	s	15 × 60	15 × 60	
Two-leg curl	s	12 × 75	12 × 75	12 × 75
Slideboard	s	30 crosses	30 crosses	
Cylinder circuit #1				
Manual neck				

Conditioning training · E

	WR, DB, RB	LB, TE, FB	Line
3 × 200 (short, 100 yd and back)	:30	:32	:34
Rest between sets	Time required for next two groups to run		

Resistance training · E

TUESDAY

Exercise		Repetitions × % 1 RM		
Bench press	b	8 × 75	8 × 75	8 × 75
Close-grip lat	b	8 × 75	8 × 75	8 × 75
Military press	b	10 × 65	10 × 65	
Free-weight upright row	b	10 × 65	10 × 65	
Close-grip bench	b	8 × 75	8 × 75	
Straight-bar curl	b	8 × 75	8 × 75	
Two-leg extension	s	15 × 60	15 × 60	
Two-leg curl	s	12 × 75	12 × 75	12 × 75
Slideboard	s	30 crosses	30 crosses	
Cylinder circuit #1				
Manual neck				

Conditioning training · E

	WR, DB, RB	LB, TE, FB	Line
4 × 100 (long, sprint entire field)	:13	:15	:17
Rest between sets	Time required for next two groups to run		

Rest: b (basic)—1:30 between sets

s (supporting)—1:00 between sets

Take 1:30 between exercises

Conditioning training   Ⓔ

8 × 50 all-out effort

Rest 2:00 after every 4 sprints.

Resistance training   Ⓔ

Exercise		Repetitions × % 1 RM		
Incline bench press	b	10 × 65	10 × 65	10 × 65
One-arm dumbbell row	b	8 × 75	8 × 75	8 × 75
Alternating dumbbell press	s	10 × 65	10 × 65	
Bar shrug	s	20 × 50	20 × 50	
Preacher curl (cable)	s	10 × 65	10 × 65	
Triceps push-down	s	10 × 65	10 × 65	
Alternating leg lunge	b	15 reps	15 reps	
Two-leg curl	s	12 × 70	12 × 70	12 × 70
Ab-ad	s	25 × 45		
Cylinder circuit #2				
Manual neck				

Resistance training   Ⓔ

Exercise		Repetitions × % 1 RM		
Bench press	b	8 × 75	8 × 75	8 × 75
Close-grip lat	b	8 × 75	8 × 75	8 × 75
Military press	b	10 × 65	10 × 65	
Free-weight upright row	b	10 × 65	10 × 65	
Close-grip bench	b	8 × 75	8 × 75	
Straight-bar curl	b	8 × 75	8 × 75	
Two-leg extension	s	15 × 60	15 × 60	
Two-leg curl	s	12 × 75	12 × 75	12 × 75
Slideboard	s	30 crosses	30 crosses	
Cylinder circuit #1				
Manual neck				

MONDAY

Resistance training   (T)

Exercise		Repetitions × % 1 RM		
Bench press	b	8 × 65	8 × 70	8 × 75
Incline dumbbell press	b	10 × 65	10 × 65	
Close-grip lat	b	8 × 75	8 × 75	
Two-arm dumbbell press	b	8 × 65	8 × 70	8 × 75
Cable upright row (superset)	s	10 × 65	10 × 65	
Dumbbell shrug (superset)	s	15 × 60	15 × 60	
EZ-bar curl	b	8 × 75	8 × 75	
Dumbbell French press	b	8 × 75	8 × 75	
Squat	b	8 × 70	8 × 70	8 × 70
Two-leg curl	s	12 × 70	12 × 70	12 × 70
Cylinder circuit #2				
Manual neck				

Resistance training   (N)

Exercise		Repetitions × % 1 RM		
Bench press	b	8 × 65	8 × 70	8 × 75
Incline dumbbell press	b	8 × 65	8 × 70	8 × 75
Dip	b	max reps	max reps	
Military press	b	10 × 65	8 × 70	8 × 75
Side dumbbell raise	s	10 × 60	10 × 60	
Straight-bar curl	b	8 × 75	8 × 75	
Alternating dumbbell curl	b	8 × 75	8 × 75	
Standing calf raise		25 × 45		
Cylinder circuit #1				
Manual neck				

Conditioning training   (E)

	WR, DB, RB	LB, TE, FB	Line
3 × 200 (short, 100 yd and back)	:30	:32	:34
Rest between sets	Time required for next two groups to run		

Rest: b (basic)—1:30 between sets
      s (supporting)—1:00 between sets
      Take 1:30 between exercises

Resistance training · N

TUESDAY

Exercise		Repetitions × % 1 RM			
Close-grip lat	b	8 × 65	8 × 70	8 × 75	
High lat front	s	8 × 70	8 × 70	8 × 70	
Free-weight upright row	b	12 × 65	12 × 75		
Dumbbell shrug	s	15 × 60	15 × 60		
Dumbbell French press	b	8 × 75	8 × 75		
Squat	b	8 × 60	8 × 65	8 × 70	8 × 75
Alternating leg lunge	s	12 reps	12 reps		
Two-leg curl	s	10 × 60	10 × 60	10 × 60	10 × 60
Cylinder circuit #2					

Conditioning training · E

	WR, DB, RB	LB, TE, FB	Line
4 × 100 (short, 50 yd and back)	:14	:16	:18
Rest between sets	Time required for next two groups to run		

Conditioning training · E

WED.

8 × 40 all-out effort
Rest 1:00 after every 4 sprints.

Resistance training · T

THURSDAY

Exercise		Repetitions × % 1 RM		
Incline bench press	b	10 × 65	10 × 65	10 × 65
High lat front	s	10 × 65	10 × 65	
Behind neck press	b	8 × 65	8 × 70	8 × 75
Bent dumbbell raise	s	12 × 60	12 × 60	12 × 60
Preacher curl (cable)	s	10 × 65	10 × 65	
Triceps push-down	s	10 × 65	10 × 65	
Two-leg extension	s	12 × 65	12 × 65	
Alternating leg lunge	s	15 reps	15 reps	
One stiff leg dead	s	12 × 70	12 × 70	12 × 70
Cylinder circuit #3				
Manual neck				

Resistance training · N

Exercise		Repetitions × % 1 RM		
Flat dumbbell press	b	8 × 65	8 × 70	8 × 75
Incline bench press	b	10 × 65	10 × 65	
High lat rear	s	10 × 65	10 × 65	10 × 65
Behind neck press	b	8 × 65	8 × 70	8 × 75
Cable upright row	s	8 × 75	8 × 75	
Preacher curl (cable)	s	8 × 75	8 × 75	
Triceps push-down	s	8 × 75	8 × 75	
Leg press	b	10 × 70	10 × 70	10 × 70
Two-leg curl	s	12 × 75	12 × 75	12 × 75
Standing calf raise		25 × 45		
Cylinder circuit #4				
Manual neck				

Phase 6 ▪ Week 40

September

SUNDAY

Conditioning training	E
12-minute run	

MONDAY

Resistance training				T
Exercise		**Repetitions × % 1 RM**		
Bench press	b	8 × 65	8 × 70	8 × 75
Incline dumbbell press	b	10 × 65	10 × 65	
Close-grip lat	b	8 × 75	8 × 75	
Two-arm dumbbell press	b	8 × 65	8 × 70	8 × 75
Cable upright row (superset)	s	10 × 65	10 × 65	
Dumbbell shrug (superset)	s	15 × 60	15 × 60	
EZ-bar curl	b	8 × 75	8 × 75	
Dumbbell French press	b	8 × 75	8 × 75	
Squat	b	8 × 70	8 × 70	8 × 70
Two-leg curl	s	12 × 70	12 × 70	12 × 70
Cylinder circuit #4				
Manual neck				

Resistance training				N
Exercise		**Repetitions × % 1 RM**		
Bench press	b	8 × 65	8 × 70	8 × 75
Incline dumbbell press	b	8 × 65	8 × 70	8 × 75
Dip	b	max reps	max reps	
Military press	b	8 × 65	8 × 70	8 × 75
Side dumbbell raise	s	10 × 60	10 × 60	
Straight-bar curl	b	8 × 75	8 × 75	
Alternating dumbbell curl	b	8 × 75	8 × 75	
Standing calf raise		25 × 45		
Cylinder circuit #4				
Manual neck				

Rest: b (basic)—1:30 between sets
s (supporting)—1:00 between sets
Take 1:30 between exercises

Resistance training (N)

Exercise		Repetitions × % 1 RM			
Close-grip lat	b	8 × 65	8 × 70	8 × 75	
High lat front	s	8 × 70	8 × 70	8 × 70	
Free-weight upright row	b	12 × 65	12 × 75		
Dumbbell shrug	s	15 × 60	15 × 60		
Dumbbell French press	b	8 × 75	8 × 75		
Squat	b	8 × 60	8 × 65	8 × 70	8 × 75
Alternating leg lunge	s	12 reps	12 reps		
Two-leg curl	s	10 × 60	10 × 60	10 × 60	10 × 60
Cylinder circuit #2					

TUESDAY

Conditioning training (E)

8 × 50 all-out effort; rest 1:00 after every 4 sprints.

Resistance training (T)

Exercise		Repetitions × % 1 RM		
Incline bench press	b	10 × 65	10 × 65	10 × 65
High lat front	s	10 × 65	10 × 65	
Behind neck press	b	8 × 65	8 × 70	8 × 75
Bent dumbbell raise	s	12 × 60	12 × 60	12 × 60
Preacher curl (cable)	s	10 × 65	10 × 65	
Triceps push-down	s	10 × 65	10 × 65	
Two-leg extension	s	12 × 65	12 × 65	
Alternating leg lunge	s	15 reps	15 reps	
One stiff leg dead	s	12 × 70	12 × 70	12 × 70
Cylinder circuit #5				
Manual neck				

WEDNESDAY

Conditioning training (E)

	WR, DB, RB	LB, TE, FB	Line
3 × sideline ladders	:34	:35	:36
Rest between sets	1:10	1:10	1:10

Resistance training (N)

Exercise		Repetitions × % 1 RM		
Flat dumbbell press	s	8 × 65	8 × 70	8 × 75
High lat rear	s	10 × 65	10 × 65	10 × 65
Behind neck press	b	8 × 75	8 × 75	
Preacher curl (cable)	s	8 × 75	8 × 75	
Triceps push-down	s	8 × 75	8 × 75	
Leg press	b	10 × 70	10 × 70	10 × 70
Two-leg curl	s	12 × 75	12 × 75	12 × 75
Standing calf raise		25 × 45		
Cylinder circuit #5				
Manual neck				

THURSDAY

Phase 6 ■ Week 41

Resistance training   T

SUNDAY

Exercise		Repetitions × % 1 RM	
Bench press	c	8 × 75	8 × 80
Close-grip lat	c	8 × 75	8 × 75
Alternating dumbbell press (hard)	c	8 × 75	8 × 80
Dumbbell snatch	c	10 × 65	10 × 65
Roll-out	c	15 × 60	15 × 60
EZ-bar curl	c	8 × 75	8 × 75
Dumbbell French press	c	8 × 75	8 × 75
Squat	c	8 × 70	8 × 70
Two-leg curl	c	12 × 70	12 × 70
Cylinder circuit #4			
Manual neck			

Conditioning training   E

12-minute run

Resistance training   N

MONDAY

Exercise		Repetitions × % 1 RM			
Flat dumbbell press	b	8 × 60	8 × 65	8 × 70	8 × 75
Incline dumbbell press	b	8 × 70	8 × 70		
Behind neck press	b	8 × 65	8 × 70	8 × 75	
EZ-bar curl	b	8 × 70	8 × 70		
Dumbbell French press	b	8 × 70	8 × 70		
Squat	b	8 × 65	8 × 70	8 × 75	
Two-leg curl	s	12 × 75	12 × 75	12 × 75	
Standing calf raise		25 × 45			
Cylinder circuit #1					
Manual neck					

Resistance training   N

TUESDAY

Exercise		Repetitions × % 1 RM		
Push-up	s	20 reps	20 reps	20 reps
Close-grip lat	b	8 × 65	8 × 70	8 × 75
High lat front	s	8 × 75	8 × 75	8 × 75
Close low lat	s	10 × 65	10 × 65	
Free-weight upright row	b	10 × 70	10 × 70	
Medicine ball circuit				
Two-leg extension		10 × 70	10 x70	
Cylinder circuit #1				

Conditioning training   E

	WR, DB, RB	LB, TE, FB	Line
2 × 200 yd shuttle	:32	:34	:36
Rest	1:12	1:14	1:16

Rest: b (basic)—1:30 between sets   c (circuit—0:45 between sets
     s (supporting)—1:00 between sets   Take 1:30 between exercises

Resistance training   (T)

Exercise*		Repetitions × % 1 RM			
Incline bench press	s	8 × 75	8 × 75	8 × 80	
High lat front	s	10 × 65	10 × 65	10 × 65	
Flat dumbbell press	s	8 × 75	8 × 75	8 × 80	
Pull-up	s	max reps	max reps	max reps	
Rear deltoid swim	s	10 reps	10 reps		
Bent dumbbell raise	s	12 × 60	12 × 60	12 × 60	
Alternating dumbbell curl	s	10 × 65	10 × 65		
Reverse dip	s	10 reps	10 reps		
One-leg extension	s	12 × 65	12 × 65		
Musketeer lunge	s	15 reps	15 reps		
Two-leg curl	s	12 × 70	12 × 70	12 × 70	
Cylinder circuit #5					
Manual neck					

* Push-pull all upper body by alternating each set of a push-pull pair. For example, do a set of incline bench press followed by a set of high lat front. Repeat the cycle until you complete all sets of both exercises.

Conditioning training   (E)

	WR, DB, RB	LB, TE, FB	Line
3 × 100 yd (long)	:13	:15	:17
Rest between sets	:32	:34	:36

Resistance training   (N)

Exercise		Repetitions × % 1 RM			
Bench press	b	8 × 55	8 × 60	8 × 65	8 × 70
Incline dumbbell fly	s	10 × 65	10 × 65		
High lat rear	s	10 × 70	10 × 70	10 × 70	
Dumbbell pull press	s	10 × 70	10 × 70		
Roll-out	s	10 × 65	10 × 65		
Leg press	b	8 × 60	8 × 65	8 × 70	
Two-leg curl	s	12 × 75	12 × 75	12 × 75	
Jump rope	b	100 reps	100 reps		
Cylinder circuit #2					
Manual neck					

WEDNESDAY

THURSDAY

Phase 6 ■ Week 42

SUNDAY

Resistance training					T

Exercise		Repetitions × % 1 RM			
Bench press	c	8 × 75	8 × 80		
Close-grip lat	c	8 × 75	8 × 75		
Alternating dumbbell press (hard)	c	8 × 75	8 × 80		
Dumbbell snatch	c	10 × 65	10 × 65		
Roll-out	c	15 × 60	15 × 60		
EZ-bar curl	c	8 × 75	8 × 75		
Dumbbell French press	c	8 × 75	8 × 75		
Squat	c	8 × 70	8 × 70		
Two-leg curl	c	12 × 70	12 × 70		
Cylinder circuit #4					
Manual neck					

Conditioning training	E

12-minute run

MONDAY

Resistance training					N

Exercise		Repetitions × % 1 RM			
Flat dumbbell press	b	8 × 60	8 × 65	8 × 70	8 × 75
Incline dumbbell press	b	8 × 70	8 × 70		
Behind neck press	b	8 × 65	8 × 70	8 × 75	
EZ-bar curl	b	8 × 70	8 × 70		
Dumbbell French press	b	8 × 70	8 × 70		
Squat	b	8 × 65	8 × 70	8 × 75	
Two-leg curl	s	12 × 75	12 × 75	12 × 75	
Standing calf raise		25 × 45			
Cylinder circuit #1					
Manual neck					

TUESDAY

Resistance training				N

Exercise		Repetitions × % 1 RM		
Push-up	s	20 reps	20 reps	20 reps
Close-grip lat	b	8 × 65	8 × 70	8 × 75
High lat front	s	8 × 75	8 × 75	8 × 75
Close low lat	s	10 × 65	10 × 65	
Free-weight upright row	b	10 × 70	10 × 70	
Medicine ball circuit				
Two-leg extension	s	10 × 70	10 x70	
Cylinder circuit #1				

Conditioning training			E

	WR, DB, RB	LB, TE, FB	Line
2 × 150 yd shuttle			
(50 yd and back; 25 yd and back)	:30	:32	:34
Rest	1:10	1:12	1:14

Rest: b (basic)—1:30 between sets   c (circuit—0:45 between sets
s (supporting)—1:00 between sets   Take 1:30 between exercises

Resistance training   T

Exercise*		Repetitions × % 1 RM			
Incline bench press	s	8 × 75	8 × 75	8 × 80	
High lat front	s	10 × 65	10 × 65	10 × 65	
Flat dumbbell press	s	8 × 75	8 × 75	8 × 80	
Pull-up	s	max reps	max reps	max reps	
Rear deltoid swim	s	10 reps	10 reps		
Bent dumbbell raise	s	12 × 60	12 × 60	12 × 60	
Alternating dumbbell curl	s	10 × 65	10 × 65		
Reverse dip	s	10 reps	10 reps		
One-leg extension	s	12 × 65	12 × 65		
Musketeer lunge	s	15 reps	15 reps		
Two-leg curl	s	12 × 70	12 × 70	12 × 70	
Cylinder circuit #5					
Manual neck					

* Push-pull all upper body by alternating each set of a push-pull pair. For example, do a set of incline bench press followed by a set of high lat front. Repeat the cycle until you complete all sets of both exercises.

Conditioning training   E

	WR, DB, RB	LB, TE, FB	Line
3 × 100 yd (long)	:13	:15	:17
Rest between sets	:32	:34	:36

Resistance training   N

Exercise		Repetitions × % 1 RM			
Bench press	b	8 × 55	8 × 60	8 × 65	8 × 70
Incline dumbbell fly	s	10 × 65	10 × 65		
High lat rear	s	10 × 70	10 × 70	10 × 70	
Dumbbell pull press	s	10 × 70	10 × 70		
Roll-out	s	10 reps	10 reps		
Triceps push-down	s	10 × 65	10 × 65		
Leg press	b	8 × 60	8 × 65	8 × 70	
Two-leg curl	s	12 × 75	12 × 75	12 × 75	
Jump rope	b	100 reps	100 reps		
Cylinder circuit #2					
Manual neck					

WEDNESDAY

THURSDAY

Phase 6 ■ Week 43

Resistance training   (T)

Exercise		Repetitions × % 1 RM	
Bench press	c	8 × 75	8 × 80
Close-grip lat	c	8 × 75	8 × 75
Alternating dumbbell press (hard)	c	8 × 75	8 × 80
Dumbbell snatch	c	10 × 65	10 × 65
Roll-out	c	15 × 60	15 × 60
EZ-bar curl	c	8 × 75	8 × 75
Dumbbell French press	c	8 × 75	8 × 75
Squat	c	8 × 70	8 × 70
Two-leg curl	c	12 × 70	12 × 70
Cylinder circuit #4			
Manual neck			

Resistance training   (T)

Exercise*		Repetitions × % 1 RM			
Bench press	s	8 × 60	8 × 65	8 × 70	8 × 75
Pull-up	s	10 reps	10 reps	10 reps	10 reps
Push press	s	8 × 65	8 × 70	8 × 75	
Free-weight upright row	s	8 × 65	8 × 70	8 × 75	
Dumbbell French press	s	8 × 75	8 × 75		
Hammer curl	s	8 × 75	8 × 75		
Squat	b	8 × 65	8 × 70	8 × 75	
Box squat	s	10 reps	10 reps	10 reps	
One stiff leg dead	s	12 reps	12 reps	12 reps	
One-legged hop		100 left leg		100 right leg	
Cylinder circuit #4					
Manual neck					

* Push-pull all upper body by alternating each set of a push-pull pair. For example, do a set of incline bench press followed by a set of high lat front. Repeat the cycle until you complete all sets of both exercises.

Conditioning training   (E)

	WR, DB, RB	LB, TE, FB	Line
1 mile	8:30	9:00	11:00

Resistance training   (N)

Exercise		Repetitions × % 1 RM	
Incline bench press	c	8 × 70	8 × 70
Close-grip lat	c	8 × 65	8 × 75
Ham 10 chest	c	10 × 70	10 × 70
Dip	c	max reps	max reps
Close low lat	c	10 × 65	10 × 65
Dumbbell upright row	c	10 × 70	10 × 70
Alternating dumbbell press	c	10 × 65	10 × 65
Rear deltoid swim	c	10 × 65	10 × 65
Squat	c	10 × 70	10 × 70
Alternating leg lunge	c	12 × 65	12 × 65

Conditioning training   (E)

	WR, DB, RB	LB, TE, FB	Line
2 × 300 yd shuttle	:58	1:02	1:05
Rest between sets	2:15	2:15	2:15

SUNDAY   **TUESDAY**

Phase 6 ■ Week 44

Resistance training ⓣ

Exercise*		Repetitions × % 1 RM		
Incline bench press	s	8 × 75	8 × 75	8 × 80
High lat front	s	10 × 65	10 × 65	10 × 65
Flat dumbbell press	s	8 × 75	8 × 75	8 × 80
Pull-up	s	max reps	max reps	max reps
Rear deltoid swim	s	10 reps	10 reps	
Bent dumbbell raise	s	12 × 60	12 × 60	12 × 60
Alternating dumbbell curl	s	10 × 65	10 × 65	
Reverse dip	s	10 reps	10 reps	
One-leg extension	s	12 × 65	12 × 65	
Musketeer lunge	s	15 reps	15 reps	
Two-leg curl	s	12 × 70	12 × 70	12 × 70
Cylinder circuit #5				
Manual neck				

* Push-pull all upper body by alternating each set of a push-pull pair. For example, do a set of incline bench press followed by a set of high lat front. Repeat the cycle until you complete all sets of both exercises.

Conditioning training ⓔ

	WR, DB, RB	LB, TE, FB	Line
1 × 100 (long)	:13	:15	:17
Rest between sets	:32	:34	:36
2 × 50	:08	:08	:09
Rest between sets	:25	:25	:25
5 × 20	All-out effort		

Resistance training ⓝ

Exercise		Repetitions × % 1 RM		
Incline dumbbell fly (superset)	s	10 × 65	10 × 65	
Incline dumbbell press (superset)	b	8 × 55	8 × 60	
High lat rear	s	10 × 70	10 × 70	10 × 70
Smith behind neck	s	8 × 70	8 × 70	8 × 70
Cable upright row	s	10 × 70	10 × 70	
Preacher curl (cable)	s	10 × 65	10 × 65	
Triceps push-down	s	10 × 65	10 × 65	
Leg press	b	8 × 60	8 × 65	8 × 70
Two-leg curl	s	12 × 75	12 × 75	12 × 75
Standing calf raise		25 × 45		
Manual neck				
Cylinder circuit #5				

Rest: b (basic)—1:30 between sets

s (supporting)—1:00 between sets

c (circuit)—0:45 between sets (or only enough time for your partner to complete his reps)

Take 1:30 between exercises

WEDNESDAY

THURSDAY

Phase 6 ■ Week 44

Resistance training (T)

SUNDAY

Exercise		Repetitions × % 1 RM		
Bench press	b	8 × 65	8 × 75	8 × 80
Close-grip lat	b	8 × 75	8 × 75	
Behind neck press	b	8 × 65	8 × 75	8 × 80
Dumbbell pull press	b	10 × 65	10 × 65	
Free-weight upright row	s	10 × 65	10 × 65	
EZ-bar curl	b	8 × 75	8 × 75	
Dumbbell French press	b	8 × 75	8 × 75	
Squat	b	8 × 70	8 × 70	8 × 70
Box squat	s	15 reps	15 reps	
Cylinder circuit #3				
Manual neck				

Resistance training (N)

Exercise*		Repetitions × % 1 RM			
Bench press	s	8 × 60	8 × 65	8 × 70	8 × 75
Pull-up	s	10 reps	10 reps	10 reps	10 reps
Push press	s	8 × 65	8 × 70	8 × 75	
Free-weight upright row	s	8 × 65	8 × 70	8 × 75	
Dumbbell French press	s	8 × 75	8 × 75		
Hammer curl	s	8 × 75	8 × 75		
Squat	b	8 × 65	8 × 70	8 × 75	
Box squat	s	10 reps	10 reps	10 reps	
One stiff leg dead	s	12 reps	12 reps	12 reps	
One-legged hop		100 left leg		100 right leg	
Cylinder circuit #3					
Manual neck					

* Push-pull all upper body by alternating each set of a push-pull pair. For example, do a set of incline bench press followed by a set of high lat front. Repeat the cycle until you complete all sets of both exercises.

Conditioning training (E)

	WR, DB, RB	LB, TE, FB	Line
1 mile	8:30	9:00	11:00

Resistance training (N)

TUESDAY

Exercise		Repetitions × % 1 RM	
Incline bench press	c	8 × 70	8 × 70
Close-grip lat	c	8 × 65	8 × 75
Ham 10 chest	c	10 × 70	10 × 70
Dip	c	max reps	max reps
Close low lat	c	10 × 65	10 × 65
Dumbbell upright row	c	10 × 70	10 × 70
Alternating dumbbell press	c	10 × 65	10 × 65
Rear deltoid swim	c	10 × 65	10 × 65
Squat	c	10 × 70	10 × 70
Alternating leg lunge	c	12 × 65	12 × 65

Conditioning training (E)

	WR, DB, RB	LB, TE, FB	Line
2 × 150 yd shuttle	:30	:32	:34
Rest between sets	1:10	1:12	1:14

Resistance training   (T)

Exercise		Repetitions × % 1 RM		
Incline dumbbell press	b	8 × 70	8 × 70	8 × 70
High lat front	s	10 × 65	10 × 65	
Dip	s	max reps	max reps	max reps
Bent dumbbell raise	s	12 × 60	12 × 60	12 × 60
Alternating dumbbell curl	s	10 × 65	10 × 65	
Close-grip pushup	s	10 × 70	10 × 70	
Two-leg extension	s	12 × 65	12 × 65	
Side lunge	s	15 reps	15 reps	
Two-leg curl	s	12 × 70	12 × 70	12 × 70
Cylinder circuit #4				
Manual neck				

WEDNESDAY

Conditioning training   (E)

	WR, DB, RB	LB, TE, FB	Line
1 × 200 yd (short, 2 × 50 yd and back)	:34	:36	:38
1 × 100 yd (short, 50 yd and back)	:15	:17	:19

Resistance training   (N)

Exercise		Repetitions × % 1 RM		
Incline dumbbell fly (superset)	s	10 × 65	10 × 65	
Incline dumbbell press (superset)	b	8 × 55	8 × 60	
High lat rear	s	10 × 70	10 × 70	10 × 70
Smith behind neck	s	8 × 70	8 × 70	8 × 70
Cable upright row	s	10 × 70	10 × 70	
Preacher curl (cable)	s	10 × 65	10 × 65	
Triceps push-down	s	10 × 65	10 × 65	
Leg press	b	8 × 60	8 × 65	8 × 70
Two-leg curl	s	12 × 75	12 × 75	12 × 75
Standing calf raise		25 × 45		
Cylinder circuit #5				
Manual neck				

THURSDAY

Phase 6 ■ Week 45

Rest: b (basic)—1:45 between sets for (T) players; 1:30 between sets for (N) players

s (supporting)—1:00 between sets

c (circuit)—0:45 between sets (or only enough time for your partner to complete all reps)

Take 1:30 between exercises

SUNDAY

Resistance training (T)

Exercise		Repetitions × % 1 RM		
Bench press	b	8 × 65	8 × 75	8 × 80
Close-grip lat	b	8 × 75	8 × 75	
Behind neck press	b	8 × 65	8 × 75	8 × 80
Dumbbell pull press	b	10 × 65	10 × 65	
Free-weight upright row	s	10 × 65	10 × 65	
EZ-bar curl	b	8 × 75	8 × 75	
Dumbbell French press	b	8 × 75	8 × 75	
Squat	b	8 × 70	8 × 70	8 × 70
Box squat	s	15 reps	15 reps	
Cylinder circuit #3				
Manual neck	s			

Resistance training (N)

Exercise*		Repetitions × % 1 RM			
Incline dumbbell press	s	6 × 65	6 × 70	6 × 75	6 × 80
High lat rear	s	8 × 75	8 × 75	8 × 75	8 × 75
Incline dumbbell fly	s	8 × 75	8 × 75		
Dumbbell shrug	s	30 × 50	30 × 50		
Behind neck press	s	6 × 65	6 × 75	6 × 80	
Straight-bar curl	s	8 × 70	8 × 70		
Bar triceps extension	s	8 × 70	8 × 70		
Squat	b	6 × 65	6 × 75	6 × 80	
Two-leg curl	s	12 × 75	12 × 75	12 × 75	
Calf raise/leg press		25 × 45			
Cylinder circuit #2					
Manual neck					

* Push-pull all upper body by alternating each set of a push-pull pair. For example, do a set of incline bench press followed by a set of high lat front. Repeat the cycle until you complete all sets of both exercises.

Conditioning training (E)

	WR, DB, RB	LB, TE, FB	Line
1 mile	8:30	9:00	11:00

TUESDAY

Resistance training (N)

Exercise		Repetitions × % 1 RM		
Pull-up	b	max reps	max reps	max reps
High lat front	s	8 × 75	8 × 75	8 × 75
Close low lat	s	10 × 65	10 × 65	
Hang clean (light)	b	8 × 75	8 × 75	8 × 75
Preacher curl (cable)	s	10 × 65	10 × 65	
Triceps push-down	s	10 × 65	10 × 65	
Kickback	s	10 × 65	10 × 65	
One-leg press	s	10 × 70	10 × 70	
One stiff leg dead	s	12 × 65	12 × 65	
Cylinder circuit #3				
Manual neck				

Conditioning training (E)

	WR, DB, RB	LB, TE, FB	Line
3 × 100 yd shuttle (long)	:13	:15	:17
Rest between sets	Time required for next two groups to run		

Resistance training   T

Exercise		Repetitions × % 1 RM		
Incline dumbbell press	b	8 × 70	8 × 70	8 × 70
High lat front	s	10 × 65	10 × 65	
Dip	s	max reps	max reps	max reps
Bent dumbbell raise	s	12 × 60	12 × 60	12 × 60
Alternating dumbbell curl	s	10 × 65	10 × 65	
Close-grip push-up	s	10 × 70	10 × 70	
Two-leg extension	s	12 × 65	12 × 65	
Side lunge	s	15 reps	15 reps	
Two-leg curl	s	12 × 70	12 × 70	12 × 70
Cylinder circuit #4				
Manual neck				

Conditioning training   E

	WR, DB, RB	LB, TE, FB	Line
3 × 100 yd gasser (all-out sprint)	:15	:17	:19
Rest between sets	Time required for next two groups to run		

Resistance training   N

Exercise		Repetitions × % 1 RM			
Bench press	b	6 × 65	6 × 70	6 × 75	6 × 80
Incline dumbbell press	s	8 × 70	8 × 70		
Close incline press	s	8 × 75	8 × 75	8 × 75	
Dumbbell push press	b	8 × 75	8 × 75	8 × 75	
Dumbbell snatch	b	8 × 75	8 × 75		
Hammer curl	b	10 × 65	10 × 65		
Leg press	b	6 × 65	6 × 70	6 × 75	
Side lunge	s	12 reps	12 reps	12 reps	
Three-sided square drills		30 sec	30 sec	30 sec	30 sec
Cylinder circuit #5					
Manual neck					

Rest: b (basic)—1:30 between sets
s (supporting)—1:00 between sets
Take 1:30 between exercises

WEDNESDAY

THURSDAY

Phase 6 ■ Week 46

Resistance training   **T**

Exercise		Repetitions × % 1 RM		
Bench press	b	6 × 70	6 × 80	6 × 85
One-arm dumbbell row	b	8 × 75	8 × 75	
Push press	b	8 × 70	8 × 70	6 × 75
Hang clean (light)	b	8 × 70	8 × 70	8 × 70
Close-grip bench	b	8 × 75	8 × 75	
Straight-bar curl	b	8 × 75	8 × 75	
Leg press	b	8 × 65	8 × 70	8 × 75
Two-leg curl	s	12 × 75	12 × 75	12 × 75
Cylinder circuit #4				
Manual neck				

SUNDAY

Resistance training   **N**

Exercise		Repetitions × % 1 RM			
Incline dumbbell press	s	6 × 65	6 × 70	6 × 75	6 × 80
High lat rear	s	8 × 75	8 × 75	8 × 75	8 × 75
Incline dumbbell fly	s	8 × 75	8 × 75		
Dumbbell shrug	s	30 × 50	30 × 50		
Behind neck press	s	6 × 65	6 × 75	6 × 80	
Straight-bar curl	s	8 × 70	8 × 70		
Bar triceps extension	s	8 × 70	8 × 70		
Squat	b	6 × 65	6 × 75	6 × 80	
Two-leg curl	s	12 × 75	12 × 75	12 × 75	
Calf raise/leg press		25 × 45			
Cylinder circuit #2					
Manual neck					

Conditioning training   **E**

	WR, DB, RB	LB, TE, FB	Line
1 mile	8:30	9:00	11:00

Resistance training   **N**

Exercise		Repetitions × % 1 RM		
Pull-up	b	max reps	max reps	max reps
High lat front	s	8 × 75	8 × 75	8 × 75
Close low lat	s	10 × 65	10 × 65	
Hang clean (light)	b	8 × 75	8 × 75	8 × 75
Preacher curl (cable)	s	10 × 65	10 × 65	
Triceps push-down	s	10 × 65	10 × 65	
Kickback	s	10 × 65	10 × 65	
One-leg press	s	10 × 70	10 × 70	
One stiff leg dead	s	12 × 65	12 × 65	
Cylinder circuit #3				
Manual neck				

TUESDAY

Conditioning training   **E**

	WR, DB, RB	LB, TE, FB	Line
3 × 200 yd	:34	:36	:38
Rest between sets	Time required for next two groups to run		

Resistance training					T
Exercise		*Repetitions × % 1 RM*			
Ham decline	c	8 × 65	8 × 70		
Close low lat	c	10 × 70	10 × 70		
Dumbbell push press	c	8 × 70	8 × 70		
Manual rear deltoid	c	12 reps	12 reps		
Preacher curl (cable)	c	10 × 65	10 × 65		
Triceps push-down	c	8 × 75	8 × 75		
Dumbbell dead lift	c	10 × 70	10 × 70		
Backward lunge	c	15 reps	15 reps		
One stiff leg dead	c	12 reps	12 reps		
Cylinder circuit #5					
Manual neck					

WEDNESDAY

Conditioning training			E

	WR, DB, RB	**LB, TE, FB**	**Line**
1 × 150 yd shuttle	:30	:32	:34
Rest between sets	Time required for next two groups to run		
1 × 100 yd shuttle			
(10 yd and back; 40 yd and back)	:15	:17	:19

Resistance training						N
Exercise		*Repetitions × % 1 RM*				
Bench press	b	6 × 65	6 × 70	6 × 75	6 × 80	
Incline dumbbell press	s	8 × 70	8 × 70			
Close incline press	s	8 × 75	8 × 75	8 × 75		
Dumbbell push press	b	8 × 75	8 × 75	8 × 75		
Dumbbell snatch	b	8 × 75	8 × 75			
Hammer curl	b	10 × 65	10 × 65			
Leg press	b	6 × 65	6 × 70	6 × 75		
Side lunge	s	12 reps	12 reps	12 reps		
Three-sided square drills		30 sec	30 sec	30 sec	30 sec	
Cylinder circuit #5						
Manual neck						

THURSDAY

Rest: b (basic)—1:30 between sets for (T) players; 1:45 between sets for (N) players
     s (supporting)—1:00 between sets
     c (circuit)—0:45 between sets (or only enough time for your partner to complete all reps)
     Take 1:30 between exercises

Phase 6 ■ Week 47

Resistance training (T)

Exercise		Repetitions × % 1 RM		
Bench press	b	6 × 70	6 × 80	6 × 85
One-arm dumbbell row	b	8 × 75	8 × 75	
Push press	b	8 × 70	8 × 70	6 × 75
Hang clean (light)	b	8 × 70	8 × 70	8 × 70
Close-grip bench	b	8 × 75	8 × 75	
Straight-bar curl	b	8 × 75	8 × 75	
Leg press	b	8 × 65	8 × 70	8 × 75
Two-leg curl	s	12 × 75	12 × 75	12 × 75
Cylinder circuit #4				
Manual neck				

Resistance training (N)

Exercise*		Repetitions × % 1 RM			
Incline dumbbell press	s	6 × 65	6 × 70	6 × 75	6 × 80
High lat rear	s	8 × 75	8 × 75	8 × 75	8 × 75
Incline dumbbell fly	s	8 × 75	8 × 75		
Dumbbell shrug	s	30 × 50	30 × 50		
Behind neck press	s	6 × 65	6 × 75	6 × 80	
Straight-bar curl	s	8 × 70	8 × 70		
Bar triceps extension	s	8 × 70	8 × 70		
Squat	b	6 × 65	6 × 75	6 × 80	
Two-leg curl	s	12 × 75	12 × 75	12 × 75	
Calf raise/leg press		25 × 45			
Cylinder circuit #2					
Manual neck					

* Push-pull all upper body by alternating each set of a push-pull pair. For example, do a set of incline bench press followed by a set of high lat front. Repeat the cycle until you complete all sets of both exercises.

Conditioning training (E)

Stadium run for 20:00

Resistance training (N)

Exercise		Repetitions × % 1 RM		
Pull-up	b	max reps	max reps	max reps
High lat front	s	8 × 75	8 × 75	8 × 75
Close low lat	s	10 × 65	10 × 65	
Hang clean (light)	b	8 × 75	8 × 75	8 × 75
Preacher curl (cable)	s	10 × 65	10 × 65	
Triceps push-down	s	10 × 65	10 × 65	
Kickback	s	10 × 65	10 × 65	
One-leg press	s	10 × 70	10 × 70	
One stiff leg dead	s	12 × 65	12 × 65	
Cylinder circuit #3				
Manual neck				

Conditioning training (E)

Four-section fartlek for 10:00 (a jog-sprint combination run with four sprint sections)

SUNDAY

TUESDAY

Resistance training   T

Exercise		Repetitions × % 1 RM			
Ham decline	c	8 × 65	8 × 70		
Close low lat	c	10 × 70	10 × 70		
Dumbbell push press	c	8 × 70	8 × 70		
Manual rear deltoid	c	12 reps	12 reps		
Preacher curl (cable)	c	10 × 65	10 × 65		
Triceps push-down	c	8 × 75	8 × 75		
Dumbbell dead lift	c	10 × 70	10 × 70		
Backward lunge	c	15 reps	15 reps		
One stiff leg dead	c	12 reps	12 reps		
Cylinder circuit #5					
Manual neck					

WEDNESDAY

Conditioning training   E

	WR, DB, RB	LB, TE, FB	Line
1 × 100 yd gasser (all-out)	:15	:17	:19
Rest between sets	Time required for next two groups to run		

Resistance training   N

Exercise		Repetitions × % 1 RM			
Bench press	b	6 × 70	6 × 75	4 × 80	4 × 85
Incline dumbbell press	s	8 × 70	8 × 70		
Close incline press	s	8 × 75	8 × 75	8 × 75	
Dumbbell push press	b	8 × 75	8 × 75	8 × 75	
Dumbbell snatch	b	8 × 75	8 × 75		
Hammer curl	b	10 × 65	10 × 65		
Leg press	b	6 × 65	6 × 70	6 × 75	
Side lunge	s	12 reps	12 reps	12 reps	
Three-sided square drills		30 sec	30 sec	30 sec	30 sec
Cylinder circuit #5					
Manual neck					

THURSDAY

Rest: b (basic)—1:30 between sets for (T) players; 1:45 between sets for (N) players
      s (supporting)—1:00 between sets
      c (circuit)—0:45 between sets (or only enough time for your partner to complete all reps)
      Take 1:30 between exercises

Phase 6 ■ Week 48

Phase 6 ■ Week 49

SUNDAY

Resistance training (T) — T

Exercise		Repetitions × % 1 RM		
Bench press	b	10 × 65	6 × 80	4 × 90
One-arm dumbbell row	b	8 × 75	8 × 75	
Behind neck press	b	10 × 65	6 × 80	4 × 90
Dumbbell pull press	b	8 × 75	8 × 75	
Dumbbell lunge/upright row	b	8 × 75	8 × 75	
Squat/press	b	8 × 75	8 × 75	
Kickback	b	12 × 65	12 × 65	
Hammer curl	b	8 × 75	8 × 75	
One-leg press	b	8 × 65	8 × 75	8 × 80
Cylinder circuit #1				
Manual neck				

Resistance training — N

Exercise		Repetitions × % 1 RM			
Incline bench press	b	6 × 70	6 × 75	4 × 80	4 × 85
Power clean or power row	b	8 × 75	6 × 80	4 × 85	
Dumbbell pull press	b	8 × 75	8 × 75	8 × 75	
Split dumbbell pullover	b	8 × 75	8 × 75		
One-arm dumbbell triceps extension	b	10 × 70	10 × 70		
Snatch squat with stick	b	15 reps	15 reps	15 reps	
Two-leg curl	s	12 × 75	12 × 75	12 × 75	
Standing calf raise		25 × 45			
Cylinder circuit #2					
Manual neck					

Conditioning training — E

Stadium run for 20:00

TUESDAY

Resistance training — N

Exercise		Repetitions × % 1 RM		
Two-arm dumbbell row	s	8 × 75	8 × 75	8 × 75
Close low lat	s	10 × 65	10 × 65	
One-arm dumbbell row	b	8 × 75	8 × 80	
Free-weight upright row	b	8 × 75	8 × 80	
EZ-bar curl	b	8 × 75	8 × 80	
Close-grip push-up	s	8 × 70	8 × 70	
One-leg extension	s	10 × 70	10 × 70	10 × 70
Two-leg curl	s	12 × 65	12 × 65	
Cylinder circuit #2				
Manual neck				

Conditioning training — E

Indian run for 10:00

Resistance training   (T)

Exercise		Repetitions × % 1 RM			
Incline bench press	b	6 × 75	6 × 80	6 × 80	
Pull-up	b	10 reps	10 reps	10 reps	
Push-up	s	20 reps	20 reps		
Close high lat	s	10 × 70	10 × 70		
Free-weight upright row	s	8 × 75	8 × 75		
Dumbbell push press	s	8 × 75	8 × 75		
Side dumbbell raise	s	10 × 70	10 × 70		
Bent dumbbell raise	s	12 × 60	12 × 60		
Alternating dumbbell curl	s	10 × 65	10 × 65		
Triceps push-down	s	8 × 75	8 × 75		
Two-leg extension	s	10 × 70	10 × 70		
Slideboard	s	30 crosses		30 crosses	
Two-leg curl	s	12 × 70	12 × 70	12 × 70	
Cylinder circuit #2					
Manual neck					

WEDNESDAY

Resistance training   (N)

Exercise		Repetitions × % 1 RM			
Bench press	b	6 × 65	6 × 70	4 × 75	4 × 80
Ham 10 chest	s	10 × 70	10 × 70		
High lat rear	s	8 × 75	8 × 75	8 × 75	
Push press	b	6 × 80	6 × 80	6 × 80	
Manual upright row	s	8 reps	8 reps		
Preacher curl (cable)	s	8 × 70	8 × 70		
Triceps push-down	s	8 × 70	8 × 70		
Leg press	b	6 × 65	6 × 75	6 × 80	
Two-leg curl	s	12 × 75	12 × 75	12 × 75	
Standing calf raise		25 × 45			
Cylinder circuit #2					
Manual neck					

THURSDAY

Phase 6 ▪ Week 49

Rest: b (basic)—1:30 between sets for (T) players; 1:45 between sets for (N) players
s (supporting)—1:00 between sets
c (circuit)—0:45 between sets (or only enough time for your partner to complete all reps)
Take 1:30 between exercises

SUNDAY

Resistance training — T

Exercise		Repetitions × % 1 RM		
Bench press	b	10 × 65	6 × 80	4 × 90
One-arm dumbbell row	b	8 × 75	8 × 75	
Behind neck press	b	10 × 65	6 × 80	4 × 90
Dumbbell pull press	b	8 × 75	8 × 75	
Dumbbell lunge/upright row	b	8 × 75	8 × 75	
Squat/press	b	8 × 75	8 × 75	
Kickback	b	12 × 65	12 × 65	
Hammer curl	b	8 × 75	8 × 75	
Leg press	b	8 × 65	8 × 75	8 × 80
Cylinder circuit #1				
Manual neck				

Resistance training — N

Exercise		Repetitions × % 1 RM			
Incline bench press	b	6 × 70	6 × 75	4 × 80	4 × 85
Power clean or power row	b	8 × 75	6 × 80	4 × 85	
Dumbbell pull press	b	8 × 75	8 × 75	8 × 75	
Split dumbbell pullover	b	8 × 75	8 × 75		
One-arm dumbbell triceps extension	b	10 × 70	10 × 70		
Snatch squat with stick	b	15 reps	15 reps	15 reps	
Two-leg curl	s	12 × 75	12 × 75	12 × 75	
Standing calf raise		25 × 45			
Cylinder circuit #3					
Manual neck					

Conditioning training — E

	WR, DB, RB	LB, TE, FB	Line
1-mile campus run	8:30	9:00	11:00

TUESDAY

Resistance training — N

Exercise		Repetitions × % 1 RM		
Two-arm dumbbell row	s	8 × 75	8 × 75	8 × 75
Close low lat	s	10 × 65	10 × 65	
One-arm dumbbell row	b	8 × 75	8 × 80	
Free-weight upright row	b	8 × 75	8 × 80	
EZ-bar curl	b	8 × 75	8 × 80	
Close-grip push-up	s	8 × 70	8 × 70	
One-leg extension	s	10 × 70	10 × 70	10 × 70
One-leg curl	s	12 × 65	12 × 65	
Cylinder circuit #2				
Manual neck				

Conditioning training — E

	WR, DB, RB	LB, TE, FB	Line
1 × 1,000 yd shuttle	3:30	3:45	3:55

Resistance training (T)

Exercise*		Repetitions × % 1 RM			
Incline bench press	b	6 × 75	6 × 80	6 × 80	
Pull-up	b	10 reps	10 reps	10 reps	
Push-up	s	20 reps	20 reps		
Close high lat	s	10 × 70	10 × 70		
Free-weight upright row	s	8 × 75	8 × 75		
Dumbbell push press	s	8 × 75	8 × 75		
Side dumbbell raise	s	10 × 70	10 × 70		
Bent dumbbell raise	s	12 × 60	12 × 60		
Alternating dumbbell curl	s	10 × 65	10 × 65		
Triceps push-down	s	8 × 75	8 × 75		
Two-leg extension	s	10 × 70	10 × 70		
Slideboard	s	30 crosses		30 crosses	
Two-leg curl	s	12 × 70	12 × 70	12 × 70	
Cylinder circuit #2					
Manual neck					

* Push-pull all upper body by alternating each set of a push-pull pair. For example, do a set of incline bench press followed by a set of high lat front. Repeat the cycle until you complete all sets of both exercises.

WEDNESDAY

Resistance training (N)

Exercise		Repetitions × % 1 RM			
Bench press	b	6 × 65	6 × 70	4 × 75	4 × 80
Ham 10 chest	s	10 × 70	10 × 70		
High lat rear	s	8 × 75	8 × 75	8 × 75	
Push press	b	6 × 80	6 × 80	6 × 80	
Manual upright row	s	8 reps	8 reps		
Preacher curl (cable)	s	8 × 70	8 × 70		
Triceps push-down	s	8 × 70	8 × 70		
Leg press	b	6 × 65	6 × 75	6 × 80	
Two-leg curl	s	12 × 75	12 × 75	12 × 75	
Standing calf raise		25 × 45			
Cylinder circuit #5					
Manual neck					

THURSDAY

Rest: b (basic)—1:30 between sets for (T) players; 1:45 between sets for (N) players
   s (supporting)—1:00 between sets
   c (circuit)—0:45 between sets (or only enough time for your partner to complete all reps)
   Take 1:30 between exercises

Phase 6 ■ Week 50

SUNDAY

Resistance training   (T)

Exercise		Repetitions × % 1 RM		
Bench press	b	10 × 65	6 × 80	4 × 90
Close low lat	b	8 × 75	8 × 75	
Clean and jerk (light)	b	8 × 75	8 × 75	
Reverse dip	b	15 reps	15 reps	
Straight-bar curl	b	8 × 75	8 × 75	
Squat	b	8 × 65	8 × 75	8 × 80
Cylinder circuit #3				
Manual neck				

Resistance training   (N)

Exercise		Repetitions × % 1 RM			
Ham decline	b	6 × 70	6 × 75	6 × 80	6 × 80
Flat dumbbell press	b	6 × 60	6 × 70	6 × 75	
Behind neck press	b	6 × 70	6 × 80	6 × 85	
Alternating dumbbell press	b	8 × 75	6 × 80		
Side dumbbell raise	b	8 × 65	6 × 80		
Squat	b	6 × 70	6 × 80	6 × 85	
Two-leg curl	s	12 × 75	12 × 75	12 × 75	
Jump rope	b	100 reps	100 reps		
Cylinder circuit #4					
Manual neck					

Conditioning training   (E)

	WR, DB, RB	LB, TE, FB	Line
1-mile campus run	8:30	9:00	11:00

TUESDAY

Resistance training   (N)

Exercise		Repetitions × % 1 RM		
Pull-up	s	max reps	max reps	max reps
Close high lat	s	10 × 65	10 × 65	
One-arm dumbbell row	b	8 × 75	8 × 75	
Power clean or power row	b	8 × 75	6 × 80	4 × 85
Incline curl	s	8 × 70	8 × 70	
Dumbbell French press	s	8 × 70	8 × 70	
Backward lunge	s	10 reps	10 reps	
Two-leg curl	s	12 × 65	12 × 65	
Cylinder circuit #3				
Manual neck				

Resistance training   (T)

Exercise		Repetitions × % 1 RM			
Incline bench press	c	6 × 75	6 × 80		
High lat rear	c	10 × 70	10 × 70		
Alternating dumbbell press	c	8 × 75	8 × 75		
Side dumbbell raise	c	10 × 70	10 × 70		
Dumbbell upright row	c	8 × 75	8 × 75		
Nautilus multishrug	c	20 reps	20 reps		
Rear deltoid swim	c	20 reps	20 reps		
Incline curl	c	10 × 65	10 × 65		
One-arm dumbbell triceps extension	c	8 × 75	8 × 75		
Two-leg extension	c	10 × 70	10 × 70		
Alternating leg lunge	c	15 reps	15 reps		
One stiff leg dead	c	12 × 70	12 × 70		
Cylinder circuit #3					
Manual neck					

WEDNESDAY

Resistance training   (N)

Exercise		Repetitions × % 1 RM			
Bench press	b	4 × 65	4 × 70	4 × 80	4 × 85
Dip	b	max reps	max reps	max reps	
High lat rear	s	8 × 75	8 × 75	8 × 75	
Alternating dumbbell press	s	6 × 80	6 × 80	6 × 80	
Roll-out	s	10 reps	10 reps	10 reps	
Alternating dumbbell curl	b	8 × 70	8 × 70		
Two-arm dumbbell triceps extension	s	8 × 70	8 × 70		
Leg press	b	6 × 70	6 × 75	4 × 90	
Two-leg curl	s	12 × 75	12 × 75	12 × 75	
Standing calf raise		25 × 45			
Cylinder circuit #5					
Manual neck	s				

THURSDAY

Rest: b (basic)—1:30 between sets for (T) players; 2:00 between sets for (N) players
s (supporting)—1:00 between sets
c (circuit)—0:45 between sets (or only enough time for your partner to complete all reps)
Take 1:30 between exercises

Phase 6 ▪ Week 51

Phase 6 ■ Week 52

SUNDAY

Resistance training (T)

Exercise		Repetitions × % 1 RM			
Bench press	b	10 × 65	6 × 80	4 × 90	
Close low lat	b	8 × 75	8 × 75		
Clean and jerk (light)	b	8 × 75	8 × 75		
Reverse dip	b	15 reps	15 reps		
Straight-bar curl	b	8 × 75	8 × 75		
Squat	b	8 × 65	8 × 75	8 × 80	
Cylinder circuit #3					
Manual neck					

Resistance training (N)

Exercise		Repetitions × % 1 RM			
Ham decline	b	6 × 70	6 × 75	6 × 80	6 × 80
Flat dumbbell press	b	6 × 60	6 × 70	6 × 75	
Behind neck press	b	6 × 70	6 × 80	6 × 85	
Alternating dumbbell press	b	8 × 75	6 × 80		
Side dumbbell raise	b	8 × 65	6 × 80		
Squat	b	6 × 70	6 × 80	6 × 85	
Two-leg curl	s	12 × 75	12 × 75	12 × 75	
Jump rope	b	100 reps	100 reps		
Cylinder circuit #4					
Manual neck					

TUESDAY

Resistance training (N)

Exercise		Repetitions × % 1 RM		
Pull-up	s	max reps	max reps	max reps
Close high lat	s	10 × 65	10 × 65	
One-arm dumbbell row	b	8 × 75	8 × 75	
Power clean or power row	b	8 × 75	6 × 80	4 × 85
Incline curl	s	8 × 70	8 × 70	
Dumbbell French press	s	8 × 70	8 × 70	
Backward lunge	s	10 reps	10 reps	
Two-leg curl	s	12 × 65	12 × 65	
Cylinder circuit #3				
Manual neck				

Resistance training — T

Exercise		Repetitions × % 1 RM			
Incline bench press	c	6 × 75	6 × 80		
High lat rear	c	10 × 70	10 × 70		
Alternating dumbbell press	c	8 × 75	8 × 75		
Side dumbbell raise	c	10 × 70	10 × 70		
Dumbbell upright row	c	8 × 75	8 × 75		
Nautilus multishrug	c	20 reps	20 reps		
Rear deltoid swim	c	20 reps	20 reps		
Incline curl	c	10 × 65	10 × 65		
One-arm dumbbell triceps extension	c	8 × 75	8 × 75		
Two-leg extension	c	10 × 70	10 × 70		
Alternating leg lunge	c	15 reps	15 reps		
One stiff leg dead	c	12 × 70	12 × 70		
Cylinder circuit #3					
Manual neck					

WEDNESDAY

Resistance training — N

Exercise		Repetitions × % 1 RM			
Bench press	b	4 × 65	4 × 70	4 × 80	4 × 85
Dip	b	max reps	max reps	max reps	
High lat rear	s	8 × 75	8 × 75	8 × 75	
Alternating dumbbell press	s	6 × 80	6 × 80	6 × 80	
Roll-out	s	10 reps	10 reps	10 reps	
Alternating dumbbell curl	b	8 × 70	8 × 70		
Two-arm dumbbell triceps extension	s	8 × 70	8 × 70		
Leg press	b	6 × 70	6 × 75	4 × 90	
Two-leg curl	s	12 × 75	12 × 75	12 × 75	
Standing calf raise		25 × 45			
Cylinder circuit #5					
Manual neck					

THURSDAY

Phase 6 ■ Week 52

Rest: b (basic)—1:30 between sets
s (supporting)—1:00 between sets
c (circuit)—0:45 between sets (or only enough time for your partner to complete all reps)
Take 1:30 between exercises

PART II

Exercises and Drills

The exercises and drills presented in the workouts in phases 1 through 6 provide constructive stress to the body of the football athlete. I have chosen and blended resistance exercises to provide general increases in strength and power in every major muscle group, in three dimensions. This produces integrity of strength among muscle groups, thus reducing the risk of injury. By varying the intensity and number of repetitions and sets, the resistance exercises address the entire spectrum of muscle-fiber types.

I have selected the conditioning exercises to help players achieve a strong foundation of cardiorespiratory fitness. Conditioning exercises attempt to simulate the typical football game. Composed primarily of anaerobic exercises, the conditioning program helps the athlete better tolerate activity that produces high levels of lactic acid. The workouts include endurance activity at low levels primarily to provide active recovery from the more intense conditioning workouts.

Exercises that address power, function, and agility round off the program. These exercises help the athlete move from a generalized state of strength and conditioning to a state of physical preparedness for football.

CHAPTER 7

Flexibility Exercises

Flexibility refers to the ability to move a joint and the surrounding muscles through a full range of motion. Flexibility is critical in all sports activities because athletes stress their joints in many different positions during competition. If an athlete's muscles are inflexible, he is more likely to become injured. Preventing injury should be the primary objective of every coach and athlete. Therefore, flexibility work is a crucial component of a complete training program.

How to Become More Flexible

Range of motion is limited by ligamentous joint capsules, tendons, and muscle. You can successfully stretch each of these tissues using a variety of techniques that improve range of motion. Two types of tissue elongation can occur as a result of flexibility training. *Plastic elongation* is a more permanent lengthening of tissue; *elastic elongation* is less permanent. To increase range of motion, you should promote plastic elongation by holding stretches for longer periods. Many athletes have experienced an inability to maintain range of motion. One day after they stretch they seem as inflexible as they were the day before. This occurs because they are not holding the stretch long enough to promote plastic elongation of the muscle and connective tissue.

Plastic Elongation

Stretching techniques that promote plastic elongation are impractical as a prepractice stretch routine because of the time required to make such stretches effective. These methods of stretching, however, are a useful program addition for the athlete having difficulty improving his flexibility. This type of stretching is excellent for muscle groups that are highly inflexible.

First, thoroughly warm up the muscle with about 5 minutes of gentle calisthenics or 10 to 15 minutes of submersion in a hot bath. By thoroughly warming the muscle, you can achieve a greater range of motion. Then, to facilitate plastic elongation, perform each stretching exercise to a point of mild discomfort. Once you feel discomfort, stop and release the stretch. This type of stretching is termed *static* because of its stop-and-hold style. Repeat the stretch-and-release method as many times as necessary until you feel comfortable holding the stretch for a count of 10. At each added level of the stretch you will find yourself naturally tensing the muscle to protect it from discomfort. When first trying to increase flexibility, take 20 minutes to teach your body to relax, and thus reduce your tendency to tense the muscle while stretching. As you become more experienced it may not require as much time to achieve *relaxability*. Understand that using one stretching exercise can facilitate the performance of another. For this reason, performing exercises back and forth, in pairs, or in circuits will improve your ability to stretch. This may require more time, extending the stretching session to 30 minutes or more. At the completion of the stretching session, cool the muscle with ice for about 15 minutes to avoid excessive muscle soreness and promote muscle repair.

Elastic Elongation

Like plastic elongation, static stretching techniques that promote elastic elongation apply a stop-and-hold style of stretch. This type of stretch requires less time, however, making it less a plastic elongation (which can promote temporary muscle laxity or looseness) and more an elastic elongation of the muscle tissue. Therefore, this stretch is excellent for prepractice warm-up routines or anytime you need a quick stretch. Overstretching the muscle or having it become too loose before a practice session may cause more harm than good. Elastic elongation will not provide the permanent flexibility gains that plastic elongation stretching will. The primary purpose of elastic elongation is maintenance—a means of reminding the muscle how far it can stretch as a result of performing the more permanent style of stretching.

When performing elastic elongation, stretch to the point of muscle discomfort, move back just slightly to where there is no pain, and hold that position for 6 to 10 seconds. Then resume the stretch by attempting to stretch the muscle slightly farther to the next point of discomfort, backing off slightly, and then holding again for 15 to 20 seconds. Then move to the next stretching exercise. You can hold these stretches for longer periods depending on the time available before practice.

You may also consider performing prepractice stretches with the help of a partner. Stretching with a partner can serve several purposes:

1. Motivation—One or both athletes in a stretching pair may need a partner to ensure that they push themselves as far as they physically can.
2. To push past equipment—Bulky football equipment may hinder the lone athlete from stretching thoroughly. In such a case a partner may be of service.
3. Style of stretch—Some styles of static stretching, such as PNF stretching, require a partner (see below).

Releasing Methods

Pain keeps us shackled to our state of inflexibility. Being able to release ourselves from the discomfort associated with muscle lengthening is essential to reaching our full potential and reducing risk of injury. You can apply several techniques to release yourself from pain barriers. I discuss two below.

Proprioceptive Neuromuscular Facilitation

Proprioceptive neuromuscular facilitation (PNF) techniques attempt to train the brain to send a message to the muscle being stretched that tells it to

© Active Images

relax. The basis behind PNF techniques is that contraction of a muscle (or its antagonist) can make the stretch easier. For example, just before stretching the quadriceps, make the stretch easier by first contracting the quadriceps (or the quadriceps antagonists, the hamstrings) and then beginning the stretch. You should therefore perform these stretching exercises in pairs or in a series (quadriceps and hamstrings; biceps and triceps; and so forth). One stretch enhances the performance of another.

Rocking or Rolling During the Stretch

An excellent method to release pain during the stretch is to use subtle rocking or rolling movements. Please note that this does not mean bouncing. Rocking is a method every mother uses to ease the baby's discomfort and pain. People in great pain often hug and rock themselves to reduce their discomfort. Rocking during the early portion of either plastic or elastic static stretching can reduce discomfort and allow you to return to a level of muscle elongation you obtained during previous stretching sessions. Many athletes complain at the beginning of a stretching session that they are as tight as they were the last session. Often the nervous system is reluctant to release its initial protective hold on the muscle tissue. By placing the muscle in a pain-free position and then slowly introducing it to greater levels of tension by rocking into the stretching position, you can advance through the pain to the muscle's fullest stretching potential for that stretching session.

During forward flexion exercises, for example, you lean forward from the waist with your back completely straight through the spinal column and your feet in front of you, *gently* rocking from your left to right buttocks. If you can lean forward enough to grab the back of your calves, you can then use your elbows as bumpers, rocking and allowing your elbows to touch the floor on either side of your outstretched legs. With each rocking motion you allow your legs to extend toward their full and locked-out position. The objective of this stretch is to stretch the hamstrings and lower back. This exercise, though excellent for improving flexibility of these two body segments, should be approached with caution because of the high stress forward flexion places on the lower lumbar spine.

Dynamic Stretching

Dynamic flexibility refers to flexibility during a movement. This type of flexibility is critical to any movement, especially sports-related movement. The less hindered the movement is by inflexible muscles or joints, the more efficient that movement will be. You often see kickers and punters warming up by swinging their kicking legs up and back. This swinging motion is a dynamic stretch because it stretches the muscle through an exaggerated range of motion. In such an exercise, the rapid swinging of the leg creates momentum that stretches the muscle farther than other techniques would stretch it. Movements in sports require us to move our legs and arms rapidly. If the muscle is not prepared to reach the particular length that might be caused by momentum, injury may occur.

Type of stretch	When to stretch
Plastic elongation	Any time you can
Elastic elongation	In-season prepractice
Releasing techniques	During static routines
Dynamic stretching	In-season prepractice or pregame

Use dynamic stretching during the in-season phases of training. Use this stretching technique with caution and *only after a thorough warm-up*. The potential for injury is increased when movement is at a higher speed and the muscles are rapidly being lengthened to their limit.

Warm-Up Stretching Routine

Use this routine before any conditioning workout and as a pregame stretch. Stretch to a point of mild discomfort, back off slightly, and then hold for 15 to 30 seconds. Before any stretching session, perform a warm-up consisting of some jogging, calisthenics, or form running to prepare the muscle for the stretching session. Each of these stretches can be performed incorporating the releasing, partner-assisted and dynamic methods.

Neck Stretch

Sit in a chair and apply *light,* steady pressure to your neck in each direction: forward, to each side, and backward.

Windmills

To warm up the shoulder girdle, rotate both arms in circles forward and backward. This dynamic rotation of the shoulder helps reduce resistance throughout the shoulder girdle. Perform windmills in a variety of directions and planes.

Trunk Stretch

While standing, bend at the waist to stretch in all directions and rotate in full circles. This stretch promotes mobility throughout the circumference of the trunk.

Feet Together Hamstring Stretch

Start in a standing position. Bend your left leg slightly, keep the right leg straight, and bend at the waist. Attempt to place your head on your knee. Return to the starting position and start again bending your right leg slightly and keeping your left leg straight. Finally repeat the stretch keeping both legs straight.

Legs Apart Hamstring Stretch

To stretch the hamstring and groin, stand with your feet a little more than shoulder-width apart. Keep your knees locked and attempt to place your head on your right knee, then switch to the left, and then to the middle. Reach as far back through your legs as possible.

Groin and Hamstring Stretch

Standing with your feet more than shoulder-width apart, lunge left so that you extend your right leg. Keep the extended leg straight. After a 15-second count turn the toe upward on the right leg and lean toward the toe. Repeat with the other leg.

Lunge

Lunge forward with your right leg in front and bent at a 90-degree angle. Place your hands on your hips and push the hips forward. You'll feel this stretch in the upper hip area of the left leg. After a 15-second count, rock back, extending the right leg in front. Lean forward and move your head to your toe. You'll feel the stretch in the hamstring of the right leg. Repeat with the left leg in front.

Dynamic Stretches for In-Season Warm-Up

Do these additional stretches as needed in your preworkout warm-up. Perform these movements only when you have warmed up thoroughly and prestretched using the stretches described earlier. Use caution with these stretches. Injury can occur if the muscle is not warm or if you attempt too much range of motion at one time. Work progressively to extend range of motion over a period of weeks or months.

Midrange and High Swings

Hamstrings and glutes

Standing and holding a support, think of your leg as a pendulum. Keeping the kicking leg and the support leg straight, swing the leg forward and upward to about waist level (midrange swings). After each upward swing, reset the leg by stopping briefly on the floor behind you. Perform this movement just as you did the previous exercise but now attempt to swing to a point above waist level (high swings).

Lateral Swings

Inner thigh and groin

The leg again acts as a pendulum, this time swinging out to the side to a comfortable height. Upon resetting the kicking leg, allow it to swing in front of the support leg.

Rotational Swings

Hip

Rotational swings help release resistance within the full range of the hip. The lateral kick originates from behind the body, kicks to the inside, and moves to the outside of the body, and then moves in a natural arc back to its point of origin.

Midline Swings

Chest, back, and shoulder

This stretch is a dynamic opening and closing of the arms. As you cross your hands over your body, they can end their arc by slapping the shoulder blades. This provides kinesthetic feedback as to the depth of the stretch.

Windmills

Shoulder girdle

Rotate your arms both forward and backward. This dynamic rotation of the shoulder helps reduce resistance throughout the shoulder girdle. Perform windmills in a variety of directions and planes.

Stretching Exercises for the Off-Season

I recommend these stretches for the off-season, but you can do them at other times of the year as well. During the season, however, avoid using these stretches aggressively because of the soreness that can result. Such soreness might lead to poor sports performance or injury. When performing these exercises on your own, take your time. Don't push too far into the painful areas of the stretch. Learn to relax. Imagine both ends of the muscle being stretched, and subsequently relaxing, thus making the middle of the muscle loose. Try to wriggle your toes and fingers when in a stretched position to help you relax during the stretch. These stretches, when performed in this manner, are best at enhancing a plastic elnogation of the muscles.

Hamstring Stretches

Bar Work 1

With one leg extended to the bar, stretch the hamstring and lower back by pointing the toe high and then leaning forward.

Bar Work 2

Rotate the leg on the bar inward, sliding the emphasis to the groin.

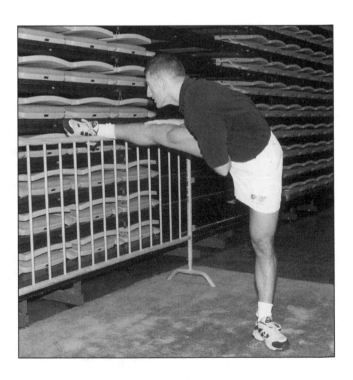

Bar Work 3

Lean forward toward the outside of the leg on the bar.

Bar Work 4

Lean forward toward the inside of the leg on the bar.

Feet Together Hamstring

Facilitate this hamstring and lower-back stretch by gently rocking from elbow to elbow.

Partner Stretch 1

Lying flat on your back, place your arms straight out from your sides and keep your legs straight. Have your partner raise and push one leg toward your torso while holding the other leg flat on the ground. Be sure to keep both legs straight throughout the stretch. You can easily apply PNF techniques to this stretch.

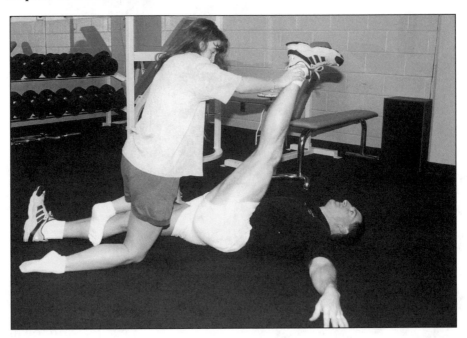

Partner Stretch 2

This stretch position is the same as the previous stretch, but requires the stretching leg to bend. Again, the hamstrings are the primary concern. You can apply PNF techniques here as well.

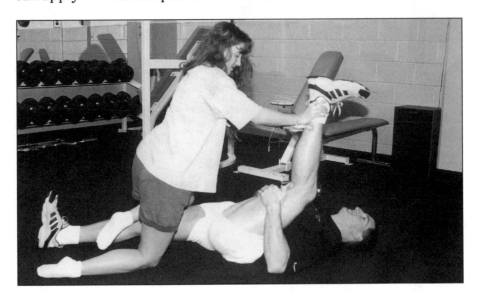

Lower-Back Stretches

Cannonball

Perform this stretch simply by lying on your back, creating a ball with your body, and stretching your back muscles.

Chair

Sitting on a chair, lean forward between your legs and gently stretch the lower back. Slight variations on the stretch (such as sitting on the floor with legs straddled, knees bent, and pulling your torso forward) can help some individuals with tightness or discomfort find a more relaxed posture upon which to stretch.

Partner Cannonball

This stretch is similar to the cannonball. Be sure to avoid overstretching. The partner cannonball is excellent for players with bigger thighs or torsos who cannot acquire a range of motion without assistance.

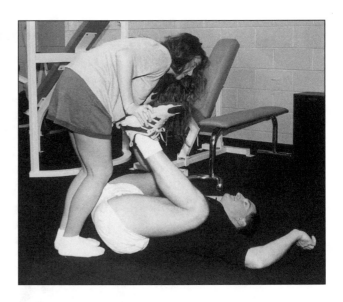

Gluteal and High Hamstring Stretches

Cross Legs– Ankle to Face

Lying on your back, cross one leg over the other so that the ankle of the top leg rests on the knee of the lower leg. Stretch the top leg by bringing the knee of this leg to the pit of the arm and the ankle toward your face.

Standing Face to Foot

Standing, place the foot of one leg on a support that is a little greater than hip height, bending the knee to the side. With the upper leg supported, lean forward. Move your chest toward your calf.

Gluteal, Hip, and Lower-Back Stretches

Reverse Twist

Sitting on the floor, legs straight in front of you, bend your right leg and cross it over the left. Place your left elbow on the outside of your right knee and twist your torso to the right. Repeat on other side. Perform this stretching exercise to rotate the spine and subsequently stretch the muscles of the lower back, hips, and torso.

Lying Twist

Lying on your back with legs extended, cross one knee over your body to the floor. Keep your elbows, head, and shoulders flat on the floor.

Groin Stretches

Butterfly

Perform this traditional groin stretch by sitting, bending the knees, and placing the feet together. Use your elbows to push down your knees and promote the stretch to a new depth.

Side Lunge

This is a great stretch for the Achilles tendon and quadriceps as well as the groin. Lunge to the side and balance yourself on the toe of your bent leg to facilitate the stretch.

Reverse Butterfly

The objective of this difficult stretch is to lower the pelvis all the way to the floor while keeping the feet in contact with the floor. Wedging the feet against a wall and placing the knees on a cushion or stretching mat can reduce discomfort and enhance relaxation. Using PNF techniques lightly press the legs together isometrically, then relax them and push your pelvis as close to the floor as you can. As you get better at this stretch your knees should slide wider apart such that your chest, pelvis and inner thigh rest flat on the floor.

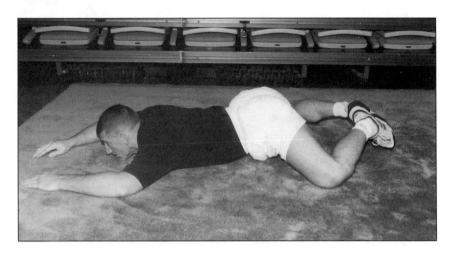

Split With Slow Rotations

Use caution with this stretch because it places heavy demand on the inner knee. Stand in a straddle position with feet more than shoulder-width apart and rotate first facing to the left and then to the right. Allow the hips to turn in the direction you are facing. The rotations stretch all the muscles of the groin.

Quadriceps and Hip Flexor Stretches

Lying Quad Stretch

This is a traditional quadriceps stretch done lying on your side. To maintain balance, lean on the outstretched arm while pulling your foot to your buttocks.

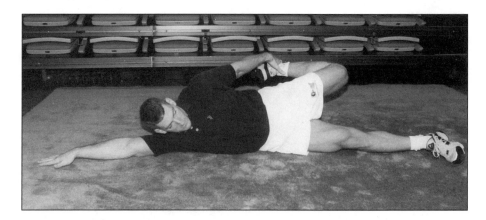

Chair to Chair Lunge

This stretch is excellent for the hip flexors as well as the quadriceps. Kneel on one knee between two chairs. Place you hands on the chair seat in front of you and place the foot of your kneeling leg on the chair seat behind you. Push the hip forward to promote the stretch.

Calf Stretches

Runner's Stretch

Using a chair or other support, stretch the calf by driving the heel into the ground while maintaining a straight leg.

Hanging Calf Stretch

In this stretch you use your body weight to press the heel to the floor. Standing on a ledge or step with your heels hanging over the edge, be sure the ball of your foot is firmly placed on the step and slowly drop your heel as far below the edge of the step as possible.

Shoulder and Chest Stretches

Front Shoulder and Chest

Using a stationary object to grip with your hand, twist your body away from the object, stretching your arm.

Rear Shoulder

From a standing position, pull your arm across your body and turn your head away from the shoulder being stretched.

Front and Rear Shoulder and Chest With Rope

Holding a stick or rope at arm's length above your head, arch your back and push the rope behind you. Place the rope behind your back and then lean forward, pulling the rope up toward your head.

Right and Left Upper Back

Grasp a stationary object and cross your arm over your body. Bend your knees slightly and twist your body away from the outstretched, anchored hand.

Trunk Stretch

Stretch by leaning in all directions—front, sides, and back. Next rotate in full circles (not pictured).

Arm Stretches

Triceps

Using one arm to pull the other, grab the elbow behind your head and pull.

Biceps

Using a rope (or a weight plate), stretch the biceps by pointing one wrist downward while the crook of the other arm is outstretched and facing upward.

To improve your performance on the field and prevent injury, incorporate flexibility exercises into your training program. The first concern of an athlete or strength coach should be to minimize injury. Flexibility is the key to longevity in your sport. If you are injury free, you can spend more time on the field, and therefore contribute more to your team.

CHAPTER 8

Strength and Power Exercises

In this chapter, I detail the various resistance exercises incorporated in the 52-week program. Base your selection of resistance exercises and the level of specificity on the equipment available and the general layout of the workout facility. As detailed in chapters 1 through 6, the phase of training also determines which exercises you should select over others.

The exercises have been categorized as supercore, core, supporting, and assisting (table 8.1). These terms describe the number of muscle and joint segments involved in the performance of an exercise, not that one group of exercises is better than the next. Because the body's musculoskeletal structure is a system in which the actions of one movement affect the actions of another, each exercise plays an important role in strengthening your body.

Supercore Exercises

Supercore exercises are complex. If you cannot perform these exercises properly or are unable to display functional flexibility in the various supercore positions, you may suffer physically by attempting them. As a result of individual body mechanics, some athletes should probably never attempt the supercore exercises. Instead, such athletes should use the core exercises to achieve the power improvements they are seeking.

Table 8.1   Exercise Classification

Supercore	Core	
Multiple muscle	*Multiple muscle*	
Unisolated	*Semi-isolated*	

Supercore	Core	
Push press	Bench press	Squat
Dumbbell snatch	Incline bench press	One- or two-leg press
Medicine ball circuits	Flat dumbbell press	Alternating leg lunge
Dumbbell pull press	Incline dumbbell press	Lunge—3 pumps
Power pull	Dip	Backward lunge
Power clean	Ham decline	Musketeer lunge
Power row	Close incline press	One stiff leg dead
Hang clean	Ballistic push-up	Box squat
	Moon push-up	Snatch squat with stick
Combo supercore	Close-grip lat	Dead lift
Dumbbell lunge, dumbbell upright row	Two-arm dumbbell row	Dumbbell squat
Dumbbell snatch, dumbbell push press	One-arm dumbbell row	Dumbbell dead lift
Step up, shoulder fly	Pull-up	Side lunge
Backward lunge, dumbbell upright row	EZ-bar pullover	
Step up, side dumbbell raise	Roll-out	
Side lunge, shoulder fly	Military press	
Squat-press	Behind neck press	
Dumbbell squat, two-arm dumbbell press	Smith military press	
	Smith behind neck	
Additional exercises	Alternate dumbbell press	
Functional exercises	Two-arm dumbbell press	
Support and balance	Free-weight upright row	
	Straight-bar curl	
Fourth-quarter tour	EZ-bar curl	
Crabbing	Reverse dip	
Leg dragging	Wall explosion	
Wrist flex	Close-grip push-up	
Jump rope	Close-grip bench	

Core Exercises

Core exercises involve several muscle groups and joint combinations working together to perform the movement. You will commonly use heavy resistance with these exercises. Coordination of the muscles and joint groups is the key to success when performing core lifts. Performing core exercises combined with supporting exercises will build muscular strength and size to optimal levels.

Supporting Exercises

Supporting exercises involve mostly a single joint and the action of a single muscle or muscle group. This isolation stimulates a large number of muscle fibers because the work being performed is not distributed as it is in supercore and core exercises. Because you use fewer muscle groups during supporting exercises, you will use less resistance. Your objective in performing supporting exercises is to move the resistance with perfect

Supporting *Single muscle* *Isolated*		Assisting *Support and balance* *Isolated*	
Ham 10 chest	Dumbbell French press	Bar shrug	Standing calf raise
Flat dumbbell fly	Triceps push-down	Cable shrug	Calf raise/leg press
Incline dumbbell fly	Kickback	Dumbbell shrug	BW one-leg calf
High lat front	One- or two-leg extension	Nautilus multishrug	Manual neck
High lat rear	One- or two-leg curl	Dumbbell stroll	
Close high lat	Ab-ad	Hammer curl	
Close low lat	Slideboard	Sit-up	
Straight dumbbell pullover	Step up	One-quarter sit-up	
Split dumbbell pullover		Ball throw	
Side dumbbell raise		Hanging abs	
Front dumbbell raise		Hyperextension	
Shoulder fly		Glute-ham raise	
Manual side raise		Butt row	
Manual front deltoid		Reverse sit-up	
Cable upright row		Hip-up	
Manual upright row		Side push-up	
Bent dumbbell raise		Elbow hip dip	
Manual rear deltoid		Clock work	
Rear deltoid swim		Reverse hyperextension	
Alternating dumbbell curl		Hi ya	
Preacher curl (cable)		Bye ya	
Incline curl		Skydiver	
Bar triceps extension		Superman	
One- or two-arm dumbbell triceps extension		Nautilus multicalf	

technique. The application of a deliberate flexion of the muscle during the performance of a supporting exercise can increase the muscle tension even further and subsequently promote muscle growth. These exercises are good for correcting muscular imbalance, as well as indirectly improving your ability to do supercore and core lifts. Supporting exercises are also good for the rehabilitation of injuries because they provide direct stimulation to the muscles surrounding the joint. This, in turn, stabilizes the injured joint area.

Assisting Exercises

Assisting exercises increase the stability of the body by addressing the core (abdominal muscles and other muscles of the midsection and lower back). Assistance exercises also address the calves, neck, and muscles of the forearms. These muscular areas assist you with balance and support during sports movements. By including assistance exercises in your routine, you can improve neural pathways throughout the body.

© Anthony Neste

Chest Exercises

Bench Press and Incline Bench Press

Core

Lying on your back (or on an incline bench), plant your feet firmly on the floor. Grip the bar with your hands shoulder-width apart and support the bar at arm's length. Lower the bar to your upper chest with your elbows out, then press the bar up by extending the arms.

Flat and Incline Dumbbell Press

Core

Lying on your back on a bench (or on an incline bench), plant your feet firmly on the floor. Grip a dumbbell in each hand and support each at arm's length and shoulder width apart. Bend the elbow to lower both dumbbells to your upper chest, then press them up by extending the arms.

Dip

Core

Support yourself on dip bars with straight arms. Leaning slightly forward as you descend, bend your elbows to lower your body until you feel a stretch in your shoulder muscles. Point your elbows in the same direction as the bars are pointing. Press upward to the starting position.

Ham Decline

Core

With your back flat against the seat back, grasp the handles with each hand and extend both arms by pressing forward. Slowly bend your elbows to bring the handles back to your chest.

Close Incline Press

Core

Lying back on an incline, plant your feet firmly on the floor. Grip the bar with your hands closer than shoulder-width apart and support the bar at arm's length. Lower the bar to your upper chest, then press the bar upward by extending the arms. By moving the hands closer together, you emphasize the muscles along the midline of the upper chest. Here the exercise is performed on a Smith machine. You can perform it on a regular incline bench if you desire.

Ham 10 Chest

Supporting

Lying on your back, rest the pads of the machine on your upper arm. Raise your arms simultaneously in a semicircular movement until the pads touch over your chest. Return to the starting position.

Flat and Incline Dumbbell Fly

Supporting

Lying on a flat bench (or on an incline bench), place your feet flat on the floor. Hold the dumbbells at arm's length above your shoulders with the palms facing each other and the dumbbells nearly touching. Lower the dumbbells in a semicircular path to your chest level by bending the elbows. Return to the starting position following the same semicircular path.

Ballistic Push-Up

Core

Perform this push-up much like a regular push-up. However, after the descending phase of the movement rapidly extend the arms and push the body upward toward the starting position so that your hands leave the floor. As you become secure with this movement, try clapping your hands together while suspended in air.

Moon Push-Up

Core

This is the Navy Seals' push-up of choice. Assume a push-up position, but bend your body at the waist with the buttocks angled above the head (1). Bend the elbows while moving the head toward the floor as if diving (2). Then move your face forward along the floor while extending the arms to full lock out (3). Once the arms are fully extended, be sure your shoulders and upper torso are angled slightly in front of your hands. To return to the starting position, bend the elbows and lower yourself to the floor as with a regular push-up.

1

2

3

Back Exercises

Close-Grip Lat

Core

Kneeling with legs secure, grasp the bar with both hands using an underhand grip. Keep hands 6 to 10 inches apart. Use your back muscles by squeezing your shoulder blades together, while bending the elbows to enhance the contraction of the back muscles and pull the bar to your chest. Return to the starting position.

Two-Arm Dumbbell Row

Core

Standing with your feet together and knees bent, bend slightly at the waist. Hold a dumbbell in each hand. Use your back muscles by squeezing your shoulder blades together and slowly pull your elbows upward until your upper arms are parallel to the floor. Slowly return to the starting position.

One-Arm Dumbbell Row

Core

With the knee and arm on the side of your nonlifting arm on a bench, bend slightly at the waist. Holding a dumbbell in the other hand, slowly pull your elbow upward until your upper arm is parallel to the floor. Return to the starting position. After completing all repetitions on one arm, switch arms.

High Lat Front

Supporting

Kneeling with legs secure, grasp the bar with both hands using an overhand grip. Keep hands 8 to 12 inches apart. Use your back muscles by squeezing your shoulder blades together. Arch your back as you bend the elbows and pull the bar to your chest to contract the back muscles. Return to the starting position.

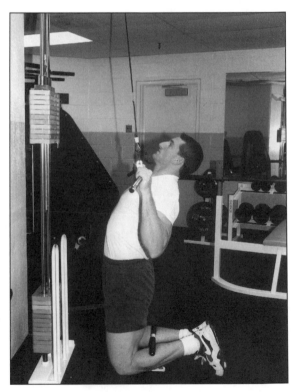

Pull-Up

Core

Grasp a pull-up bar with an underhand grip. Cross your legs behind you and pull your body up until your chin reaches the bar. Return to the starting position.

High Lat Rear

Supporting

Kneeling with legs secure, grasp the bar with both hands using an overhand grip. Keep hands 8 to 12 inches apart. Use your back muscles by squeezing your shoulder blades together. Arch your back as you bend the elbows and pull the bar behind your head to your shoulders. Return to the starting position.

Close High Lat

Supporting

Kneeling with legs secure, grasp a V-shaped bar with both hands, palms facing one another. Use your back muscles by squeezing your shoulder blades together. Arch your back as you bend the elbows and pull the bar to your chest. Return to the starting position.

Close Low Lat

Supporting

Sit with your back straight and legs in front and knees slightly bent. Grasp a cable with both hands. Use your back muscles by squeezing your shoulder blades together. Arch your back as you bend the elbows and pull the cable toward your stomach. Return to the starting position.

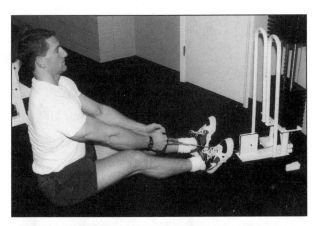

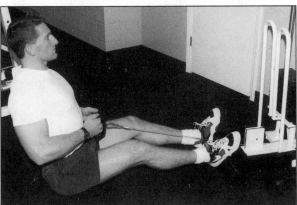

Straight Dumbbell Pullover

Supporting

Lie on your back on a bench with feet flat on the ground. Hold a dumbbell with both hands above your chest. Use your back muscles to lower the dumbbell to a point above your head and parallel to the floor. Return to the starting position.

 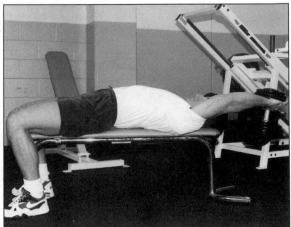

Split Dumbbell Pullover

Supporting

Lie on your back on the floor with legs straight and both arms at your side. Holding a dumbbell in each hand raise one arm up and place it back behind the head (forming a 180° arc with your arm). At the same time you return that arm to the starting position raise the other arm up and place it behind the head. Repeat, alternating arms.

EZ-Bar Pullover

Core

Lie on your back on a bench with your feet on the ground. Hold a barbell over your chest using an overhand grip with hands six to eight inches apart. Extend your arms up and over your head until the barbell is behind your head. Return to the starting position.

Roll-Out

Core

Kneeling on a mat on the floor, grasp the bar with both hands shoulder-width apart. Keeping your back straight, roll the bar forward until arms are outstretched as far as they will go. Use your arms to press down onto the bar while flexing the abdominal muscles forward to roll back up to the starting position.

Shoulder Exercises

Military Press

Core

Sitting in an upright position with your back straight, plant your feet firmly on the floor. Grip the bar with your hands shoulder-width apart and support the bar at arm's length. Lower the bar to your upper chest then press the bar up by extending the arms.

Behind Neck Press

Core

Sitting in an upright position with your back straight, plant your feet firmly on the floor. Grip the bar with your hands at shoulder-width apart and support the bar at arm's length. Lower the bar to a point behind the head at ear level, then press the bar upward by extending the arms.

Smith Behind Neck and Military Press

Core

Using a Smith machine to increase linear overload, sit in an upright position with your back straight. Plant your feet firmly on the floor. Grip the bar with your hands shoulder-width apart and support the bar at arm's length. Lower the bar to a point behind the head at ear level then press the bar upward by extending the arms. When performing the military press assume the same body position, but slide the bench back to allow the bar to move in front of the chin just above the collar bone.

Alternating Dumbbell Press

Core

To perform the hard version of this exercise, start with both arms extended overhead. Lower one arm to the shoulder while keeping the other arm extended overhead. Switch arms. To perform the easy version, start with both dumbbells resting at shoulder level. Extend one dumbbell to arm's length while keeping the other at the shoulder. Alternate.

Two-Arm Dumbbell Press

Core

Perform this exercise similarly to the alternating dumbbell press, however extend both dumbbells upward at the same time. Attempt to push the chest forward as the dumbbells ascend just slightly above and behind the head.

Push Press (Dumbbell or Barbell)

Supercore

Stand resting a barbell or dumbbells at shoulder level with your feet firmly planted shoulder-width apart. Quickly bend the knees about two to three inches to allow the weights to gain a downward momentum, then rapidly extend the knees and press the weight upward by extending the arms to a point over and slightly behind the head. Return to the starting position by slowly lowering the weights.

Dumbbell Snatch

Supercore

Assume a squatting position with the back straight, eyes focused up, and arms reaching to dumbbells on floor. Rapidly pull the dumbbells from the floor by fully extending the knees and hips. Keep your back straight and the head and eyes angled slightly upward during the entire pull to avoid lower back stress. As you extend the legs, pull the dumbbells upward toward your forehead. Remember to keep your elbows higher than your wrist during the pull. When the dumbbells have reached their maximum height, flip the wrists under, securely catching the dumbbells and extend the arms fully above your head.

As the exercise resistance increases, the height you can pull the dumbbells will become less and less. To safely finish the movement, you will have to squat lower to secure the dumbbells at full arm extension.

Side Dumbbell Raise

Supporting

Perform this exercise either standing or sitting. Sitting versions of any upper body exercise allow less lower body involvement and result in greater upper body exertion. Begin with the dumbbells at arm's length in front of the lower torso (if standing) or at the sides of the seat (if sitting). Slightly bend the elbows in throughout the movement to reduce stress on the elbow joint and keep palms facing the floor. Slowly raise the dumbbells upward and out from the sides of the body. Once parallel to the floor the dumbbells should be slightly in front of the body in a place where they can be seen in your peripheral vision. Then slowly turn the dumbbells forward so that the thumb on each hand faces downward (as if pouring water from a pitcher) and return the weights to the starting position.

Front Dumbbell Raise

Supporting

Perform this exercise either standing or sitting. Begin with the dumbbells at arm's length in front of the lower torso (if standing) or at the sides of the seat (if sitting). With palms facing inward toward one another, slowly raise the dumbbells upward and out to arm's length in front of the body, parallel to the floor. Twist the wrist at the top of the movement to add additional muscle exertion. At this point the dumbbells can be lowered to their starting position. Perform this movement alternating arms or moving both arms simultaneously.

Shoulder Fly

 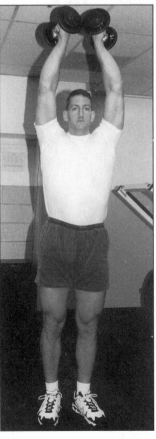

Supporting

Perform as if you are doing a side dumbbell raise (see p. 163) but instead of stopping the dumbbells at a point parallel to the floor, bring them above the head. Then return them slowly to the beginning position. Use this exercise during heavy training. Performing it in a standing position allows you to use heavier resistance; use the legs to make the movement more complex.

Manual Side Raise

Supporting

Sit with your back to your partner, who will stand and provide resistance. Position your arms to the side and slightly to the front of your body slightly bending the elbows. Your partner applies upward pressure just below the elbows while you resist the pressure by pressing your arms down toward your sides. Once your arms reach your sides, press them upward while your partner applies downward resistance (pictured). Your arm movement should be the same speed moving up as it was going down.

Manual Front Deltoid

Supporting

Sit facing a partner who will stand and provide resistance. Position your arms to the side and slightly to the front of your body slightly bending the elbows Using the same resistance methods as described in manual side raise, work to thoroughly fatigue the front deltoid muscle area.

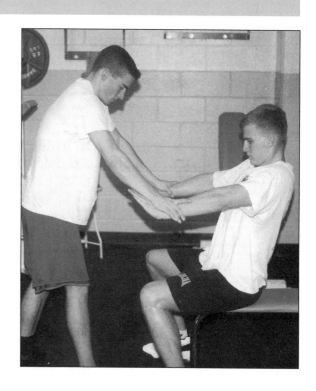

Medicine Ball Circuit

Supercore

This is a series of multijoint functional movements performed with a medicine ball in a circuit.

1. **Wood chop.** Hold the ball with two hands above the head at arm's length. Bring the ball to a point between the legs just above the floor, using a squatting motion. Keep your back straight and tilt your chin slightly upward. Perform 10 to 15 repetitions.

2. **Circular rotation.** Extend the ball above the head at arm's length. Bring the ball down to your right in a clockwise direction. As the ball reaches the far right, squat with the ball just above the floor. Keep the back straight and tilt your chin slightly upward. Continue the circle to the left as you move up and out of the squat. Completing the circle and ending in full extension above the head counts as one repetition. Perform 10 to 15 repetitions clockwise and 10 to 15 more counterclockwise.

3. **Side woodchop.** Extend the ball at arm's length above and to the far left of the head. Squat as you bring the ball to a point outside the right ankle just above the floor. Keep your back straight and tilt your chin slightly upward. Complete the repetition by moving the ball back to its starting point. Perform 10 to 15 repetitions from upper left to lower right and from upper right to lower left. This circuit is a great lower and upper body combination exercise; you will feel it profoundly in the shoulder area.

Dumbbell Pull Press

Supercore

Assume a squatting position with the back straight and the eyes looking forward. Rapidly pull the dumbbells from the floor by extending the knees and hips fully. As you extend the legs, pull the dumbbells upward toward the forehead. Keep your elbows higher than your wrist during the pull. When the dumbbells have reached their maximum height, flip the wrist under to securely catch the dumbbells at the level of the shoulders. Once the dumbbells are secure, extend the arms fully above and slightly behind the head. As the exercise resistance increases, the height the dumbbells can be pulled toward the forehead will be less; to safely finish the movement, squat lower to catch the dumbbells at the shoulders. (See facing page.)

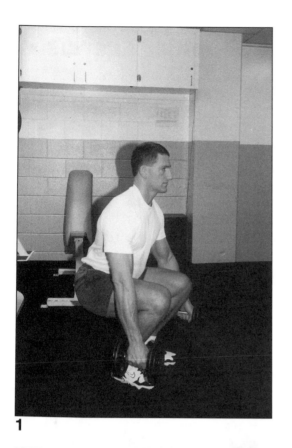

1

2

3

4

Trapezius and Posterior Shoulder Exercises

Power Pull

Supercore

An exaggerated version of the bar shrug, this exercise uses the legs more. Standing, hold a barbell at arm's length in front of the hips. Bend the knees two to three inches to allow the bar to gain a downward momentum. Straighten the knees and at the same time pull the bar upward as if to shrug the shoulders. Keep the arms straight. Since the weight is heavier, it is safer to allow the knees to bend slightly as the bar descends. Catch the bar on the upper thighs to prevent the lower back from having to fully decelerate the momentum of the weight. Stand straight again and repeat the process.

Power Clean

Supercore

Perform this exercise with the press overhead to make it a clean and jerk. Grasp the bar just outside your shins with an overhand, closed-thumb grip. Be sure the buttocks are in a perfect parallel squat position, the back is straight, and the head is tilted slightly up. Rapidly pull the bar from the floor by extending the knees and hips fully. As you extend the legs, pull the bar toward the upper chest, keeping your elbows higher than your wrist during the pull. When the bar has reached its maximum height, flip the wrist under, securely catching the bar at chin level. To ensure the catch, keep the elbows high and to the front of the body. As the resistance increases, the height the bar can be pulled will be less; to safely finish the movement you will have to squat lower to securely catch the bar.

Free-Weight Upright Row

Core

Hold a barbell at arm's length in front of the hips. Bend the arms at the elbow, keeping the elbows always higher than the wrist. Pull the bar to chin level and slowly return to the starting position.

Power Row

Supercore

An exaggerated version of the free-weight upright row, the power row uses the legs more. Hold a barbell at arm's length in front of the hips. Bend the knees two to three inches, allowing the bar to gain downward momentum. Straighten the knees while pulling the bar upward with the arms. Bend the arms at the elbow, keeping the elbows higher than the wrist. Pull the bar to chin level and slowly return to the starting position. Since the weight is heavier than in the free-weight upright row, it is safer to bend the knees slightly as the bar descends. Catching the bar on the upper thighs prevents the lower back from fully decelerating the momentum of the weight. Stand up and repeat the process.

Hang Clean

Supercore

Hang cleans are performed similarly to the power row, but instead of pulling the bar to the chin and returning to the start, flip the wrists under as during the power clean movement, and catch the bar at chin level. Slowly return the bar to hip level.

Cable Upright Row

Supporting

Hold a bar and cable at arms length in front of the hips. Bend the arms at the elbow, and keep the elbows higher than the wrists. Pull the bar to chin level and slowly return to the starting position.

Manual Upright Row

Supporting

Stand facing your partner. Grasp a towel with both hands and hold at hip level while your partner holds the other end. Pull the towel upward toward the chin, keeping your elbows higher than your wrist. As you pull up on the towel, your partner resists by pulling downward. Once you reach chin level, your partner should reverse the resistance and pull upward while you pull the towel down toward your hips. Keep the speed of movement the same in both directions.

Dumbbell Shrug

Assisting

Hold a pair of dumbbells at arm's length in front of the hips. Keep the arms perfectly straight and use the upper shoulder muscles to pull the weight upward as if to shrug. Keep your chin tucked to the upper chest to allow the upper shoulders to reach their maximum height. Slowly lower the dumbbells to complete the first repetition.

Bar or Cable Shrug

Assisting

Hold a barbell or cable bar at arm's length in front of the hips. Keep the arms perfectly straight and use the upper shoulder muscles to pull the weight upward as if to shrug. Tuck the chin to the upper chest to allow the upper shoulders to reach their maximum height. Slowly lower the bar to complete the first repetition. The cable provides a more constant resistance than the free weights.

Nautilus Multishrug

Assisting

Using a Nautilus multi-machine, hold the machine's lever at arm's length in front of the hips. Loop your hands through the straps attached to the cross bar, keep your arms straight, and pull the cross bar and level upward by shrugging the shoulders. Tuck the chin to the upper chest to allow the upper shoulders to reach their maximum height. Slowly lower the cross bar and lever to complete the first repetition.

Dumbbell Stroll

Assisting

Carry a dumbbell in each hand for a given distance while walking. The natural vertical rise and fall of the body while striding create a small shrugging motion that strengthens the upper shoulders and trapezius muscle group. The gripping strength of the forearms and hands is also profoundly effected. This is a great exercise to measure the psychological willingness to complete the distance without stopping.

Bent Dumbbell Raise

Supporting

With the feet pressed firmly together, bend both knees two to three inches; both of these techniques reduce pressure on the lower back. Bend at the waist until the upper back is parallel to the floor, and allow the dumbbells to hang freely and perpendicular to the floor. Arch the middle back just below the shoulder blades and slowly pull the dumbbells upward and to the sides of the body, with the palms facing downward. The dumbbells should reach their end point when they are parallel to the floor and just slightly in front of the shoulders. You should see them in your peripheral vision.

Manual Rear Deltoid

Supporting

Using a partner to apply resistance from behind, cross your arms in front of your body at upper chest level. While your partner applies forward pressure on your elbows, push your elbows back against the resistance. Upon reaching the furthermost point that your elbows can travel, push forward against your partner's backward resistance.

Rear Deltoid Swim

Supporting

Perform this exercise with or without weights. Lying on your stomach, with your feet elevated two inches from the floor, stretch your hands in front of you, palms down, two inches from the floor. Bring both hands in an arc along the sides of the body without touching the floor. Turn the hands palm up as they reach the buttocks. Return to the starting position. Do not bend the elbows at any time.

Arm Exercises

Alternating Dumbbell Curl

Supporting

Stand grasping a dumbbell in each hand; allow the dumbbells to hang freely at each side of the body. Lift one dumbbell upward toward the shoulder by flexing the arm at the elbow. Return the dumbbell slowly to your side before lifting the other dumbbell. Continue to alternate lifting the dumbbells.

Straight-Bar Curl

Core

Starting with the bar at your upper thigh, pull it toward the chin by flexing the arms at the elbows. Keep the elbows close to the sides and slightly in front of the body. Never lean back to lift the weight.

Preacher Curl (Cable)

Supporting

Sit on the preacher bench with the back of the upper arms resting securely on the pad. Grasp the bar attached to the cable and lift the bar toward the chin by flexing the arms at the elbows. Return the bar slowly to the starting position to complete the repetition. You can also perform this exercise using a free-weight bar.

EZ-Bar Curl

Core

Start with the EZ bar at the upper thigh level and pull the bar toward the chin by flexing the arms at the elbows. Keep the elbows close to the sides and slightly in the front of the body. Do not lean back to lift the weight.

Incline Curl

Supporting

Sit on an incline bench with your back resting securely on the pad. Grasp a dumbbell in each hand, and allow them to hang freely at each side of the body. Lift one dumbbell upward toward the shoulder by flexing the arm at the elbow. Return the dumbbell slowly to your side before lifting the other dumbbell. Continue to alternate lifting the dumbbells.

Hammer Curl

Assisting

Stand with a dumbbell in each hand and allow the dumbbells to hang freely at each side of the body. Lift one dumbbell upward toward the shoulder by flexing the arm at the elbows. Face your palms inward as if holding a hammer during the entire movement. Return the dumbbell slowly to your side before lifting the other dumbbell. Continue to alternate lifting the dumbbells.

Bar Triceps Extension

Supporting

Lying on a bench, grip a straight or EZ-curl bar with your hands slightly closer than shoulder-width. Extend the bar at arm's length above the upper chest. Bend at the elbows and allow the bar to descend to a point at the top of the forehead or just above the head. Keep the upper arms perpendicular to the floor and stationary throughout the movement of the elbows. To complete the repetition, extend the arms to the starting position.

Two-Arm Dumbbell Triceps Extension

Supporting

Lying on a bench, grasp a dumbbell in each hand and extend the arms above the upper chest. Bend at the elbows and allow both dumbbells to descend to a point beside the head. Keep the upper arms perpendicular to the floor and stationary throughout the movement. To complete the repetition, extend the arms to the starting position.

Dumbbell French Press

Supporting

Sitting or standing, grasp the end of one dumbbell and extend it above the head at arm's length. Lower the dumbbell until the lower head of the weight is even with the ears. Extend the dumbbell upward toward the starting position. Keep the elbows close to the head at all times. It is safer to used fixed dumbbells for this exercise; weights with removable collars may detach and cause injury.

Triceps Push-Down

Supporting

Grasp a bar attached to a high cable with a close grip. Start with the fore-arms parallel to the floor making a 90-degree angle between the upper arm and forearm. Keep the elbows tucked tightly to the sides and just slightly in front of the body. Extend the elbow downward to full extension. Return to the starting position to complete the movement.

Kickback

Supporting

Bend the knees two to three inches and bend forward at the waist, as if skiing downhill. Grasp a dumbbell in each hand and tuck your upper arms against your sides. For maximum effect keep your upper arms parallel to the floor throughout the movement (see photo at right). Extend the dumbbells to full arm extension (see photo, top of page 181). You can apply various hand positions at this point in the movement; palms can end facing inward toward

the hips, upward, or downward. The variation in hand positions affects the different parts of the triceps muscle. Lower the dumbbells to the starting position by bending only the elbow.

One-Arm Dumbbell Triceps Extension

Supporting

Sitting or standing, extend a dumbbell above the head at arm's length. Lower the dumbbell until the lower head of weight is even with the ears; then extend the dumbbell upward to the starting position. Keep the working arm's elbow close to the head at all times. It is safer to used fixed dumbbells for this exercise; weights with removable collars may detach and cause injury.

Wall Explosion

Core

Place your hands on the wall with your thumbs fully extended and touching. Place your nose two inches from the wall in the space between your hands. Lean your body headfirst toward the wall making sure your feet are secure and on a nonslip surface. The further your feet are from the wall the more difficult the movement will be. Tuck the elbows toward the centerline of your body and quickly extend the arms with enough force to push you to a standing position. If you cannot push yourself to a standing position start with your feet closer to the wall. Slowly return to the wall by placing your hands on the wall first before lowering your head toward the wall. This is an easier version of the ballistic push-up.

Reverse Dip

Core

With your back to a securely positioned bench, place the heels of your palms on the edge of the bench so the fingers extend over the edge. Vary leg position to vary the intensity of the exercise; the farther your feet are from you the more difficult it is. Add even more resistance by placing the feet on another bench or exercise ball in front of you. Once you choose you body position, fully extend the elbows. Slowly bend the elbows to lower your body. Complete the movement by fully extending the arms.

Close-Grip Push-Up

Core

Place hands on the floor with the thumbs fully extended and touching each other. Bend elbows and do a push-up. Keep your elbows close to your sides during this version of the push-up to ensure that the triceps are emphasized rather than the chest and shoulders.

Close-Grip Bench

Core

Perform this exercise just as you would a regular bench press, except move the hands in about six to eight inches apart. Lower the weight to your chest with the elbows tucked tightly against the sides of the body. Fully extend the arms to complete the movement.

Leg Exercises

Squat and Smith Squat

Core

The core squat movement is the same whether you use free weights or a Smith machine. Stand inside a squat rack with your feet shoulder-width apart and toes turned slightly out. Take the weight from the stands and look straight ahead at a point on the wall that you are facing. Keep the back completely straight so that the spine is in a natural alignment. Descend by flexing the knees and sitting back so that the buttocks move to a point well behind the heels. This will keep the shins perpendicular to the floor, and prevent the knees from extending too far over the toes. Descend to a point where your hamstrings are parallel to the floor or farther if you can. Do not bounce off the bottom when returning to the starting position. Bring your hips slightly forward to place the back in perfect alignment.

One- or Two-Leg Press

Core

Two leg: Place the feet flat and firmly in the middle of the platform. Turn the toes slightly outward. Push the weight to full leg extension, and turn the platform supports to their unlocked position. Begin to lower the weight by flexing the knees to a point where the upper and lower leg perform a right angle. Then, extend the knees to push the platform back to its starting position.

One leg: Place the foot in the same position on the platform as for a two-leg press. Let the free leg occupy the space between the slides, or keep it tucked up and close to your abdomen.

One- or Two-Leg Extension

Supporting

Extend the knee(s) to a full and locked position using the upper thigh muscles (quadriceps). Pause just briefly, and slowly lower the weight back to its starting point

One- or Two-Leg Curl

Supporting

Using either a lying or seated version of the leg-curl machine, flex the knee(s) and bring the heel(s) toward the buttocks. If lying, keep the hips firmly against the bench to provide maximum muscle contraction in the hamstrings.

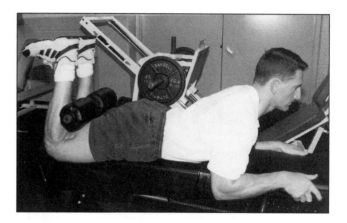

Ab-Ad

Supporting

Perform using an inner-outer thigh machine. Spread the legs apart against resistance (abduction) to work the outer thighs. Change the machine resistance direction and squeeze the legs together (adduction) to work the inner thighs. Keep the buttocks firmly against the seat to provide the maximum result during the lifts.

Alternating Leg Lunge

Core

Standing with both legs together, step forward with one leg and bend that knee to 90 degrees. Be sure the shin of your forward leg is perpendicular to the floor. Allow the back leg to bend also when first learning the exercise; as you become more advanced, keep the back leg straight, forcing the front leg to step out from the standing position even farther. Push back to a standing position off the front leg. Alternate legs throughout the exercise; you can also perform these as walking lunges, moving from one point to another.

Lunge—3 Pumps

Core

Another variation of the lunge involves 3 pumps of the leg (see phase 1 workouts). As you step out from the standing position, keep the leg out front and then straighten it and bend it three times before pushing yourself back to a standing position. This pumping of the leg emphasizes the level of muscle fatigue, the objective in phase 1.

Backward Lunge

Core

From a standing position step backward with one leg. Bend the front knee 90 degrees and lower the body toward the floor. Allow the back leg to bend when first learning the exercise. As you become more advanced, keep the back leg straight, forcing it to step back from the standing position even further.

Musketeer Lunge

Core

From a standing position step with one leg behind the other leg. Like performing a carioca or grapevine maneuver, the front leg is the supporting leg during the repetition. Bend the knee of the front leg, lower the body and keep the back leg as straight as possible. Push the front leg back up to a standing position while bringing the back leg beside the front leg to finish the repetition. Alternate the leg that steps behind during the exercise.

One Stiff Leg Dead

Core

Standing on one leg, bend forward at the waist. As the upper body bends forward, keep the support leg straight and move the free leg behind the buttocks. Attempt to touch the floor or shoe of the support leg with your fingertips. Return to the starting position. Once upright, bend the knee of the support leg four to five inches and return the leg to full extension. Repeat all the repetitions on one support leg before switching to the other leg.

Box Squat

Core

Stand on one leg on a box or raised surface. Perform a squat. You can practice this exercise by holding a stable object for support or supporting your free leg on a stable object. As you become better at this exercise, perform it by holding the free leg and arms straight in front of the body while the support leg performs a squat until the buttock touches the heel on the support leg. Keep the foot of the support leg flat on the floor and the knee of the support leg behind the toe by pushing the buttocks to a point well behind the heel.

Snatch Squat With Stick

Core

Perform a squat while holding a light stick or piece of PVC above your head. This exercise can help you learn the position required for the snatch by positioning the body to improve ankle, knee, hip, back, and shoulder flexibility.

Dead Lift

Core

With your feet slightly narrower than shoulder width, grasp a weighted barbell. Use an undergrip with your strongest hand so that the palm faces away from the shins; use an overgrip with your weaker hand so that the palm is turned toward the shins. Space your grip just outside the legs. Position the body like the bottom position of a squat; keep your back straight, your eyes focused straight ahead, your chin tilted forward, your hamstrings parallel to the floor, and the buttocks at a point behind the heels. With the arms perfectly straight, extend the knees and allow the legs to do all the work. Once in a straight and standing position, lean slightly back with the lower back. Lower the weight slowly back to the floor using the legs to control the speed of descent.

Dumbbell Dead Lift or Dumbbell Squat

Core

Grasp a dumbbell in each hand. Stand straight with the feet just inside shoulder width and the toes turned slightly out. Slowly lower the weights to one to two inches from the floor by bending the knees. Use the legs to control the speed of descent. Hold the dumbbells outside the legs at arm's length; keep your back straight, your eyes focused straight ahead, your chin tilted forward, your hamstrings parallel to the floor, and the buttocks at a point behind the heels. Extend the knees to return to the starting position.

Side Lunge

Core

From a standing position step to the right with the right leg and bend the right knee. Step far enough to the side so that the left leg is as straight as possible. Push the right leg back to a standing position with both feet ending side by side to finish the repetition. Alternate the leg that steps to the side during the exercise.

Slideboard

Supporting

Stand on one side of the slideboard. Push hard with one leg to propel yourself across the board. Once on the other side of the board use the opposite leg to push yourself back.

Step Up

Supporting

Using a box or a secure bench, step onto and off of it, alternating legs. The best height for the box allows the upper leg to be parallel to the floor when the foot is on the box. Be sure to lean forward to place all the stress on the leg on the box; do not push off the floor with the other leg.

Cylinder Circuit Exercises

This is a series of circuit exercises for the torso (cylinder). There are five circuits of five to seven exercises selected from the following, mixed up across the weeks to provide variation and changes in intensity.

Sit-Up

Assisting

Lying on the ground, place your hands over your ears and anchor your feet under an object with your knees bent. Curl the upper body, using your abdominal muscles, until your elbows come past the knees. Lower the upper body slowly—again using your abdominal muscles—until your lower to mid back touches the floor.

One-Quarter Sit-Up

Assisting

Lying on your back, bend your legs slightly so that the feet are two inches from the ground. This creates a natural arch in the lower back. Flatten the arch into the floor by lifting the hips up and contracting the abdominal muscles.

Ball Throw

Assisting

Perform sit-ups with a medicine ball. Release the ball as you come up. Have a partner catch and return the ball to you or throw the ball against a wall and catch it for the next repetition.

Hanging Abs

Assisting

Hang from a chin-up bar with your knees bent and raise your feet as high as you can. You can support yourself with your feet touching the ground after each repetition or you can try not touching the feet to the ground, which requires more body control.

Hyperextension

Assisting

Use a glute/ham or hyperextension bench and secure your legs under the supports. Bend forward from the waist toward the floor. Use your lower back to lift your body back up. Keep legs straight during the entire movement. Hold your hands over your ears.

Glute-Ham Raise

Assisting

Use a glute/ham bench and perform a hyperextension (above), but at the top of the movement when the body is suspended nearly perpendicular to the floor contract the hamstrings against the glute/ham pad. Bend the knees, thus pulling the body even higher. To return, slowly extend the legs while lowering the upper body back to the floor.

Butt Row

Assisting

Using the hands for support, bring the knees to the chest keeping your buttocks on the floor. Then push legs away and lean back.

Reverse Sit-Up

Assisting

Using the arms for support, bring the knees to the chin and lift the buttocks from the floor. Then slowly lower the buttocks while pushing the legs away until they are nearly straight with the feet held two inches from the floor.

Hip-Up

Assisting

Hold a support with the hands or place the hands on the floor at your sides to make the exercise more difficult. Keep the legs straight and raise your hips off the ground. Slowly lower them making sure to push the legs slightly away from your face to make the exercise more effective.

Side Push-Up

Assisting

Lie on your side with one foot on top of the other. Use the feet as a fulcrum. Place the forearm of the side you are lying on flat on the floor. Make a sort of tripod with the fingertips of your free hand in front of your stomach. Push the hips straight up, using the arms for support. Vary this exercise by turning the body inward so that more of the stomach is facing the ground. This shifts the emphasis from the side or oblique muscles to the intercostals around the front rib cage.

Elbow Hip Dip

Assisting

Support the body on the elbows and toes and keep the hips off the ground. Hold this position for 10 seconds and then allow the hips to dip quickly to touch the floor and return to the supported position. This is a great stabilizing exercise for the lower back and torso muscles.

Clock Work

Assisting

Lie on your back and hold a support or spread your arms out from your sides on the floor. Imagine your body is a clock. Your head is at twelve o'clock and your buttocks are at six o'clock. Start with your legs together straight above your hips. Carry your legs side to side. When the legs are carried to the side they should point toward three and nine o'clock to maximize the exercise.

Reverse Hyperextension

Assisting

Lie face down with only the upper torso supported on a high bench or table. Keep the legs and hips off the bench and the feet touching the ground. Grasp the sides of the bench firmly with the hands. Keeping the legs straight, lift the legs to a point parallel to the floor. Use the lower back and gluteal muscles to perform the lift. Lower the legs slowly to the floor.

Hi Ya

Assisting

Lie face down on the floor and extend the arms and the legs. Keeping the feet in contact with the floor, repeatedly raise one arm at a time off the floor as high as you can. Contract the lower back muscles to help provide lift. Do not twist the body to achieve height. You can push up slightly with the lowered hand to provide support during the exercise. Attempt to clear the entire chest and upper stomach from the floor before switching hands.

Bye Ya

Assisting

Lie face down on the floor, extend the legs, and start with both of them in contact with the floor. Place the hands flat on the floor beside your shoulders.

Alternate, lifting each leg several times. You can push up slightly with the lowered leg to provide support during the exercise. Attempt to clear the entire upper thigh and hip from the floor before switching legs.

Skydiver

Assisting

Lie face down on the floor. Bend the arms 90 degrees at the elbow and spread the legs apart. Lift both the arms and the legs upward, using the lower back and gluteal muscles to perform the lift. Slowly return the arms and legs toward the floor without resting them on the floor during the set. Just lightly touch the floor, using it as a point of reference for the movement.

Superman

Assisting

To make this exercise more difficult than the skydiver exercise, instead of bending arms and spreading the legs, extend the arms in front of the body and keep the legs together and fully extended as well. This adds more resistance on each end of your body, causing the lower back and gluteal muscles to work harder.

Calf Exercises

Nautilus Multicalf

Assisting

Perform a heel raise (come up on your toes) using a Nautilus multimachine. Keep the knees locked, and use only the ankle to fully emphasize the muscles of the calves.

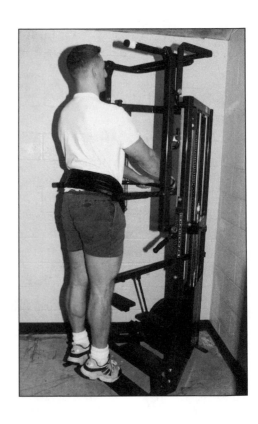

Standing Calf Raise

Assisting

Perform a heel raise (come up on your toes) using a Smith machine. If you do not have this machine, then choose another type of resistance keeping the knees locked and using the ankles to fully emphasize the calf muscles.

Calf Raise/Leg Press

Assisting

Perform a heel raise on a leg press machine. Allow the toes to rest on the bottom edge of the leg press platform, with the heels hanging off. Do not turn the platform supports out

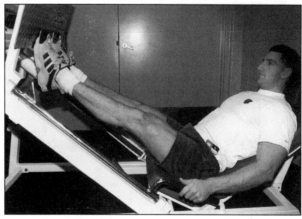

of their locked position. If the platform were to slip off the toes, serious injury could occur.

BW One-Leg Calf

Assisting

Perform this version of the calf raise with one leg at a time, using only your body weight for resistance. Again keep the knee as straight as possible and use only your ankle to move your weight.

Neck Exercises

Manual Neck

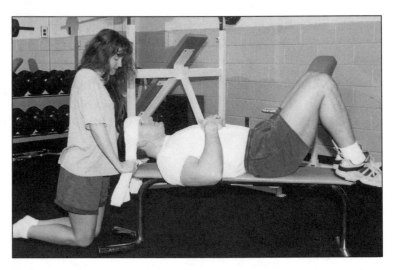

Assisting

Have a partner apply steady nonjerking manual resistance to the front, back, and sides of the neck. Manual exercises require a serious commitment to safety; both partners need to be mature and work together at all times during the exercise. The worker determines the speed and the range of motion of the movement while the resistor should be a coach or trained person who understands the limitations of the body.

Combo Exercises

Combo exercises are two or more exercises combined together to require you to coordinate movements. Combining exercise also condenses the workout and saves time. These exercises can also provide a greater demand on your cardiorespiratory system, therefore providing a conditioning effect.

Dumbbell Lunge, Dumbbell Upright Row

Supercore

Hold a dumbbell in each hand and step forward to perform an alternating leg lunge. Upon pushing back from the lunge to a standing position, perform a dumbbell upright row. Remember to keep the elbows higher than the wrist during the row. Perform one set with one leg, and switch legs for the second set.

Dumbbell Snatch, Dumbbell Push Press

Supercore

Perform a dumbbell snatch; then lower the dumbbells to the shoulders and perform a dumbbell push press. Lower the dumbbells to your sides for the next dumbbell snatch.

Step Up, Shoulder Fly

Supercore

Hold a dumbbell in each hand at your sides and perform a step up. Upon returning to the floor, perform a shoulder fly. Remember that the fly ends with the dumbbells above the head. Perform another step up with the other leg.

Backward Lunge, Dumbbell Upright Row

Supercore

Hold a dumbbell in each hand and perform a backward lunge. Upon pushing up from the lunge to a standing position, perform a dumbbell upright row. Keep your elbows higher than the wrist during the row. Perform one set with one leg stepping back and a second set with the other leg stepping back.

Step Up, Side Dumbbell Raise

Supercore

Perform a step up, shoulder fly, but bring the dumbbells parallel to the floor during the side dumbbell raise.

Side Lunge, Shoulder Fly

Supercore

Hold a dumbbell in each hand and perform a side lunge. As you lower the body to the side allow the dumbbells to meet at the center line of the body at arm's length. Upon pushing back up to a standing position, allow the dumbbells to move to the sides of the body. Then perform a shoulder fly: one set with one leg stepping to the side and a second set with the opposite leg stepping out.

Squat-Press

Supercore

Using dumbbells or a light barbell, perform a squat. Once you come up from the bottom of the squat, press the barbell above your head.

Dumbbell Squat, Two-Arm Dumbbell Press

Supercore

Perform a dumbbell squat (dumbbell dead lift) holding the dumbbells at shoulder level during this combo rather than at the waist. Upon standing up from the squat, press the dumbbells upward to arm's length. If you use the legs to press the weight above the head it becomes a dumbbell push press. However, this may be necessary if the weight becomes heavy as a result of fatigue.

Other Drills

Fourth-Quarter Tour

This is a leg combination exercise—performed on the football field or on a basketball court—consisting of walking lunges, step slides, backward walking lunges, deep-knee bends, or any plyometric exercise. Mark off a rectangle about the size of a basketball court or larger (96 ft by 50 ft). An example of a fourth-quarter tour combination might include 20 deep knee bends in each corner, lunging down the lengths of the rectangle, and step slides across the widths. Create any combination of exercises that causes fatigue. Once around the rectangle completes one repetition.

Crabbing

Assume the up position of a push-up, but spread the arms and legs apart. In this position, walk to the left by simultaneously moving your left arm and leg out to the side. Shift your weight to the left then move your right arm and leg to the left. Repeat this pattern, thus walking the body along the floor for a given distance.

Leg dragging

Assume the up position of a push-up with your feet placed on a towel or seat cushion (if on a slick surface such as a basketball court or tile floor) or on a scooter or dolly with wheels (if on a rough surface). Walk along the floor with your hands to a designated point, dragging your legs behind. Your legs will sway from left to right with each hand placement. This works the hips and lower back during the exercise.

Wrist flex

Hold a sand-filled bag or sponge and squeeze, using quick motions for 100 repetitions with each wrist.

Jump rope

Jump rope in the traditional rope skipping fashion; any and all variations can be applied.

CHAPTER

9

Running Drills

In the conditioning training section of each workout, I've provided several running drills. Running and other activities such as cycling, swimming, stair climbing, and rowing enhance your *cardiorespiratory conditioning*. We have discussed how to make your muscles bigger and more powerful by directly stimulating them with some form of resistance training. Having muscle is critical to being a successful athlete. Muscle is what enables you to move with grace and speed. But we must do more than just work the muscle directly. It is critical that we improve the other systems of the body to provide the muscles with the nutrients and oxygen that will keep them functioning optimally.

By performing cardiorespiratory exercises we can better stimulate the heart and lungs (cardiorespiratory system), kidneys (renal system), sweat glands and various other organs of the body (thermoregulation and endocrine systems) to provide support to our ever-demanding muscle. While resistance training does work these supporting systems, it places only one type of demand on them. More continuous activity, such as running, however, places different demands on these supporting systems.

During a football game, your body must respond to a variety of situations. Let's say you have trained hard with resistance exercises to become stronger and more powerful but have done little running. When the first game comes along you're the strongest, most powerful athlete on the field. Your heart and lungs, however, are so poorly conditioned that you can't get enough oxygen to your muscles to keep them functioning. You are the

© Active Images

biggest and baddest player out there, but you can't stay on the field long enough to help your team. What good is that? By incorporating cardiorespiratory conditioning into your training, you can be big and powerful and still be able to run like the wind.

Types of Cardiorespiratory Training

You can do two general types of cardiovascular conditioning depending on whether you are conditioning for power or endurance:

- *Anaerobic,* or "stop-and-go," or sprint training. This type of training is oriented to speed and power. As a football player you particularly need to incorporate anaerobic work into your training program because football games include short (under 200 yards) sprints and frequent starts and stops.
- *Aerobic,* or endurance training. Football athletes require little aerobic conditioning relative to anaerobic conditioning to meet the demands of the sport, but time-extended bouts of play may push a football athlete toward the threshold where aerobic-type conditioning is required.

Sports with similar cardiorespiratory requirements place similar physical demands on the body. If you play a combination of sports, you run a greater risk of not being as physically prepared for one sport as you are for another, unless the physical requirements of both sports are similar. Soccer, lacrosse, and basketball are closely related in their cardiorespiratory requirements; football and sprint track events have other cardiorespiratory requirements. This is not to say that a multisport athlete cannot be great at all his sports. But differences in the physical demands among sports mean that the multisport athlete may have to work twice as smart as the single-sport athlete in preparing himself physically.

Sprint Training

Stop-and-go training, or sprint or anaerobic training, is exercise that you perform at 85 percent to 125 percent of your maximum oxygen uptake ($\dot{V}O_2$max) or which pushes your heart rate around 90 percent or above of your maximal heart rate. (An approximation of your maximal heart rate in beats per minute can be determined quickly by subtracting your age from 220). *Anaerobic* means without oxygen, and during anaerobic-type exercise the intensity at which the muscles are working prevents them from fully absorbing and using oxygen from the air being breathed. Hence, anaerobic training can improve the efficiency of the anaerobic energy-producing systems and can improve muscle strength and tolerance for additional anaerobic activity.

As noted previously, in a game you will not run more than 200 yards at any one time. The field of play is only 100 yards long, and even if you had to run from one side of the field to the other while trying to avoid being tackled, you would probably not run more than 200 yards in a given play. After a play, you have around 30 seconds to recover before sprinting again. So a stop-and-go conditioning program for football should consider the total yardage run in any one play, the total yardage run during a game, and the amount of recovery between plays. Knowing these variables, you can create an exercise program that simulates a game situation.

Game Simulation Sprints

Game simulation sprints provide one method of increasing the specificity of the conditioning session. The simulators, based on the short-clock offense and defense that a football player may have to endure at the end of a half or game, consist of a series of sprints from one area of the field to the next. Each sprint is followed by a jog to the next sprint location. Each series of sprints is termed a quarter. During a conditioning session you may be required to perform one to four quarters of activity.

To perform these game simulation sprints effectively, you and your teammates should be divided into groups of five or six. On command the first group sprints to the first marker on the field (indicated by an X in the four field diagrams that follow). After the sprint, the first group continues by jogging to the next marker (indicated by an O). While the first group is jogging, the second group can line up to perform their first sprint. On the command the first group sprints to the third marker, while the second group sprints to the first marker. After each sprint the groups jog to their next starting point. Each group follows the group in front of them. On a short sprint, if the athletes sprint hard through the X marker and end at the next O marker, then no jog is necessary. Sprints can be timed to ensure intensity.

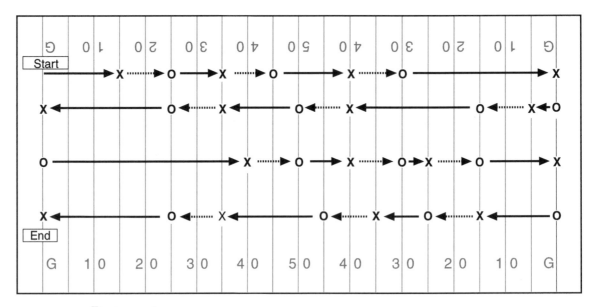

First quarter

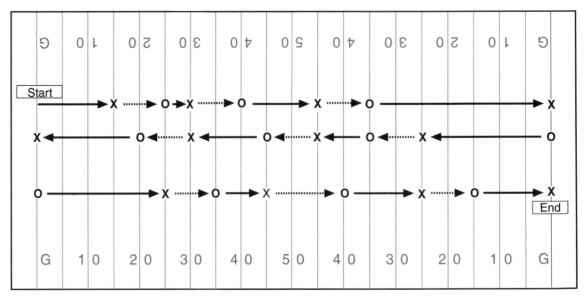

Second quarter

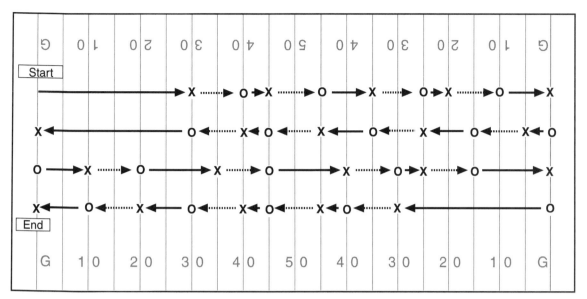

Third quarter

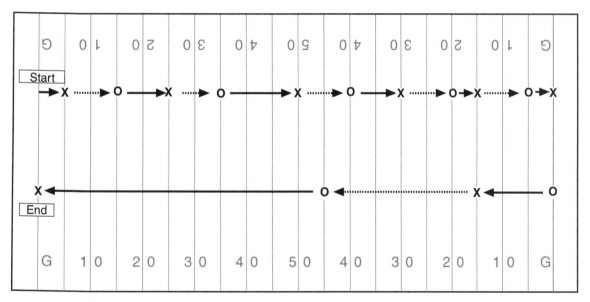

Fourth quarter

Intervals

Interval training refers to bouts of exercise that cover a given distance or a given time. These bouts of exercise are followed by periods of complete rest or exercise of a lesser intensity. This type of exercise is usually intense; you can regulate the intensity of training in three ways:

1. Increase the number of sprints or the yardage that each sprint covers. The best way to do this is to establish the total number of yards covered in a game situation. Let that amount of yardage be your goal. Gradually,

over a period of weeks, add more yardage or additional sprints until you reach your yardage goal.

2. Reduce the amount of rest between exercise bouts. This method, however, is less effective because during a game the amount of rest is relatively constant. Time-outs are usually all the same length. The time that players are on the field and the time between plays is usually about the same each game.

3. Increase the speed of the sprint by reducing the time allowed for its completion. This method of increasing intensity is also of limited value because you can only adjust the speed so much without making the sprint too easy or too difficult. Adjusting the time allowed for the activity works better for longer-distance running. Another argument for not adjusting the speed of the sprint during sprint training is the psychological effect that success and failure may have if the work is too easy or too hard.

In the weekly workouts in chapters 1 through 6, I've outlined various interval workouts as part of the conditioning program. In some instances I recommend that intervals be run on a track. (Lengths are given in yards for consistency, though tracks are now commonly measured in meters; 110 yd = 100 m, 220 yd = 200 m, 440 yd = 400 m, and so forth.) In other cases they may be run on the football field. Goal times are provided for three groups: wide receivers, defensive backs and running backs; linebackers, tight ends, and full backs; and linemen. I have also provided appropriate rest intervals. In some cases, no goal times have been noted; you should run those intervals as an all-out effort.

Crosses

Run across the football field from sideline to sideline for the number of times recommended in the workout. Rest while another group is performing.

Shuttles (Long or Short)

These sprints involve a series of down-and-back transitions on the football field for a given number of yards. For example in phase 6, the *long* 300-yard shuttle requires you to run the length of the football field (100 yards) down and back and down again before resting. In phase 5, the *short* 20-yard shuttle requires you to sprint 5 yards to a cone. Staying low, circle to the outside of the cone and sprint past your original starting spot to another cone directly in line with the first, 10 yards away. Staying low again, circle the cone and sprint back through the original starting spot. Your time on this drill should be comparable to your time in the 40-yard dash. The short shuttle drills work to improve quickness more than cardiorespiratory capacity.

Another variation of the shuttle involves sprinting down and back repeatedly to the following yard markers—10, 15, 25, 40, 40, 25, 10, 5, goal—for the length of the field. Shuttle runs are often referred to as ladders.

Sideline Ladders

Like a shuttle run, ladder drills require you to cover a given distance across the football field. Ladders usually consist of shorter transitions, which is why I have chosen to distinguish the two. During the sideline ladder, you sprint across the football field from sideline to sideline. Stop at the first hash mark and touch it with your hand, then return to the starting position and touch it with your hand. From here sprint to the next hash mark near the opposite sideline, touch it, and sprint back to the original starting line. Turn again and sprint to the opposite sideline and back, touching it and each hash with your hand. This type of exercise used to be called suicides.

Gassers

A gasser is a specific kind of shuttle run in which you run to the 10- or 20-yard line and back, 10 times. Ten times to the line and back equals 1 repetition.

Hash and Back

A variation of the gasser, in this exercise you run 10 times from sideline to hash mark and back before resting.

Combination Training

Combination training incorporates both sprint (stop-and-go) and endurance training. The different types of combination work can keep the workout fresh. This technique can help you train at a higher intensity for a longer time before fatigue causes you to request a rest period.

Combination training can be incorporated into the workout plan as a moderately intense exercise session. Stop-and-go training stresses the anaerobic capability of the body; endurance training stresses the aerobic capability of the body. Steady, easy runs make it easy for the cells to absorb oxygen. But we know that in athletics we cannot always run nice and slow. Competition demands that we push to maximal muscular effort most of the time. Combination training is one secret to developing the ability to exercise for a longer time at high intensity.

Fartlek Training

Fartlek is Swedish for speed play. This training method was developed by Gosta Holmer, who used paths in the Swedish forest. When possible, the athlete ran fast, and when the terrain became too rugged, the athlete had to run more slowly. Fartlek training uses this idea of intermingling higher-intensity surges with slower running. Running at regular speed, you can choose on impulse when to throw in short (10- to 60-second) surges or sprints, or you can designate them at specific times during your run (that is, every two to five minutes). After you finish the sprint, return to regular running speed.

Indian Running

The term "Indian running" was given to the type of exercise that Native Americans once performed at gatherings and ceremonies. This running technique was both a game and a test of endurance. Running would continue until all the participants retired due to exhaustion. The participants would begin running in a single-file line at moderate speed. The last runner in the line would sprint past all the others and take his place at the front of the line. Each runner, as he dropped to the last position in the line, would sprint to the front, creating a steady rotation. This type of running is continuous, with bursts of sprinting mixed in. It is a fartlek with a twist.

Hill Training

If you live in a hilly area, you are in luck. You can achieve the same type of cardiorespiratory work as fartlek or Indian running by running hills. As you run along at a moderate pace you build your endurance capabilities, but as you begin to run up a hill you increase the demand on your muscles. This is much like the added demand that increased speed places on the muscles. By running a trek over hills, you can simulate a fartlek run.

Stadium Runs

Like hill running, running the stairs of a football stadium can provide an excellent combination workout. Sprinting up the steps (taking 2 to 3 steps at a time) provides an increase in running resistance and the walk down allows for a moment of active recovery. Since every stadium is constructed differently, I provide a set time to do the workout (such as 20 minutes). See how many rows or steps or how many times through the course you can go in this time.

Endurance Training

Endurance, or aerobic (with oxygen), training involves activity that is not as intense as sprint training but that continues for a longer time. Because the intensity is low, the muscles do not have to work so hard. The demand for energy by the muscle is therefore lower. Simply put, endurance exercise is not as intense as stop-and-go training. Because the intensity is lower in the two-mile run, you can perform it longer before becoming exhausted. A working definition of endurance training is exercise that you can perform for 20 to 30 minutes each day. You can perform the exercise three to five days per week, at an exercise intensity of 60 percent of maximal effort.

Though football has low endurance needs, you can use endurance training to maintain fitness without further stressing your body with intense stop-and-go training. Like resistance training, cardiorespiratory conditioning can result in fatigue and overtraining. Conditioning days with lesser intensity are necessary to promote positive overall gains in conditioning. If you perform an intense stop-and-go training session on Monday and some type of lower-body resistance training on Tuesday, you can bet that your legs will be tired. Remember, you do not gain from the workout—you gain from the recovery after the workout. Endurance training can keep the muscle active, maintaining the circulation of blood to the legs at a higher level. That higher rate of circulation can promote healing of overstressed muscle tissue and thus enhance recovery. Endurance training can also improve body composition by reducing body fat. This greatly benefits most athletes, because being too fat can hinder performance.

Your conditioning program should mimic the playing style of football. Because football is a stop-and-go sport, the base of the conditioning program should center on stop-and-go, or sprint, training. For the conditioning program to be successful, consider how you will recover from workouts, with complete rest between bouts of exercise or during less intense periods of exercise. This is where you can apply your creativity to make the program fun and productive.

Speed and Power Exercises

Speed, quickness, explosiveness, power—what every athlete wants, what every athlete needs to be competitive in sports today. If you have speed and quickness, if you have that first explosive step, you can usually outrun, outjump, or overwhelm your opponent. The best assurance of having speed, quickness, and explosiveness is to be born with it. Perhaps your parents bestowed on you many fast motor neurons, which in turn gave you more fast-twitch muscle fibers. No matter how much quickness you've inherited, however, only proper training can develop it to its fullest potential.

Power is the ability to move a resistance quickly from point A to point B. To move your body weight quickly either horizontally, as in sprinting, or vertically, as in jumping, you must enhance your power. You can improve your power output by using both resistance training and specific power drills. The most important type of strength in developing power is *reactive strength*.

Improving Reactive Strength

Reactivity does not directly refer to reaction time (the time it takes to respond to a movement or signal). In the promotion of power, reactivity refers to how fast the muscle can go from a stretched position to an active position (eccentric to concentric muscle contractions). During jumping, you crouch slightly before accelerating upward. As you crouch, the muscles of your leg stretch. Then the muscles must rapidly contract to produce height. If you stretch the muscles quickly, they can help slingshot you upward. It's like stretching a rubber band and letting it go.

One method of enhancing reactivity is weight training. During the downward path of the bench press, for example, you must apply an eccentric muscle contraction to decelerate the weighted bar. At some point along the range of motion you must accelerate the bar upward from your body. If you can improve the skill of rapidly decelerating and then accelerating, you will increase your reactivity.

You often perform at high speed. In the weight room, though, the external speed of movement seems to be slower because the weight of the objects that you are moving is often much heavier than your body weight. However, internally, the muscles' contractile proteins are moving at great speeds. In this way the weight room serves its purpose by creating overload. The overloaded resistance is more weight than you would normally encounter during your athletic event. This overload therefore makes your body weight seem less a burden when you are performing on the football field.

A more athletically specific and highly reactive type of resistance training, called plyometrics, has recently become popular. By definition, plyometrics is the rapid deceleration of mass followed by an immediate and rapid acceleration of the same mass. The effects produced by plyometrics are similar to those produced by heavy resistance training, with the exception that plyometric movements result in visibly greater limb speeds.

Certain neural adaptations occur when you incorporate both methods of speed and power training into the workout program. These adaptations have been described as *intramuscular coordination* and *intermuscular coordination*. Intramuscular coordination refers to how effectively actions occur *within* the muscle (neural communication, cross-bridging of muscle fiber, chemical exchanges, and so forth). Intermuscular coordination, on the other hand, refers to the coordinated actions that occur *between* separate muscles or muscle groups.

Both plyometric and resistance training contribute to power and speed development. One is not better than the other. By employing both methods in the training regimen you will produce the highest gains. For example, you can apply both methods of training to enhance jumping ability. As you perform a traditional squat exercise with heavy resistance, the movement speed may seem slow. The motor neurons, however, are having to fire very rapidly to involve enough muscle fibers to control the weight. But squatting does not involve the ankle movement or arm action used during jumping. Squatting, then, may be an excellent *intramuscular* exercise to improve the internal workings of the muscles, while the high-speed act of jumping during a plyometric exercise can improve your *intermuscular* performance.

© Anthony Neste

Designing a Plyometric Program

Plyometrics, if performed too often or incorrectly, can cause overtraining of the nervous system. This overtraining can result in poorer performance. Keep in mind that acceleration and deceleration techniques used in plyometric training are also applied in other exercises in the training program. Overtraining with plyometrics is unlikely to occur using the workouts in this book unless the athletes are inexperienced and not yet physically mature. For these athletes the plyometric workouts may need to be scaled down in volume, with some exercises deleted entirely. To reduce the potential for injury, inexperienced athletes should use the low- to medium-intensity exercises and perform them off two feet rather the one.

Plyometric exercise is stressful to the body. But by increasing the intensity of the plyometric exercise slowly, you will reduce the risk of injury or overwork. Use plyometrics, like any exercise, in a periodization context, including in the training week both lower-intensity days and higher-intensity days.

Some plyometric exercises are easier on the body than others. Those exercises can serve as an introduction to plyometric training. The advanced athlete can incorporate the same exercises into his training program to provide a lower-stress training day. In periodization, you should consider two main principles:

1. As the exercise becomes more intense, perform fewer sets of that exercise.
2. If the exercise is less intense, you can perform more sets of that exercise.

Are You Physically Ready to Begin Plyometric Training?

Though many athletes on your team may be the same age and possess some of the same strengths, not all may be ready for the same levels of plyometric training. Weakness in primary or stabilizing muscles signals a potential for injury. The Soviet coaches who originally developed plyometric training suggested that the athlete be able to perform a 1 RM squat with a weight one and a half to two times his body weight. In *Eccentric Muscle Training in Sports and Orthopedics,* physical therapist and athletic trainer Mark Albert suggests a series of one-legged squat tests performed statically (held in place). These tests seem much more practical and can provide the athlete specific feedback about where muscular weakness exists. The tests are as follows:

1. Stand on one foot in place for 30 seconds with your eyes open. Repeat with your eyes closed. Switch legs.
2. Stand on one leg and perform a quarter squat. Hold in the bottom position for 30 seconds. Perform once with your eyes open and again with your eyes closed. Switch legs.
3. Stand on one leg and perform a half squat. Hold in the bottom position for 30 seconds. Perform once with your eyes open and again with your eyes closed. Switch legs.

If you can perform the first test, standing on one foot, and the second test, the quarter squat, without noticeable wobbling or shaking of the support leg (the leg in contact with the ground), then you're qualified to begin a progressive plyometric program. You should perform the half-squat test before starting the program and then again after you have trained for a while to measure improvement in your stability.

Guidelines for Plyometric Exercise Training

Before beginning plyometric training become knowledgeable of the following guidelines to get the most out of your training and to prevent injury.

1. Keep exercises specific to the activities performed on the field.

2. Use low-intensity exercises primarily during the off-season or other preparatory period. Use high-intensity exercises during the preseason or competitive period of training.

3. As the intensity of exercise increases, decrease the volume (sets and reps) of training.

4. If you increase the intensity of the workouts, allow more recovery time between workouts.

5. Terminate the exercise when fatigue begins to occur and you can no longer perform the exercise correctly.

6. When you do more difficult exercises that require more agility and coordination (complexity) to perform, reduce the number of sets and repetitions.

7. During the off-season, lower the complexity of the plyometric exercises.

8. During the preseason and in-season, increase the complexity of the plyometric exercises.

9. During the off-season phase of training, perform the plyometric workouts no more than three times per week. During the preseason and in-season phases of training, perform the plyometric workouts no more than twice per week. During the in-season phase of training, use discretion. Reduce plyometric workouts to zero if you feel overtired.

10. If the emphasis of the training program is endurance, the resistance-training intensity is low. In this case, perform the plyometric training before the resistance-training session. If the emphasis is on muscular power, then perform the plyometrics after the resistance-training program. If you do the plyometrics after the resistance-training session, choose a lower-intensity resistance-training day to perform the plyometric exercises or do upper-body plyometrics on a lower-body resistance-training day and vice versa.

11. Use a slow progression in plyometric training intensity. More is not necessarily better. A conservative approach to training is always advised. The SAID principle (specific adaptations to imposing demands) restated is that you should allow your body to adapt to stress—don't give it too much stress at once.

12. Use the one-leg squat test to assess strengths. Use these tests before, during, and after a training phase to track progress.

Determining the Intensity of the Plyometric Exercise

Several methods of determining the intensity of plyometric exercise are available:

- Type of exercise
- Number of exercises performed during a workout
- Increase in repetitions and sets of that exercise
- Changes in takeoff and landing surfaces
- Height of the objects jumped over or onto
- Rest period between sets of an exercise

Some plyometric exercises are low in intensity, while others are more stressful and are therefore categorized as high intensity.

1. Plyometric exercises performed on two legs are less intense than those performed on one leg.
2. Movements in place are less intense than movements that cover distance (jump rope versus triple jump).
3. Upper-body plyometrics are more intense than lower-body plyometrics.

The National Strength and Conditioning Association (NSCA) suggests performing exercises on a stress continuum divided into four levels (see table 10.1). Level I (the lowest intensity level) involves exercises performed while standing in place. The exercises within each level become progressively more intense (from low to shock).

The following exercises provide alternatives and variations for a plyometric program and illustrate the plyometric workouts set forth in chapters 1 through 6. The Thursday conditioning workout on week 11 (page 39) is one session that emphasizes plyometrics but allows for variations. For example, the power skip (leap) was varied by being performed more horizontally than vertically. It could thus enhance horizontal power for speed. Don't be afraid to use your imagination. Choose exercises in place of those listed to customize the workout plan to your liking.

In-Place Low Intensity

Ankle Bounce

Standing in place jump using only the ankles to create upward bouncing momentum. As soon as you touch the ground, rapidly rebound into another bounce. Jump on a padded surface to prevent overstressing the body and to make plyometric training more effective.

Table 10.1 Plyometric Stress Continuum

Intensity	Level I *In-place*	Level II *Short response*	Level III *Long response*	Level IV *Upper body*
Low	Ankle bounce Tuck jump Split jump Lateral bounce Skate bound Lateral hurdle hop Spin jump	Standing long jump	Leap	Overhead throw Medicine ball chest pass Half twist Full twist Walking twist and lunge Clap push-up Medicine ball push-up
Medium	Cycle jump Drop jump Jump-up Lateral hop	3 standing long jumps Standing triple jump Single hurdle jump Ski Zigzag bound Crossover lateral bound 5 alternate leg bounds	10 or more alternate leg bounds	Overhead forward throw Underhand backward throw Drop and slow return push-up
High	Hop	5 standing long jumps	10 or more hops	Drop and rebound push-up
Shock	Depth jump	Continuous hurdle jumps Box bound		One-arm push-up

Tuck Jump

Jump upward and tuck the legs against the chest while suspended in air. To emphasize the tuck, loosely hug the knees. Release the tuck before landing. Upon landing allow the knees to bend a little to absorb the landing.

Split Jump

Jump upward while straddling the legs in front of you in the air. Try to bring your outstretched legs to chest level and attempt to touch your toes. Land with both feet together. This exercise also adds dynamic flexibility to your plyometric routine.

Lateral Bounce

Stand with your legs about shoulder-width apart and quickly bounce from one foot to the other foot. The body does not travel far during this exercise; the feet leave and return to the floor in nearly the same place.

Skate Bound

This exercise is an exaggerated version of the lateral bounce and involves moving a greater distance laterally. Jump laterally from the left foot and land on the right foot. Then spring back to the left using the right foot.

Lateral Hurdle Hop

Using a small hurdle or other object as a obstacle, stand to the side of this object. Hop with feet together laterally over the object and back.

Spin Jump

Jump upward from both feet. While in the air spin the body around. You can start with a quarter turn and expand the spin into half and full turns. This exercise is a great way to develop body control, balance, and awareness.

In-Place Medium Intensity

Cycle Jump

Jump upward with one leg in front of the other. While in the air, cycle the legs so that the back leg moves to the front, and the front leg moves to the back. Cycle the arms in opposition with the legs to assist you in balancing the body while in the air.

Drop Jump

Step down from a box or similar object onto a padded floor or surface underneath. The height of the box can vary, but should be raised as you become more advanced in the exercise. Return to the box and repeat. Alternate legs each time.

Jump-Up

Stand in front of a sturdy box or platform. Using both legs, jump onto the box and land with both feet at the same time. Step off the box and repeat. Use a padded platform or box to reduce the negative stresses of plyometric training.

Lateral Hop

Hop on one foot from side to side over a line on the floor or over an object. As you become more advanced, extend the distance of the hops.

In-Place High Intensity

Hop

Hop upward on one leg. Land in the same place. Concentrate on hopping as high as you can and exploding off the ground as soon as you land.

In-Place Shock

Depth Jump

Step from a box or other object. The height of the box can vary, becoming higher as you become more advanced in the exercise. As your feet contact the ground allow your knees to give and absorb the shock of the landing. After landing, quickly rebound and jump upward off both feet.

Short-Response Low Intensity

Standing Long Jump

Stand with your feet together. Prepare to jump forward to a point well in front of you by pulling your arms back and bending the knees. Use your arms' forward movement and extend the knees as you jump to propel yourself horizontally forward.

Short-Response Medium Intensity

Three Standing Long Jumps

Perform three standing long jumps in succession. As soon as you land from each jump, rebound quickly into the next jump.

Standing Triple Jump

Stand with your feet together. Jump forward off both legs as far as you can and land on your right foot. Upon landing on your right foot immediately spring forward as far as you can and land on your left foot. After landing onto your left foot immediately spring forward onto both feet again. Repeat the action for a given number of times or for a given distance.

Single Hurdle Jump

Stand in front of a hurdle. A more advanced athlete can jump over a higher hurdle. Jump up and over the hurdle by bringing the knees high into the chest. Upon landing allow the knees to give slightly to cushion the shock of the landing. Turn around and repeat the jump over the same hurdle. Using a cushioned track or padded surface will minimize the stress of the exercise.

Ski

Jump from both feet from side to side while moving forward. If you are a beginner, jump over a line on the floor. If you are more advanced jump over a raised object, like a low hurdle or cone.

Zigzag Bound

Jump from your right leg to the right and forward. Upon landing, immediately jump with the left leg to the left and forward. Alternate legs with each jump. Jumping over a line on the floor can ensure your jumps move from one side to another.

Crossover Lateral Bound

Jump from your right leg to the left and forward. Upon landing, immediately jump with the right leg to the right and forward. Progress forward and from side to side on the same leg, Switch legs, and repeat the exercise.

Five Alternate Leg Bounds

Begin bounding by running in long exaggerated strides; work on spending more time in the air than on the ground. With each landing, explode off of your foot into the air. Alternate takeoff legs as you move forward.

Short-Response High Intensity

Five Standing Long Jumps

Perform five standing long jumps in succession. As soon as you land from each jump, rebound quickly into the next jump.

Short-Response Shock

Continuous Hurdle Jumps

Place a series of hurdles in a straight course about three to four feet apart. Perform a series of single-hurdle jumps with both feet. The hurdles can be all the same size, or the size of the hurdle can increase with each jump. The more advanced the athlete, the higher the hurdles can be adjusted.

Box Bound

Place a series of boxes about three to four feet apart. The boxes can be all the same size, or the size of the box can increase with each jump. Jump onto the box with one leg; then jump off of the box onto the ground with the other leg. Repeat this up and down cycle through the line of boxes using opposite legs as the up and down legs.

Long-Response Low Intensity

Leap (Power Skip)

Hop upward off of one foot, pulling the arms and the knee of the nonsupport leg upward quickly. Land on the same leg you took off on. Upon landing, quickly pull the arm and the knee of the opposite leg (the one that was the support leg) upward. This time hop upward off the new support leg. Repeat the action for a given distance or a given number of times. Emphasize moving vertically as high as you can.

Long-Response Medium Intensity

Ten or More Alternate Leg Bounds

Perform 10 or more alternate leg bounds. Begin bounding by running in long exaggerated strides; work on spending more time in the air than on the ground. To acquire more distance between the bounds, bring the legs higher into the chest during the hang time between landings.

Long-Response High Intensity

Ten or More Hops

Hop forward 10 or more times on one leg. Concentrate on hopping as high as you can and exploding off the ground as soon as you land. Repeat the exercise on the opposite leg.

Upper-Body Low Intensity

Overhead Throw

You can perform this exercise with a partner or a pitch-back device designed for heavy medicine balls. Stand with a medicine ball at arm's length above your head. Place one foot in front of the other to provide support. Keeping the arms straight and above your head, throw the ball. Catch the ball high above the head. Allow the arms to give to absorb the incoming weight of the ball.

Medicine Ball Chest Pass

You can perform this exercise with a partner or a pitch-back device designed for heavy medicine balls. Pushing with both hands at the same time, pass the medicine ball forward. When catching the ball, allow the arms to give to absorb the incoming weight of the ball.

Half Twist

Perform this exercise with a partner. Stand back to back. As one twists to the right to hand the ball off, the other must twist to the left to receive the ball. Reverse directions to pass and receive the ball on the other sides of your bodies. To make this exercise more challenging, stand farther apart so that you have to reach out farther to pass and receive the ball.

Full Twist

Perform this exercise with a partner. Stand back to back. Both twist to the right at the same time reaching all the way across your backs to give and receive the ball. Reverse directions to pass and receive the ball on the other sides of your bodies. To make this exercise more challenging, stand farther apart so that you have to reach out farther to pass and receive the ball.

Walking Twist and Lunge

Lunge forward with your right leg, while twisting your body to the left. Then lunge forward with your left leg and twist your body to your right. Repeat this pattern while walking forward. Hold a medicine ball in your hands to make the exercise more challenging. This movement can also be performed while lunging backward.

Clap Push-Up

Perform a regular push-up but push up with enough force for your hands to leave the ground during the up phase of the movement. While suspended in air, clap your hands together, and quickly place them back on the ground to catch yourself.

Medicine Ball Push-Up

Start in a down push-up position with one hand on the floor and the other hand on a medicine ball. Push yourself up rapidly, so that your hands leave the floor. When you push up, push at an angle so that your body moves from one side of the medicine ball to the other. While in the air, and moving over the ball, switch hands, so that the hand that was on the floor moves to the medicine ball, and the hand that was on the ball moves to the floor. Once both hands are placed, move into the bottom phase of the push-up. Remember: the ball is unstable. A beginner may choose a small box or another stable object on which to place his upper hand. Later, as he becomes more advanced, he can introduce the medicine ball.

Upper-Body Medium Intensity

Overhead Forward Throw

Assume a squatting position with your back straight and your chin tilted slightly upward. Place a medicine ball between your legs and grasp it with two hands. Rapidly extend the legs and jump up slightly while bringing the arms above the head. At the body's fullest extension, release the ball so it flies upward to its maximum height. The ball should land in front of you. A partner or coach can time how long the ball stays in the air. Begin with a light medicine ball; as you become advanced, use a heavier ball.

Underhand Backward Throw

Assume a squatting position with your back straight and your chin tilted slightly upward. Place a medicine ball between your legs and grasp it with two hands. Rapidly extend the legs and jump up slightly while bringing the arms over the head and arching the back slightly. At the body's full extension, release the ball so it flies upward to its maximum height. The ball should land behind you. A partner or coach can time how long the ball stays in the air. Begin with a light medicine ball; as you become advanced, use a heavier one.

Drop and Slow Return Push-Up

Support your hands on sturdy boxes, chairs, or benches. The height of the supports can vary. The beginner might choose a four- to five-inch support from which to drop and increase the distance as he becomes more experienced. If the supports are too high for your level, you could be injured while performing this exercise. Assume a push-up position on the support. Then drop free of the support and land your hands on the ground. Landing on a pad will minimize the shock of the exercise. As the shoulders and arms bend to absorb the landing, continue lowering as if performing a regular push-up. Once at the bottom of the push-up, slowly move to your knees and assume the starting position.

Upper-Body High Intensity

Drop and Rebound Push-Up

Support your hands on sturdy boxes, chairs, or benches. Assume a push-up position on the support. Then drop free of the support and land your hands on the ground. Landing on a pad will minimize the shock of the exercise. As the shoulders and arms bend to absorb the landing continue lowering as if performing a regular push-up. Once at the bottom of the push-up, rapidly drive the arms upward. The object is to push yourself high enough to land back on the supports.

Upper-Body Shock

One-Arm Push-Up

Assume a push-up position, but tuck one arm behind your back. Spread your legs apart. Keeping your chest and shoulders square to the ground, lower your body toward the ground. The more advanced you become, the closer together you will be able to move your feet while performing the movement.

Speed Training

Speed training is not cardiorespiratory training. Rather, it reinforces the basic skills of starting, accelerating, striding, and sprinting. Speed training involves high-intensity exercises of less than 10 seconds or less than 20 meters. Team sports like football demand little pure, linear speed. Most of the speed requirements are for lateral speed or change-of-movement speed (agility). But because coaches depend on the 40-yard dash as a testing tool, regardless of its applicability to the sport, we need to work on linear speed.

Phase 2 workouts address linear speed on Thursdays. During phase 4, starting at week 28, we work on the cutting and acceleration components of speed. By week 30 of phase 4, and through phase 5, we approach the linear aspects of speed again.

Stride Length

Speed can be improved by increasing the distance between foot falls. If you can cover more distance with each foot fall without sacrificing their frequency over a designated distance, then you should arrive at the finish line in less time. To increase the distance with each stride (and not overstride), you must improve your power output. This is the strength of a good sprinter. The sprinter's hips need to be powerful churning machines that propel his entire body horizontally through space. By performing resistance exercises on your upper body, lower body, and core, you can increase your muscular power. The parts of your body must work together to achieve the most efficient results. An increase in power output allows the trailing leg to drive the body forward during sprinting. The more powerful you are, the farther forward your body will travel with each push from the trailing leg. You will thus increase your stride length and speed.

With an increase in stride length comes an increase in the twisting motion of the body (torque). The twisting motion is centered in the hip area but can be seen more prominently in the shoulders. For you to achieve the best potential for speed, you must minimize the torque or twisting of your body. Your goal is to have all your body's movement centered in the direction of the finish line. If you begin to overstride, or if your upper body and trunk muscles (abdominals and lower back) are not powerful enough to counterbalance the twisting motion, you hinder your speed. You use your upper body and trunk muscles to counteract the twisting motion created by the movement of the lower body. To see the effects of trunk and upper-body involvement during a sprint, try running at high speed with your arms crossed over your chest—be careful, keeping your balance might be difficult. Some other drills you can use to focus and emphasize your stride length include the following:

- Downhill running
- Towing (pictured on next page)
- Target striding
- Overstriding

Even though overstriding is not the running form that produces ultimate speed, controlled overstriding in workouts can help you gain the feel of the increased stride length.

Stride Frequency

The next concern in developing speed is to increase the number of strides from start to finish. You can best accomplish this through overspeed work. Overspeed work may include downhill running (on a moderate downhill grade, perhaps three degrees) or towing with elastic ropes or cords. It is important during these drills that you do not alter your running style. If the overspeed work is too severe, you may have to compensate by leaning too far forward, too far backward, or by twisting too much. Emphasize sprinting form during stride frequency work.

Power is still important, but the emphasis on power must shift from pushing the body forward and off the ground to pulling the trailing leg upward toward the chest and pulling the heel toward the buttocks. This powerful action prepares the leg to extend outward on the ground again. The following drills and exercises for improving stride frequency are designed to increase your ability to pull the knee forward and high, and to promote the action of the heel being brought to the buttocks. By bringing the heel to the buttocks, rather than letting the heel drop away, the knee can swing forward and allow the leg to extend faster. The high knee and close heel act to increase foot speed during a sprinting activity. Emphasize your stride frequency during the following drills or exercises:

- Downhill running
- Towing
- Butt kicks
- Flexibility work

Starting Stance and Starting Posture

An effective start is essential for good performance in any timed sprint. In the 40-yard sprint the start can make the difference between a 4.6 and a 5.0. The key to a timed sprint is achieving full acceleration and maintaining it as long as you can before fatigue sets in. If you have difficulty starting, you can lose .3 to .8 seconds between the start and full acceleration. Because success is often measured in tenths of a second, that can mean the loss of playing potential. The difference between making it to the pros or not can sometimes come down to whether you can perform the sprint as well as the other guy at your position. You should not lose the opportunity for success because of a poor starting stance.

During the workout, phases 2, 4, and 5 emphasize starting stances. Week 33 of phase 5 contains a good example of start work (p. 84)—Thursday's 10 × 10-yard thrusts. This exercise is a 10-yard sprint with total concentration applied to the starting stance and that critical first explosive step.

In the starting posture for the sprint, place the front foot 2 to 6 inches from the starting line, with the back foot 12 to 18 inches behind the heel of the front foot. Place the hand opposite the front foot on the ground just behind the starting line. Place the other hand behind the hip with the arm extended straight. Lean the weight of your body forward so your head and shoulders are over the starting line. Your front leg supports most of your body weight. Face your head and eyes forward toward the finish line.

As you start, you bring the hand positioned at the hip rapidly forward and out in front, as if to reach and grasp an imaginary rope suspended in midair. Your front leg pushes your body forward and outward as if to long jump. The hand originally in front swings rapidly back as if to push the ground under it back and away from your body. You must bring the back leg forward, with the knee high and the heel of the foot brought close to the buttocks. You should maintain a forward lean until acceleration begins to peak, usually at three to six yards.

The best method of improving a start is to break it down and work on each aspect individually. Improve the general stance by assuming the starting position whenever you can during running or conditioning workouts. This will help you become comfortable with the stance and perform a more comfortable transition from the starting stance to the sprint.

Another aspect of the start is an effective first step. This step is similar to a horizontal bound. Pull your knees high into the chest while at the same time pulling back equally hard with your arms. To help improve the forward lean required for increased acceleration, extend your arms in front of you for the initial six yards of the sprint. Having your arms out in front ensures that you maintain a forward lean. This technique is not beneficial to your running form, so use such an exercise sparingly. This is true also for specific resistance exercises designed to build strength and power while sprinting.

Specific Resistance Exercises for Sprinting

Resistance exercises should become more specific as your in-season period or event approaches. In chapter 3 we discussed specificity in exercise. What follow are methods of increasing the resistance during the specific activity of sprinting:

- Partner-resisted sprints
- Sled pulling (below)
- Parachutes (see p. 224)
- Sprints with weighted pants and vest (see p. 224)
- Uphill or stadium stair sprints

You need not incorporate all these activities into your program. Some may better suit your needs and available time; all can be effective if performed properly.

After you have developed your body's power and learned to engage it in sprinting by using proper starts and running form, the last concern is to build acceleration. Reaccelerating on the fly provides your body with the feel of acceleration and thus helps you recognize the need to accelerate during a timed sprint.

You can also develop acceleration using the sleds and chutes to develop specific sprint strength. By beginning the sprint with the sled or chute attached, and at a given distance detaching from the apparatus, you will gain the perception of acceleration.

Football-Specific Agility Exercises

Your body is unique in the way that it performs sports-related movements. For this reason you should explore various methods that can teach your body how to perform a movement. Effortless movements result from time invested in a workout program. Gifted athletes may not have to invest as much time to be good, but they would undoubtedly be better if they demonstrate the desire to improve and make the effort to keep practicing.

Sports-related movements are complex combinations of smaller, simpler movements. The reason some athletes are better at performing certain movement skills is that they more easily bring together all the smaller movements and coordinate them. Some athletes seem to be born with the gift of coordination. That might be true, but anyone can improve if he learns the correct methods and is willing to evaluate himself constructively.

These drills work the smaller or individual skills necessary for you to play your position better. They allow you to concentrate on individual movement patterns that the position might require, while not having to worry about the entire position's movement responsibilities. Now that we have an understanding of the importance of the smaller component parts of movement patterns, let's investigate some of these smaller parts of movement—balance, foot speed, and agility. Then we'll coordinate these smaller movements to explore combination movements and reaction and quickness drills.

Balance

Balance is critical to being able to move gracefully and quickly. The human body depends on the senses of sight and touch and the faculties of the inner ear to achieve balance. Balance is a fundamental ability and, sadly, often overlooked.

You can improve and develop your balance, as you can any physical ability. The following drills are designed to improve your balance during movement and while standing still. You perform most of the drills on one foot. If you can improve your balance on one foot, you can more easily balance yourself on two feet. If your body is orthopedically sound, perform the drills barefoot. By performing the movements with your shoes off, you will force the small stabilizing muscles of the ankle and knee to work harder to maintain balance. Working with your shoes off can also strengthen weak muscles in the ankles and knees, thus preventing further injury. If your knees and ankles are injured, then perform the movements with your shoes on. The shoe acts as a stabilizer that provides additional balance and support to your already balanced body.

You perform some balance exercises with your eyes closed. Without sight you must depend more on feedback from muscles and joints. You can develop a higher level of kinesthetic sensory information (motor feedback) by relying more on how your body feels and less on your other senses. The sense of sight helps balance the body, so if you can develop balance proficiency while performing a movement with your eyes closed, then you will be even more balanced when you perform the movement with your eyes open.

Balance Drills

Perform each of these drills barefoot on the left foot and then the right.

Balance Drill #1

1. Stand on one foot with the foot flat on the ground for 30 seconds.
2. Then stand on the same foot on your toes for 30 seconds.
3. Bring up the knee of your free leg and kick it to the front. Remain on one foot for 10 kicks with each leg.
4. Standing on one foot, hold the free leg out to the back for 30 seconds.
5. Standing on one foot, hold the free leg out to the front for 30 seconds.

Balance Drill #2

1. Stand on one foot with your eyes closed for 30 seconds.
2. Stay on the same foot and make quarter turns, pausing for 10 seconds at each turn.
3. Stay on the same foot and hold your free leg out to the side for 30 seconds.
4. Bring your knee up, rotate the support leg, and kick the free leg to the side for 10 kicks.
5. Finally, stand on the same foot on your toes for 30 seconds.

Balance Drill #3

1. Stand on one foot and push the opposite leg behind (10 times each leg).
2. Hop on the same foot. Do a three-quarter turn and kick to the side slowly (5 times each leg).
3. Hop sideways after each hop and add a side kick (10 times each leg).
4. Stand on one foot, perform a three-quarter turn, and then kick slowly out to the side (10 times each leg).

Balance Drill #4

1. Hop on one foot sideways, maintain your balance, and reach down and touch the floor. Balance and hop again, trying not to double hop (10 times each leg).
2. Stand on one foot, push your free leg out in front of you, and lean back as far as you can without falling (10 times each leg).
3. Stand on one foot, lean to the side, push the free leg out to the side, and then try to touch the floor to the side (10 times each leg).
4. Stand on one foot and then lean your upper body in all directions as far as you can without falling (5 times each leg).

Foot Speed

Everyone talks about foot speed and quickness. Everyone wants to know how he can get it. The question is *what is it?* Foot speed is the ability to touch the foot quickly to the ground while reducing the time that the foot is in contact with the ground.

Try tapping your hand on your leg. Slowly increase the rate of the tapping until it is as fast as you can tap. You'll probably find that you can tap faster if your hand makes light contact rather than contact with a greater force. Now try the same thing with your foot to the ground. You will probably find it difficult to tap your foot as quickly as you tapped your hand. This is because the hand has a greater number of nerve fibers activating a smaller number of muscle fibers. The hand is designed for more delicate and faster work than the foot. Another reason that the foot cannot move as quickly is that it is seldom required to. What if the foot were trained to act like the hand regarding speed? The foot may never be as fast as the hand, but I would bet that you would see an increase in its agility.

The following drills address the smaller, more basic components of hip, knee, and ankle movement to produce greater foot speed. I have arranged the drills to address the most simple foot movements first, adding more complex foot movement patterns later. These drills should help you perform more complex movements with softer and faster foot falls.

Foot-Speed Drills

The first foot-speed drill addresses the most basic speed components—the cadence of the foot, ankle, knee, and hip movements. How fast you become is ultimately determined by how efficiently the joints of the lower body work with one another. You can facilitate faster joint actions by applying tapping routines to each joint area. *Tapping* is synchronization exercise that you perform by tapping the floor or some other surface with your foot. You tap your foot by moving your ankle, knee, or hip.

In some cases an athlete's lack of movement coordination could be the result of one or more of his joints being out of cadence with other joint segments. If, for example, you are having trouble during a sprint at high speed, the problem may not be at the hip or knee. Instead, the ankle might be losing the ability to retain the higher speed movement pattern. The tapping exercises may help correct this and improve your synchronization.

The following workouts are included in the weekly workouts under the headings "on your own" and "by position."

Foot-Speed Workout #1

Tap as fast as you can without losing rhythm.

1. Sit in a chair. Moving only the ankle (let the heels remain in contact with the floor), tap your *toes* on the floor, alternating legs. Tap for 30 seconds, three times.

2. Sit in a chair. Moving only the ankle (let the toes remain in contact with the floor), tap your *heels* on the floor, alternating legs. Tap for 30 seconds, three times.

3. Sit in a chair. Moving only the ankle, tap the heel of one foot and the toes of the other foot to the floor in an alternating fashion. Tap for 30 seconds, three times.

4. Sit in a chair facing a wall one foot away. Moving only the knee, tap your *toes* on the wall in an alternating fashion. Tap for 30 seconds, three times.

5. Sit on a plyometric box with your feet on the floor. Moving only the knee, tap your *heels* on the box in an alternating fashion. Tap for 30 seconds, three times.

6. Lie on your back on the floor. Keeping your legs straight and moving only your hips, tap the floor with your *heels* in an alternating fashion. Tap for 30 seconds, three times.

7. Lie on your stomach on the floor. Keeping your legs straight and moving only your hips, tap the floor with your *toes* in an alternating fashion. Tap for 30 seconds, three times.

Foot-Speed Workout #2

The second foot-speed workout uses slightly more complex movement patterns. Also you incorporate your entire body weight into the exercises—having to manage body weight is the most critical aspect of athletic movements. You perform these exercises in a contained area, and they involve more cyclic, alternating, and dancelike movement patterns. This teaches the ankles, knees, and hips to act naturally in a variety of situations, while at the same time maintaining cadence.

1. **Wall running.** Stand facing a wall and place both hands on the wall for support. Stand on one foot. With the free leg, bring the knee up toward the chest. Then push the free leg slightly out in front of you, and downward toward the ground. When the foot touches the ground, slide it lightly backward and up as if you were a bull pawing the ground. Perform this movement in slow motion for the first few repetitions and gradually increase speed without losing the coordination of the movement. Perform for 30 seconds, three times with each leg.

2. **Russian hops.** Mark a straight line on the floor six feet long. Stand on one foot on the line. Slowly begin to perform very small, short hops. As you move down the line, attempt to hop faster and faster with lighter contact to the floor. Perform as many hops within that six-foot margin as possible. Perform three times with each leg.

3. **Box running.** Place a small sturdy box, 6 to 12 inches high, on the floor. Place one foot lightly on the box while allowing the opposite foot to remain on the floor as if to step up on a step. Quickly begin to alternate the position of the feet. The foot on the floor moves to the box while the foot on the box moves to the floor. Attempt to keep foot contact, both on the floor and on the box, light and quiet. Perform for 30 seconds, three times.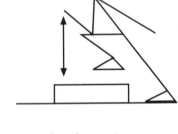

4. **Box shuffle.** You perform this drill much as you do the box-run drill previously described. Place one foot on the box and allow the other to remain in light contact with the floor. The foot on the floor will move up to the box, while at the same time the foot on the box will move to the floor on the opposite side of the box. This drill 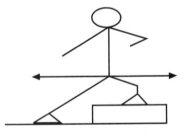 is like stepping up on a step, sideways and back off again. Quickly alternate feet back and forth. Perform for 30 seconds, three times.

5. **Three-sided square.** The three-sided square is a foot pattern drill. Place three strips of tape on the floor forming a square with only three sides. The object is to step quickly in and out of the square in various patterns. You can also form the square with string or rope raised slightly off the ground to force yourself to raise your knees higher.

- *Pattern 1.* Start by standing on the right foot, then step into the square with the left foot, then bring the right foot into the square while simultaneously moving the left foot to the opposite side of the square. Pick up the right foot; then put it back down into the square. Next, bring the left foot into the square while moving the right foot to where it originally began. Repeat this one-two-three, one-two-three pattern for 30 seconds; stop; repeat for 30 seconds more.

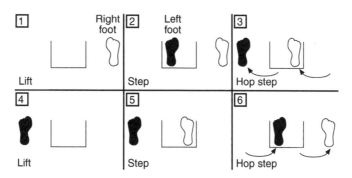

- *Pattern 2.* Start by standing on the right foot; then step into the square with the left foot. Next bring the right foot into the square while simultaneously moving the left foot to the opposite side of the square. Pick up the right foot and move it to the outside of the square beside the left foot. Next bring the right foot back into the square, and then the left foot. Next, return the right foot to where it originally began. Follow by bringing the left foot out of the square beside it. Repeat this one-two-three-four, one-two-three-four pattern for 30 seconds; stop; repeat 30 seconds.

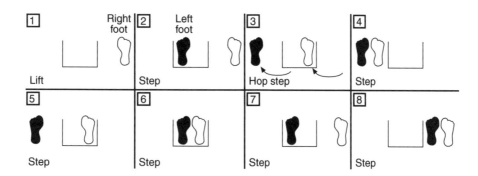

Foot-Speed Workout #3

The third foot-speed workout involves even more complex movements by having you perform foot patterns while at the same time moving forward and laterally. You will also need to do cutting drills to get your movements under control and maintain balance while still being able to change directions rapidly.

1. **Ladder drills.** You perform these drills on a five-yard-long rope ladder lying on the floor. You can perform a variety of drills on the three-sided square and the ladder mentioned earlier. Use your imagination to create new drills for yourself or refer to agility ladder workouts provided by Randy Smythe at Speed City Incorporated, 16650 SW 72nd Ave., Portland, OR 97224; 800-225-9930.

   - Using the ladder, use the same foot pattern you did in the three-sided square drill (pattern #1; previous page) except perform the drill horizontally in and out of each hole created by the ladder—one-two-three, one-two-three, and so on. Perform this three times as quickly as you can.

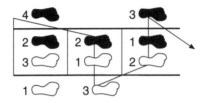

   - Move sideways through the ladder, placing two feet in each hole, then stepping out of the ladder with both feet—one-two-in, one-two-out, and so on down the ladder. Perform this three times as quickly as you can.

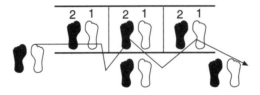

2. **Tiny hurdle drills.** Set 10 to 12 small one-foot hurdles two feet apart. Hurdle drills help develop hip flexion and coordination of movement at the hip joint. At the same time you are moving in a horizontal direction, which relates more to athletic movement requirements.

   - Quickly step over each hurdle with each foot moving in a straight line. Step over 10 to 12 hurdles, five times.
   - Moving laterally, quickly step over each hurdle with each foot. You should never cross your feet while performing this drill. Step over 10 to 12 hurdles, five times.
   - Moving laterally, quickly step over each hurdle with each foot. Move back and forth for 30 seconds.

3. **Cutting quickness.** To develop more athletic movements, you must be able to change direction rapidly while remaining under control.

   - Transitional carioca. Perform a carioca movement. Upon command, rapidly change direction, back and forth for 30 seconds. Coaches can give the commands at different intervals to keep athletes guessing and avoid establishing a set movement pattern.

- Sprint forward 10 yards. Rapidly change direction and backpedal to the starting point. Perform three sets of 10 transitions.
- Shuffle or step slide 10 yards. Rotate your body and plant your inside foot to the outside and shuffle back. Continue for 5 transitions. Then adjust so that you plant the opposite foot to the outside for 5 transitions. Do three sets.
- Sprint in a zigzag pattern. At each zig cut off the outside leg. At each zag cut off the inside leg. You will be doing the cutting with the same leg. Switch legs. Complete three sets of 10 cuts with each leg.

Quick Feet Drills

These drills improve foot quickness by drilling hopping or stepping over a rope or line on the ground. If you are using a rope, you can also suspend it a few inches off the ground to ensure you are evolving a high knee action.

Side-to-Side Hop

Stand on one side of the rope. Hop laterally with both feet together across the rope and back for an assigned time (30 to 60 seconds). Your coach may cue you when to hop faster or slower. You may also vary the lateral hop by having the foot closest to the rope touch the ground first at landing, followed by the opposite foot.

Front and Back Hop

Stand facing the rope. Hop forward with both feet together across the rope and then backward across the rope. Continue jumping for an assigned time (30 to 60 seconds). Your coach may cue you when to hop faster or slower. You can vary this drill by touching the ground with one foot first and then the other when hopping.

Single Side Split Hop

Stand over the rope so that one foot is on each side. Hop up; while in the air cross your legs so that upon landing the right foot is on the left side of the rope and the left foot is on the right. Alternate crossing with the right leg behind and in front of the left leg. Then hop back with both feet at the same time across the rope to their starting position. Continue for 30 to 60 seconds. Try to achieve the switch in foot placement by hopping as low to the ground as possible.

Agility

As you approach the season, you should increasingly emphasize movements specific to football. Agility movements are an excellent method of increasing the specificity of the workout session. These agility drills along with work on specific position drills will help you learn how to use your newly developed muscular size, power, endurance, and speed.

In the weekly workouts in part I, several of the following drills are presented in a four-station format. Four-station drills allow the team to be divided into four groups with each group performing a drill before moving onto the next drill. Station drills allow a coach to manage practice time more wisely, minimizing the amount of time athletes are waiting to perform the next drill. After a given number of minutes at one station the groups rotate to the next station and repeat until all athletes have performed each drill.

Agility Drills

Snake

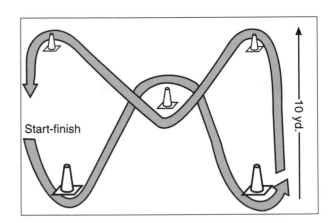

T Drill

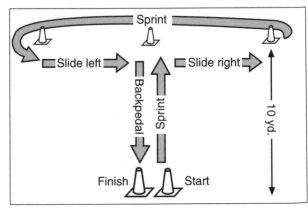

S Drill

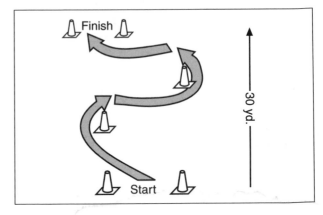

W Drill

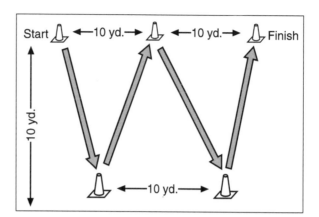

Box 1

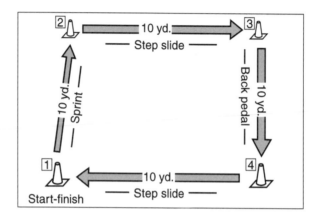

Box 2

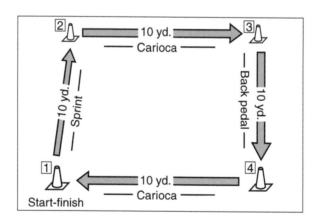

Box 3

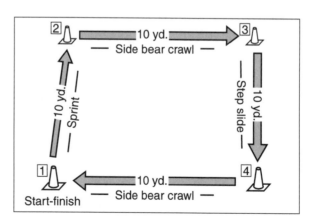

Box 4

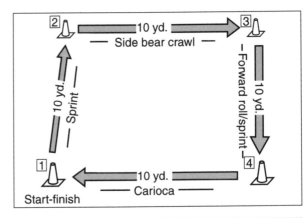

Triangle

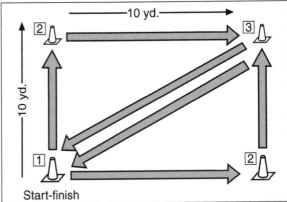

Cones

Agility Ladder Drills

Quick Run, Sprint Out

Place a ladder flat on the ground or raised a few inches to induce a high knee action. Moving forward through the length of the ladder, step one foot after the other into each space created by the rungs of the ladder. Start with the left foot first and on subsequent runs lead with the right foot. Once through the ladder, sprint to a set distance.

Lateral Quick Run, Sprint Out

Moving laterally along one side of the ladder step one foot after the other into each space created by the rungs of the ladder. Then step back out to the same side of the ladder that you started on, moving up the length. Once through the ladder, sprint to a set distance.

Lateral Two In, Two Out, Sprint Out

Starting with one side facing the top of the ladder, step laterally through the first space created by the rungs. Follow the first foot in the first space with the second foot in the same space, then move your first foot into the next rung followed by the opposite foot and continue up the ladder—two feet into the rung space, two feet out, When you reach the end of the ladder, sprint out.

One In, Three Out, Sprint Out

Perform this drill by standing to the left of the ladder's first open space created by the rungs. Place your right foot into that first space. Then tap your left foot to the ground outside the ladder near its original starting spot. Bring your right foot out of the ladder and tap it to the floor near where it originally began. Tap your left foot on the floor again before moving your right foot forward and into the next space on the ladder. In this way your right foot is always stepping in and out of the ladder and your left foot is tapping a tune as you move forward: step . . . tap, tap, tap . . . step . . . tap, tap, tap. When you reach the end of the ladder, sprint out.

Other Drills

When examining the workout plan, you will come across other agility exercises that provide variations to the movements mentioned earlier. Doing a variety of movement patterns will help prepare your body for the movement stresses that occur during a football game.

Agility Over Bags

A series of low blocking pads or bags are laid in a line across the ground. The distance between the bags varies depending on the task at hand. The idea behind performing agility over bags is that it will help you move uninhibitedly over fallen opponents. By varying the ways you get around the bags, you can increase your agility in a number of ways:

1. High knees
2. Hopping over bags
3. Zigzagging between bags
4. Shuffling laterally over bags

Cutting Inside and Outside Legs

This cutting drill conditions you to the demands of lateral movement. Perform the drill by running at 45-degree angles to the sideline or to a line straight down the field. Upon a command or whistle, drive rapidly off your outside leg. Perform the drill up and down the field. A variation to the drill is to drive off the inside leg. In doing so, you are forced to spin to go in the opposite direction that you were just running.

Lateral Shuffle Over Low Hurdle

Just as you did a lateral shuffle over bags, you can shuffle over cones and hurdles. A lateral shuffle is simply a high knee and arm run performed sideways, in which each foot lands in the space between the hurdles, one after the other.

Combination Movements

The individual movement drills just described can be mixed and matched into a workout plan called a movement course. The movement course can help you apply and blend your movement strength and balance to your game. These courses are basically obstacle courses, with the obstacles being foot-speed, cutting, and lateral-movement drills. Shifting from linear to cutting activities and from sprinting to jumping, the movement courses mimic the athletic requirements of football.

The movement courses are used during phases 2 and 5. They are performed as a team or assigned as individual or position work. These courses can be repeated several times to produce a workout effect.

Movement Course Drills

Movement Course #1

Equipment needed: 8 to 10 low hurdles, four high hurdles, and four tackle dummies

1. Start by chopping your feet.
2. Turn and sprint to a set of low hurdles.
3. Shuffle through the hurdles sideways.
4. After the last hurdle, quickly backpedal to a series of high hurdles.
5. Jump each high hurdle with a two-foot hop.
6. After the last hurdle turn and sprint to a series of four tackle dummies.

7. Forearm block each dummy and then tackle the last dummy in the series.

8. Complete the course by turning and sprinting to the finish.

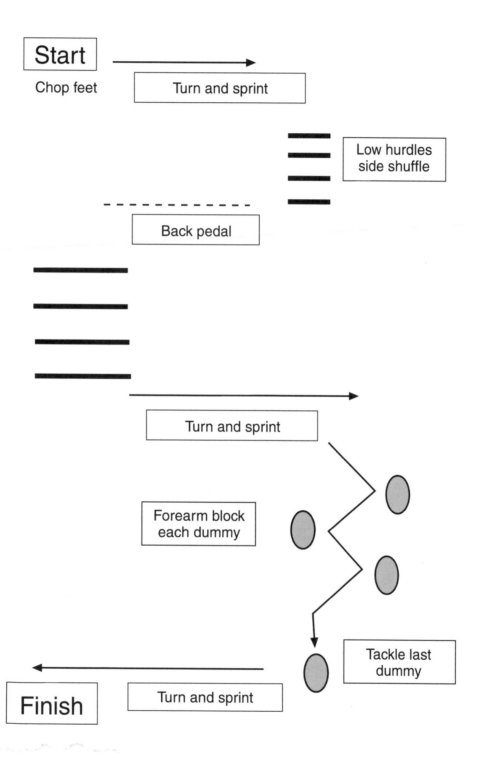

Movement Course #2

Equipment: two tackle dummies, one set of suspended rope ladders, three flat drill bags, and one agility cord laid out in a zigzag fashion.

1. Start by chopping your feet.
2. Then backpedal until the coach gives you the signal to cut left or right.
3. Once you get the signal and cut to either side, sprint back to the forearm-block tackle dummy.
4. After blocking the dummy, dive over the two or three low bags.
5. Jump to your feet and sprint through a rope ladder (one foot in each hole).
6. Shuffle along the line of the agility cord in the manner that it is staked along the ground.
7. Complete the course by turning and sprinting to, and tackling, a final tackle dummy.

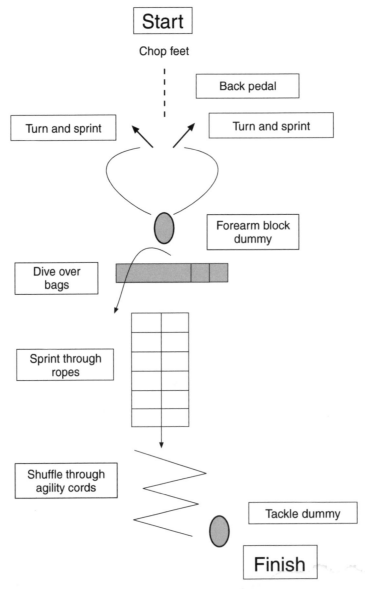

Movement Course #3

Equipment needed: four cones forming a square, four large tackle dummies or bags, one agility ladder or rope ladder laid flat to the ground, and two final cones to mark final cue location.

1. Start by chopping your feet.
2. Shuffle left to cone 1, sprint to cone 2, shuffle right to cone 3, and backpedal to cone 4.
3. Quickly change direction and sprint to the rope ladder.
4. At the rope ladder, execute a two-feet-in-each-hole-and-one-foot-out pattern down the length of the ladder (Icky shuffle) to the bags.
5. Jab into each space between the bags lying on the ground. At the last bag, sprint out. *(continued)*

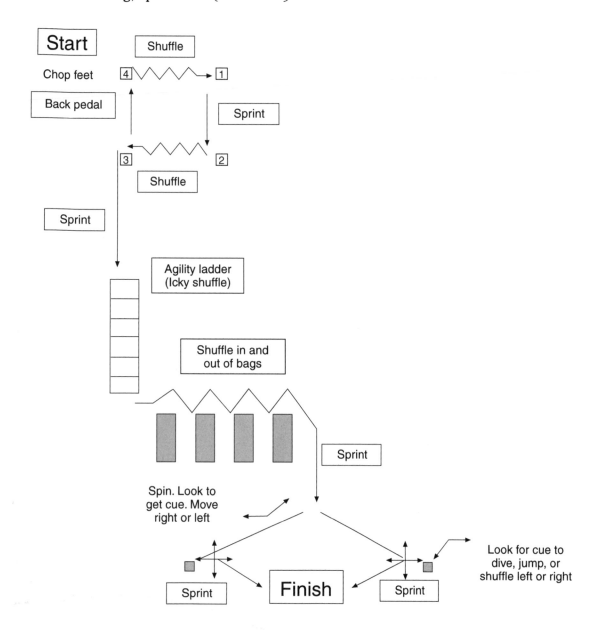

6. Spin around to receive cue from the coach to drop step and sprint either right or left to a cone.

7. Complete the course by receiving a final cue from the coach to jump or dive to the ground or to move left or right.

8. Sprint to the finish.

You can substitute other ladder drills for those just described. The following ladder drills are incorporated throughout the program. These drills are only a sample of what you can perform in the agility ladders; use your imagination to think of others.

Reaction and Quickness

Often your opponent does not beat you physically—he beats you with deception. He is able to prevent you from reading his intentions, causing you either to delay your reaction or to overreact. In either case you find yourself a split second behind, and he has gained the advantage.

Reaction Drills

Once you can efficiently perform the drills described earlier, you are ready to hone your ability to perceive and react to movement, movement that might be your opponent's initial step. The following drills are but a few exercises that you can use to sharpen your reactive abilities.

Basic Reaction Drill

Perform basic reaction drills with three or four players. The players come out of their lines chopping their feet. The coach, 10 to 15 yards away, signals the athletes to move in a given direction—left, right, backward, forward—or to jump up or hit the ground. This drill is a basic movement drill cued by sight.

Three-Cone Reaction Drill

The three-cone version of the reaction drill is similar to the basic reaction drill but is most often done one athlete at a time. Set up three sets of cones. A coach can provide instructions to three athletes at once as long as there is enough room for all three to see or hear his cues.

Each athlete is responsible for three cones, numbered 1 through 3, arranged in a straight line in front of him. Begin by chopping your feet about 10 to 15 yards from the middle cone. When the coach calls a number or points to a cone, rush to the cone and tap it. If the coach calls another number, quickly run to it; if he doesn't call a number, rush back to the starting position, still chopping your feet and waiting for the cue. Be alert—you may also receive a cue to jump and hit the ground!

Ball-Drop Reaction Drill

The ball-drop drill is the next drill along the progressive cycle of improving your reaction. Standing five yards from you, the coach holds a ball in each hand. The objective of the drill is to catch the ball before it can take a second bounce. The coach can choose to drop the ball out of either hand, thus making your job more difficult.

Coaches may choose to use several cues. Visual cues include the sight of the ball dropping or a corresponding blink of the coach's eyes or a change of body position, timed with the drop of the ball. He might also use an oral cue before dropping the ball to help improve auditory reaction. After each successful catch the coach takes one normal step back from the starting point. This will challenge you to push your first-step quickness to its highest level.

Tag Games

The next drills are games commonly played on the school yard. Still, they provide a sound way to improve your "recognize and react" skills. These games, particularly prominent in phases 2 and 5, are the next step forward in the reaction development continuum. Tag is an excellent method of working on cutting skills, reacting to an opponent, and changing direction and speed. Tag requires athletic movements and hard work but also provides a way to have fun.

Several games are provided here, but you can create others using your imagination. Perform all tag games with boundaries—a square marked off with cones will do. If an athlete about to be tagged steps out of bounds, he is out.

Dodge Ball

You can play several variations of dodge ball. In one of the safest versions, you stand with your back facing a wall as a coach or teammate rapidly issues a hand-tossed barrage of tennis balls toward you one at a time. This drill forces you to dodge and spin to avoid the projectiles. Stop the play when you are tagged by a ball or if the balls begin to gather dangerously under your feet.

Of course, you can play the larger version of the game in which one athlete serves as the thrower and the others attempt to avoid being tagged by the ball. This version can quickly get out of hand, however, so use it only with small groups.

Sharks in the Tank

Try performing these games in a 15-by-15-yard square with five or six athletes being tagged by one, or in a 30-by-30-yard square with ten or more athletes being tagged by two.

In this tag game one or two people are *it* depending on the dimensions of the tank. The objective of the game is for the person who is it to tag everyone else. The game is over when all players have been tagged.

Pick-Up Tag

Try this game in a 30-by-30-yard square. You will need 4 to 20 paper balls. Match one to three pickers with one to three taggers and blockers.

One athlete is the picker. His objective is to pick up assorted paper balls that are lying randomly on the floor or playing surface. The picker is guarded by a blocker. The blocker's job is to stay between the picker and the tagger. The tagger attempts to keep the picker from getting any of the balls by tagging him. The blocker can only shield; he cannot hold or touch the tagger.

Goal-Line Tag

The objective of this tag game is for the player to cross a goal line without being tagged by the tagger. The goal line should be about 20 feet wide so that the tagger has to work to defend it. This is a one-on-one tag game. Players line up, and the line moves forward as players who have run against the tagger become the next tagger.

Cops and Robbers

In this tag game two people are *it*. These taggers are the cops. Everyone else is a robber. The objective is for one cop to tag and jail all the robbers. Once tagged, the robbers must go to jail—a designated side of the playing area. The other robbers can break into jail and free a robber by tagging him, but only one at a time. They must, however, get by the jailer cop, who is a goal-line defender both going into and coming out of jail. The jailer is assigned to a limited area, along the goal line (jail) and cannot tag a robber unless the robber enters the area or tries to enter or leave the jail. The game is over when all robbers are jailed.

About the Author

From 1990 to 1994, Ben Cook was the assistant strength and conditioning coach for the University of North Carolina Tar heel football team. His coaching helped 27 players reach the NFL. From 1994-2001 he was the head strength coach for Tar Heel men's basketball. During his seven seasons, the teams made four Final Four appearances. Currently Ben is Manager of Exercise Programming for Carolinas Sports Performance Center and co-founder of the LINK System.

Cook holds a master's degree in exercise and sports science from UNC and is a CSCS and NSCA-CPT with the National Strength and Conditioning Association. Cook lives in Harrisburg, North Carolina.

You'll find other outstanding football resources at

http://football.humankinetics.com

In the U.S. call 1-800-747-4457

Australia 08 8372 0999 • Canada 1-800-465-7301
Europe +44 (0) 113 255 5665 • New Zealand 0064 9 448 1207

 HUMAN KINETICS
The Premier Publisher for Sports & Fitness
P.O. Box 5076 • Champaign, IL 61825-5076 USA